Gender and Devel<

Children are born into a world infused with gendered information. An understanding of what it is to be a boy or girl can be critical in forming social relationships, social identities, and learning how to think and behave. *Gender and Development* is an important new volume that charts how children practise these gendered identities at different ages and in different social contexts

Taking a socio-cognitive approach, and integrating both theoretical and applied perspectives, the book looks at a range of contexts in which gender affects development and socialization, from the child's place in the family unit and their interaction with parents and siblings, to the influence of communication with peers over the Internet. Throughout the chapters an age-old issue is addressed through a contemporary, empirically focused perspective – namely the nature and extent of equality between the genders, and how difficult it is for attitudes, perceptions and stereotypes to change. Key social issues are covered, including pro-social behaviour, career choice and academic competencies.

Gender and Development brings together some of the latest research in this important and enduring field of study. It is a timely and invaluable collection, and will be essential reading for all students and research in developmental psychology, social psychology and gender studies.

Patrick J. Leman is Professor of Psychology, Royal Holloway University of London, UK. He is Chair of the British Psychological Society Developmental Psychological Section and associate editor of the *British Journal of Developmental Psychology*. His research explores peer communication and learning in gender and ethnic interactions.

Harriet R. Tenenbaum is Reader at the University of Surrey, UK. She is the editor of the *British Journal of Educational Psychology*. Her research covers children's cognitive, social and emotional development in relationships.

Current Issues in Developmental Psychology
Series Editor: Margaret Harris
Head of Psychology, Oxford Brookes University, UK

Current Issues in Developmental Psychology is a series of edited books that reflect the state-of-the-art areas of current and emerging interest in the psychological study of human development. Each volume is tightly focused on a particular topic and consists of seven to ten chapters contributed by international experts. The editors of individual volumes are leading figures in their areas and provide an introductory overview. Example topics include: developmental disorders, implicit knowledge, gender development, word learning and categorisation.

Published titles in the series

Current Issues in Developmental Disorders
Edited by Chloë R. Marshall

Gender and Development
Edited by Patrick J. Leman and Harriet R. Tenenbaum

Gender and Development

**Edited by Patrick J. Leman
and Harriet R. Tenenbaum**

Psychology Press
Taylor & Francis Group
LONDON AND NEW YORK

First published 2014
by Psychology Press
27 Church Road, Hove, East Sussex BN3 2FA

and by Psychology Press
711 Third Avenue, New York, NY 10017

Psychology Press is an imprint of the Taylor & Francis Group, an informa business

British Library Cataloguing in Publication Data
A catalogue record for this book is available from the British Library

Library of Congress Cataloging in Publication Data
Gender and development / [edited by] Harriet Tenenbaum,
Patrick Leman.
pages cm
Includes bibliographical references and index.
1. Developmental psychology. 2. Child psychology. 3. Sex differences
(Psychology) I. Tenenbaum, Harriet. II. Leman, Patrick.
BF713.G463 2014
155.43—dc23
2013026281

ISBN: 978-1-84872-113-5 (hbk)
ISBN: 978-1-84872-143-2 (pbk)
ISBN: 978-1-315-87087-8 (ebk)

Typeset in Times New Roman
by Swales & Willis Ltd, Exeter, Devon, UK

Printed and bound in Great Britain by
TJ International Ltd, Padstow, Cornwall

To Arabella, Ella, Hannah, Jacob, Samuel, Sophie

Contents

Figures

Tables

Contributors

Margarita Azmitia, Department of Psychology, University of California, Santa Cruz, 1156 High Street, Santa Cruz, CA 95064, USA (azmitia@ucsc.edu).

Andrew Scott Baron, Department of Psychology, University of British Columbia, 2136 West Mall, Vancouver, BC V6T 1Z4, Canada (abaron@psych.ubc.ca).

Dario Cvencek, Institute for Learning & Brain Sciences, 1715 Columbia Road N, Portage, Bay Building, Box 357988, University of Washington, Seattle, WA 98195-7988, USA (dario1@u.washington.edu).

Matthew D. DiDonato, School of Social and Family Dynamics, PO Box 873701, Arizona State University, Tempe, AZ 85287, USA (matthew.didonato@asu.edu).

Dawn England, School of Social and Family Dynamics, PO Box 873701, Arizona State University, Tempe, AZ 85287, USA (dawn.england@asu.edu).

Timea Farkas, Department of Psychology, University of California, Santa Cruz, 1156 High Street, Santa Cruz, CA 95064, USA (timeafar@gmail.com).

Benjamin Hine, Department of Psychology, Royal Holloway, University of London, Egham, Surrey, TW20 0EX, UK (ben.hine@rhul.ac.uk).

Angela Ittel, Institute of Education, Berlin Institute of Technology (TUB), Marchstraβe 23, 10587 Berlin, Germany (angela.ittel@tu-berlin.de).

Melanie Killen, Department of Human Development, 3304 Benjamin Building, University of Maryland, College Park, MD 20742, USA (mkillen@umd.edu).

Campbell Leaper, Department of Psychology, University of California, Santa Cruz, 1156 High Street, Santa Cruz, CA 95064, USA (cam@ucsc.edu).

Patrick J. Leman, Department of Psychology, Royal Holloway, University of London, Egham, Surrey, TW20 0EX, UK (patrick.leman@rhul.ac.uk).

Carol Lynn Martin, School of Social and Family Dynamics, PO Box 873701, Arizona State University, Tempe, AZ 85287, USA (cmartin@asu.edu).

Dionna May, Brooklyn College, Experimental Program, 2900 Bedford Ave, New York, NY 11210, USA (mase1031@aol.com).

Andrew N. Meltzoff, Institute for Learning & Brain Sciences, 1715 Columbia Road N, Portage Bay Building, Box 357988, University of Washington, Seattle, WA 98195-7988, USA (meltzoff@u.washington.edu).

Christin R. Müller, Institute of Education, Berlin Institute of Technology (TUB), Marchstraße 23, 10587 Berlin, Germany.

Jan S. Pfetsch, Institute of Education, Berlin Institute of Technology (TUB), Marchstraße 23, 10587 Berlin, Germany (jan.pfetsch@tu-berlin.de).

Toni Schmader, Department of Psychology, 2136 West Mall, University of British Columbia, Vancouver, BC V6T 1Z4, Canada (tschmader@psych.ubc.ca).

Christine Schuette, Regent University School of Education, 1000 Regent University Drive, Virginia Beach, VA 23464, USA (cschuette@regent.edu).

Stefanie Sinno, Department of Psychology, Muhlenberg College, Allentown, PA 18104, USA (ssinno@muhlenberg.edu).

Harriet R. Tenenbaum, School of Psychology, University of Surrey, Guildford, Surrey, GU2 7XH, UK (h.tenenbaum@surrey.ac.uk).

Introduction

Patrick J. Leman and Harriet R. Tenenbaum

Throughout its history, a significant strand of psychological enquiry has sought to understand gender and its role in development. This focus may largely stem from the centrality of gender to many aspects of children's and adults' everyday lives; children are born into a world that is infused with gendered information, and as such, gender can provide a means of understanding the world and social relationships where little other information exists. Thus, the consideration or understanding of what it is to be a boy or a girl is often critical in forming social relationships, social identities, and learning how to think and behave. In fact, it is arguable that coming to understand one's own gender and to enact gender roles is a fundamental developmental achievement.

In this book we have brought together a set of contemporary contributions to this important strand of psychological research. Our objective is not just to compile contributions that constitute the best and most original current research in the area, but also to create possibilities for future work that will advance our understanding of developmental processes and help to begin to frame interventions and programmes to reduce or even eliminate gender inequality. So while this book has a clear intellectual focus, it also recognizes that this focus is most useful when it is applied to improve the quality of children's (and adults') lives. We hope that this book will not only open up new paths for research but, in time, also stimulate a new kind of emphasis for developmental psychologists who have always had an important contribution to help find solutions to social (or societal) problems.

Gender development in context

Gender development has always been a focus for psychological research. However, there is by no means consensus on what causes or promotes such development. This book will not provide any definitive resolution to theoretical debates about the influence of social, biological or cognitive processes. However, it will offer fresh perspectives on some old and new questions, and some new ways of thinking about the role and significance of gender in development. Clearly, a recent and emerging flavour to present research is a recognition that gender development happens in a variety of different contexts. Perhaps more importantly, we bring together researchers who are seeking to understand development in these contextual terms where the sorts of relationships that children encounter are considered vital for understanding development and growth. Of course, relationships are a complex matter. For a start, children typically form different types of relationships with men and women, peers and adults, parents and siblings, at school and at home. In this respect development is, at least in part, a matter of understanding that these are subtly different contexts that require different applications of gender knowledge. In some senses, understanding that gender involves basic categorical distinctions is the easy part; learning how these guide behaviour in different social situations is more complex, and learning that some of these gender rules or guidelines are associated with social inequality and even injustice, more complex still. Thus the development of gender knowledge, and the influence of gender on developmental process and social relationships, in many respects sets the stage for the myriad ways in which children will develop into competent social actors across a range of areas and domains of psychological life.

Of course, historically, research into gender and development has not always recognized the central importance of relationships and social context in the developmental process. Indeed, much early research focused on gender *differences* in ability and personality (see, for instance, Blakemore et al., 2009). Typically such differences (even if they were associated with very small effect sizes, see Hyde, 2005) were attributed to essential biological or social processes, or some combination of the two. While essentialist accounts are now widely regarded as simplistic, they persist in many widespread beliefs and often affect judgements and attributions for adults and children alike (e.g. Rangel & Keller, 2011). In this book, we see that essentialist beliefs may well underlie the judgements and behaviour of children in terms of their and their parents' beliefs about academic performance (e.g. Baron et al.; Tenenbaum & May), pro-social judgements (Hine & Leman), and family roles (Sinno et al.). In fact, even in areas where essentialist beliefs are being challenged the influence of such beliefs is arguably felt in participants' responses, justifications and interactions (see, for instance, contributions from DiDonato et al., Tenenbaum & May).

Cognitive psychology is often presented as a means of bridging the social and biological 'gap' in research. Broadly, information processing and gender schema accounts (e.g. Bem, 1981) are now dominant in the literature and there can be little objection to the assertion that their appeal lies largely as explaining development as, in part, an active process where the child's own judgement and understanding has a pivotal role in the developmental process. Thus such accounts are now dominant in the field, because they provide us with a way of understanding the intersection of social and biological processes while retaining a sense in which children themselves are active participants in their own gender knowledge and growth. Broadly, the chapters in this book articulate the socio-cognitive developmental processes that are involved in gender development in different domains. However, mapping the ways in which these divergent areas intersect is no small matter. Increasingly, researchers have recognized the complexity involved in children's understanding of their own gender group memberships and the consequences of this membership.

Nonetheless, advances in understanding developmental processes have been matched only by rather modest advances in the social arena. For example, women are still under-represented in science (and the higher echelons of other) careers. Male sportsmen still experience homophobia. When women do enter new fields, there is a feminization effect in which such a field becomes less valued. An important and distinctive feature of much new work is an emerging interest in understanding how gender influences the different paths that boys and girls may take in different domains: in school, the workplace and the home. With this new turn towards understanding 'gender development in context' comes a recognition that developmental psychologists need to consider the ways in which changes in knowledge, attitudes and reasoning come about through the actions of children themselves and the influence of the social contexts in which they are immersed.

Gender and social change

In several of the chapters in this book we see evidence that gender stereotypes and asymmetric gender attitudes are prevalent among young children and may well be the seeds for later gender differentiation (and disadvantage). For instance, Sinno et al.'s chapter in this book highlights how children pick up readily on different male and female roles and duties in the home. As we have seen, children make similar pre-judgements about careers and jobs at a young age. These early developmental origins may cast children's social attitudes into a particular mould that is hard to break in adolescence and adulthood. It is at first glance alarming that many of these attitudes and beliefs appear to have changed little over the past 40 years.

The chapters in this book are not only examples of the highest quality academic research. In common with many contemporary research contributions, underlying this empirical research is a recognition of the need for social change to bring about greater equality or equity in gender relations in society. To be sure, earlier generations of researchers have recognized this need. However, perhaps today we know more about the challenges and the complexity of working out what is to be done. Attitudes and stereotypes that are formed early are difficult to break and more resilient in the face of interventions to reverse them or limit their influence.

One important area where gender differences in performance (but not ability) are commonplace is education. The issue of the complexity of gender influences, and change, becomes very evident when considering research into the links between education, attainment and gender. For instance, during much of the twentieth century men and boys outperformed women and girls in most areas of education attainment. For some of this time, this gender difference could be attributed to differences in terms of access and opportunity: men were given an education, and women were often not or were denied the opportunities that men received. However, in the latter part of that century, patterns of educational attainment changed. In many Western countries girls began to outperform boys in school across subjects in both arts and social and natural sciences. It seems unlikely that such a change came about as a consequence of changes in essential gender differences (although some claim that changes in assessment methods may obscure differences in natural ability, e.g. Mellanby et al., 2000). It is curious that superior female performance at school is often attributed to girls' temperaments being more suited to formal education or 'school readiness' than boys, whereas explanations for differences often focused on natural ability when boys outperformed girls (Baron-Cohen, 2004; Masson et al., 2003).

There are a number of important further variations that explain why any reversal of gender differences in school attainment is not matched by equality higher up in the educational system or into work. For instance, men achieve proportionately more of the highest marks than girls at university (e.g. Leman, 2004) and particularly so in some subject areas. Moreover, the barriers to female access still exist in many careers, particularly sciences, where girls' superior performance at school is not followed by career success. The powerful influence of stereotypes (see Baron et al.'s chapter in this book) explains much of this, and these stereotypes affect not only academic performance but also choices. But other factors play their part too.

Social attitudes can also change to reinforce existing status asymmetries. For instance, that girls now typically often outperform boys at school may be seen as a sign of positive social change but might throw into question the basis for other stereotypes or undermine essentialist notions of difference between men and women. It also endangers a status quo of male superiority in educational attainment. These status asymmetries may be hard to break down. Walkerdine's (1986) identification of children's and teachers' descriptions of how success was a consequence of either 'natural male ability' or 'female hard work' in mathematics demonstrates neatly how accounts may change to accommodate a change in the empirical reality.

As we have seen, what children understand about gender, and when they understand it, is more than a matter of academic interest. Gender is also still a key source of inequality across societies. In the twenty-first century, girls and women are under-represented in science careers (science, technology, engineering and mathematics; STEM) (Greenfield et al., 2002; National Science Foundation, 2009), business (Catalyst, 2013) and in political representation throughout North America and Europe (Inter-Parliamentary Union, 2012). For example, women constitute only 18 per cent of the US Congress and 22 per cent of the UK Parliament.

One theme underlying the questions asked by the researchers in this volume is why equality appears so elusive. Several chapters in this book report research that seeks specifically to address issues of inequality. Other chapters address these issues less directly, and instead explore the development of behaviours or beliefs that create and sustain inequality. Both approaches allow us to learn more about how gender and development interrelate. By focusing on understanding this development we can begin to find ways to promote positive social change and psychological development.

Making the implicit, explicit

Why is lasting and profound change in our gender attitudes so difficult to achieve? Arguably, changes in women's and girls' achievement in education have occurred while underlying attitudes, beliefs and stereotypes about genders remain relatively unchanged. It is important to point out that broad changes in achievement are underpinned by sometimes very specific variations in achievement in different subject areas. For instance, girls' improving performance in mathematics relative to boys in some nations is not evident or is even in reverse elsewhere (Ben-Jacob et al., 2013). Charting achievement and changes in achievement is complex and, again, a matter of a diverse set of influencing factors that relate to underlying attitudes and beliefs about gender and gender differences. Yet in many instances changes in behaviour or performance of men and women are understood in ways that preserve existing essentialist beliefs. For instance, the long-standing stereotype that men (and boys) are superior in mathematical ability endures in spite of the evidence that, at least in some educational systems, girls outperform boys in school exams in the subject (see again Ben-Jacob et al., 2013).

A further reason why underlying attitude change may be difficult to achieve may relate to the distinction between explicit and implicit attitudes. While explicit attitudes may be challenged and their links to behaviour addressed more directly, implicit attitudes are by definition more difficult to detect. Moreover, implicit attitudes may be more automatic in terms of how they affect behaviour yet can be fundamentally important in framing interaction (Eagly & Karau, 2002). In the present book this distinction is (itself) addressed implicitly in several chapters: most notably, DiDonato and colleagues explore fine-grained features of children's interactions to demonstrate how gender is an important organizing determinant of synchrony between children in collaboration. However, elsewhere (e.g. Hine and Leman) we see the role of stereotypes or gendered beliefs that frame decision making and judgement. And the influence of implicit process pervades much research in to the role of stereotype threat.

One reason why gender stereotypes and gender differences may be so difficult to ignore lies in the developmental origins of children's understanding of gender. Some researchers (e.g. Gelman, 2004) have argued that children's gender and other beliefs are essentialist. While no studies in the present book directly address this distinction, the early acquisition of essentialist and implicit beliefs may well explain some of the characteristics of children's gender-linked judgements, belief and behaviour. Implicit beliefs may also be implicated in the effects of stereotypes on academic achievement (e.g. Baron et al.). By understanding more about these implicit processes we may be better able to target and make more effective interventions that are aimed at reducing inequality or prejudice associated with gender in the classroom.

Gender and the developmental process

In this book, we bring together the latest research to help frame the direction of work in the area into the future, but also extend research to tackle some old and some new social problems that are understood in terms of the development of gender knowledge, beliefs and inequality. The work reported covers many different fields. However, all chapters share a focus both on children's and adolescents' gender knowledge and on the significance of gender for development. In this respect, the work here views gender as an integral part of the developmental process. So by understanding gender we come to know much more, and more rich, information about psychological development. The status of gender as the key, binary social category (Duveen & Lloyd, 1992) has important implications for developmental and social psychological theories. From a developmental perspective, the ubiquity of information about gender in everyday life and interactions means that it is unsurprising that it is the first social category that children acquire.

Gender pervades children's social relationships. For instance, DiDonato et al.'s and Ittel et al.'s studies ably demonstrate how children can react to a peer's gender in often subtle ways, but with potentially far-reaching consequences. Adult–child (Tenenbaum and May) and sibling (Farkis and Leaper) relationships, also discussed in this book, are similarly infused with gender and messages about how to enact gender roles. If a key task for the child is not only to understand gender but also to operate as a gendered social actor, then the ways in which gender structures interactions and, in turn, relationships is something developmental researchers ought to be very concerned with. Indeed, throughout this book we see how that the enactment of gender structures children's relationships to influence who they become.

From such a sociocultural perspective (Rogoff, 1990), children's knowledge of how to enact gendered behaviour supports their active participation in daily activities whether it be discussions about science (DiDonato et al.) or conversations with parents (Tenenbaum and May). The particular ways of being in these daily events vary with the gender of the participants which is why gender adds to our understanding of development in sociocultural perspectives. Children need gender knowledge to be able to transform their participation in everyday situations.

Connectedness and independence

We do not wish to attempt a synthesis of research reported here. Rather, we wish to draw upon some themes that emerge across chapters in the anticipation that others will bring this process of synthesis and theoretical development themselves. Taken together the chapters in this book suggest that children's active participation with others contributes to the enactment of gendered ways of being. Enactment may be triggered in several ways; for example, by implicit understandings as the work of Baron et al. suggests. Through interacting with others, children appropriate ideas about gender. In conversations with parents (Tenenbaum and May), girls showed more connected speech than boys. Similarly, DiDonato and colleagues' chapter details how children engage differently with peers of different genders. Girl dyads showed greater coordination than did either mixed-gender or boy dyads. Girls learn to coordinate their interactions with other girls, but not with boys. This coordination may become stronger over time. Such differences in early interactional styles may contribute to girls' greater connection with others.

Through sibling interactions, children learn gendered messages. Indeed, Farkas and Leaper demonstrate that children with an older brother are more likely to become masculine-stereotyped than those with an older sister. However, girls are more likely to be similar to a male sibling than boys are to a female sibling. In general, then, we see a pattern for girls to be socialized towards connection and similarity in important relationships inside and outside the family. These studies raise an intriguing set of questions about how interaction dynamics map onto (or are a consequence of) the developmental process. More broadly, they point us towards considering what it is about socialization in different spheres of children's lives that seems to reinforce a message that girls need to be connected to different people, whereas boy do not (or need to do so less often and less intensely)?

Connection in and of itself may not be a negative thing. However, the work of Sinno et al. suggests that young adolescent girls are less likely to expect to work as are boys when they have a family. Girls may perceive themselves as needing to be closer to the family than do boys even at the age of ten. Moreover, children generally are more likely to judge it unfair for a father than a mother to have to take on 'second-shift parenting', that is, the burden of parenting responsibilities in addition to work. With greater connection comes a sense of responsibility for family, which may partially account for why children believe that mothers should engage in second-shift parenting more than should fathers. Perhaps because of these beliefs, mothers tend to do more 'labours of love' around the house, such as paying bills, remembering household chores and so on (Gershuny, 2008; Hall & MacDermid, 2009). Consider that these are not enjoyable activities related directly to the socialization of children. Nor do such activities confer high status. More importantly, many women will need to work to financially support their families. When girls do not plan for work, they may not pursue the educational prerequisites necessary for high-paying and flexible work.

The future of gender development

One important message from this book is that research into gender and development is alive and well! Another important message is that this research is still clearly needed because gender continues to define behaviours and shape opportunities available to boys and girls in restricting and unfair ways. Future research needs to help us understand why gender equality has proved so elusive and to devise interventions to decrease inequities. From family to school to society, women and men do not play equal roles. These differences begin early. Moreover, as suggested by Sinno and colleagues, children often endorse unequal roles for women and men from a young age. Unfortunately, these beliefs undermine equality in the family and in the workplace. In contrast, males are less likely to consider the need to balance family and work and may see their future role as breadwinner (Fulcher & Coyne, 2011).

Debate frequently occurs about women's right to work or to raise children. Our argument does not centre on whether these decisions are the only way for women to be happy. Instead, the argument is about whether what women decide to do is valued and that work, whether it be paid or unpaid, is equally shared with their partner. However simple such a proposal is we see in the popular presses a conservative backlash against equality, whether it be in the workplace or the home, as seen by the reaction to Sheryl Sandberg's (2013) *Lean In: Women, Work, and the Will to Lead*. As Sandberg argues, interests and passion need to be the deciding factor in women's and men's work- and family-related decisions rather than their gender. As research underscores, children whose fathers are involved in childcare have better outcomes than children whose fathers are not involved (Rohner & Veneziano, 2001; Yeung, 2004).

Everyday interactions may also contribute to the inequality in the shaping of the workforce rather than letting interests and passions decide. The work by Tenenbaum and May suggests that mothers continue to believe that science is a more appropriate cultural task for sons than for daughters. These messages are communicated to children in everyday interactions (Tenenbaum & Leaper, 2003), which then forms the underpinnings of children's implicit attitudes (Baron et al.). These implicit attitudes prevent girls from pursuing domains, such as mathematics. Without equal numbers of women and men pursuing these fields, only half of the potential applicants can contribute to the future of these domains.

Our hope is that this book will provide a route map for future researchers to begin to address some of these continuing issues. By exploring gender and development across domains we highlight not only what a pervasive force gender is in psychological development. We also highlight how addressing gender inequality can also be a means of promoting positive social and psychological growth.

References

Baron-Cohen, S. (2004). *The essential difference*. London, UK: Penguin Books.

Bem, S. L. (1981). Gender schema theory: a cognitive account of sex typing source. *Psychological Review, 88*, 354.

Ben-Jacob, E., Stoet, G. & Geary, D. C. (2013) Sex differences in mathematics and reading achievement are inversely related: within- and across-nation assessment of 10 years of PISA data. *PLoS ONE, 8*(3), e57988.

Blakemore, J. E. O., Berenbaum, S. A. & Liben, L. S. (2009). *Gender development*. New York: Taylor & Francis.

Catalyst (2013). Women CEOs of the Fortune 1000. Retrieved on 13 June 2013 from http://www.catalyst.org/knowledge/women-ceos-fortune-1000.

Duveen, G. & Lloyd, B. (1992). *Gender identities and education*. London: Harvester.

Eagly, A. H. & Karau, S. J. (2002) Role congruity theory of prejudice toward female leaders. *Psychological Review, 109*, 573–598.

Fulcher, M. & Coyne, E. F. (2011). Breadwinner and caregiver: a cross-sectional analysis of children's and emerging adults' visions of their future family roles. *British Journal of Developmental Psychology, 29*, 330–346.

Gelman, S. (2004). Psychological essentialism in children. *Trends in the Cognitive Sciences, 8*, 404–409.

Gershuny, J. (2008). Time-use studies: daily life and social change: full research report. ESRC End of Award Report, RES-000-23-0704-A. Swindon: ESRC.

Greenfield, S., Peters, J., Lane, N., Rees, T. & Samuels, G. (2002). A Report on women in science, engineering, and technology from the Baroness Greenfield CBE to the Secretary of State for Trade and Industry. http://extra.shu.ac.uk/nrc/section_2/publications/reports/R1182_SET_Fair_Report.pdf#search='set%20greenfield%20report'.

Hall, S. S. & MacDermid, S. M. (2009). A quantitative typology of dual-earner couples: unanswered questions about circumstance, motivations, and outcomes. *Journal of Family and Economic Issues, 30*, 215–225.

Hyde, J. S. (2005). The gender similarities hypothesis. *American Psychologist, 60*, 581–592.

Inter-Parliamentary Union. Women in National Parliaments (2012). http://www.ipu.org/wmn-e/world.htm.

Leman, P. J. (2004). And your specialist subject is . . . *The Psychologist, 17*(4), 196–198.

Masson, A. M., Cadot, M. & Ansseau, M. (2003). Failure effects and gender differences in perfectionism. *Encephale, 29*, 125–135.

Mellanby, J., Martin, M. A. & O'Doherty, J. (2000). The 'gender gap' in final examination results at Oxford University. *British Journal of Psychology, 91*, 377–390.

National Science Foundation, Division of Science Resources Statistics. (2009). Women, Minorities, and Persons with Disabilities in Science and Engineering. Retrieved on 2 June 2013 from http://www.nsf.gov/statistics/wmpd/.

Rangel, U. & Keller, J. (2011). Essentialism goes social: belief in social determinism as a component of psychological essentialism. *Journal of Personality and Social Psychology, 100*, 1056–1078.

Rogoff, B. (1990). *Apprenticeship in thinking: cognitive development in social context.* New York: Oxford University Press.

Rohner, R. P. & Veneziano, R. A. (2001). The importance of father love: history and contemporary evidence. *Review of General Psychology, 5*, 382–405.

Sandberg, S. (2013). *Lean in: women, work, and the will to lead.* New York: Random House.

Tenenbaum, H. & Leaper, C. (2003). Parent–child conversations about science: the socialization of gender inequities? *Developmental Psychology, 39*, 34–47.

Walkerdine, V. (1986). *Counting girls out: studies in mathematics education.* London: Virago.

Yeung, W. J. (2004). Fathers: an overlooked resource for children's school success. In Conley, D. & Albright, K. (Eds), *After the bell: solutions outside the school.* London: Routledge Press.

1 Gender in parent–child relationships

Harriet R. Tenenbaum and Dionna May

Parent–child relationships contribute to children's appropriation of gender-differentiated behaviours and future activities. When parents engage girls and boys differently, they provide children with gendered ways to act in social interactions. From a young age, children practise future gendered behaviours and activities with their parents. Children become more skilled and comfortable enacting behaviours that they frequently practice. For example, parents may encourage interactions involving interpersonal closeness more in daughters than sons, whereas they may engage sons more than daughters in interactions promoting autonomy (Leaper et al., 1998). Of course the exact behaviours children enact as appropriate for girls and boys differ based on the developmental stage of the children and do not exactly mirror the gendered behaviours enacted by adults (see Leman & Tenenbaum, 2011, for a review). Nonetheless, such practices likely make a substantial contribution to future gender differences in women's and men's everyday behaviours.

Engagement in such everyday interactions contributes to children's interpretation of complex messages about gender. Similar to many domains (Karmiloff-Smith, 1995), children's understanding of gendered behaviour is implicit at first. Through continued interactions with important others, children negotiate a more explicit understanding of gender. These beliefs about gender become incorporated into children's gender schemas (Berenbaum et al., 2008). However, children conform to gendered patterns before their understanding becomes explicit.

As emphasized by social-cognitive, sociocultural and eco-cultural theoretical frameworks, development occurs within children's daily lived experiences with important people. According to eco-cultural and sociocultural theories, children develop or are 'apprenticed' into activities appropriate for their cultural context (Rogoff, 2003). Parents prepare children to be successful based on their microsystem and the larger macrosystem (Ogbu, 1981). For example, parents raising children in inner-city neighbourhoods may teach children to be able to defend themselves; parents living a mile away in a more affluent neighbourhood may not teach such a skill. Of course, what may be deemed successful may well be different for girls and boys.

Generally speaking, most Western cultures expect girls and women to become affiliative and connected to others, whereas boys are expected to become assertive and autonomous (DiDonato et al., this volume; Fabes et al., 2003; Leaper & Smith, 2004). Not surprisingly, a comprehensive meta-analysis found that mothers were more affiliative with daughters than sons (Leaper et al., 1998). Mirroring this pattern, girls use more affiliative language than do boys with both parents and peers, whereas boys use more assertive language than do girls (Leaper & Smith, 2004). Moreover, girls tend to use more emotion words, a sign of connection and responsiveness, with peers than do boys (Tenenbaum et al., 2011). Thus, there is evidence in the literature that this expectation is upheld in children's everyday interactions with important others. What is unknown are some of the processes through which these expectations are communicated and enacted in parent–child interactions.

The present chapter examines two ways in which parents may contribute to children's future behaviours and activities. This first study is an interview study with parents of 11- and 13-year-old children to examine whether parents believe that girls and boys should pursue different academic domains. Parents' reasoning about whether their children should pursue science and foreign languages were examined. Science as a discipline tends to be viewed as orderly and rational, characteristics that are more masculine-stereotyped than feminine-stereotyped (Kahle, 1988; Sjøberg & Imsen, 1988). Moreover, in a comprehensive meta-analysis, Lytton and Romney (1991) found that parents encouraged gender-stereotyped activities in children. Whereas science is stereotyped as an important cultural task for men and boys (Kahle, 1988), emotions are stereotyped as appropriate for girls and women (Brody, 1985). The second study focuses on gender differences in how parents and children converse about interpersonal topics. Although these studies differ in their focus, they give wide insight into how parents' beliefs as well as parent–child talk may differ for girls and boys. These topics – science and interpersonal negotiation – are imbued with gendered connotations. Thus, we would expect that parents would encourage daughters and sons differently in these domains. Both studies contribute to a larger picture of how everyday interactions with parents give children opportunities for practising gendered behaviours and engaging in gendered activities. These studies, thus, highlight ways in which parents communicate their values about different activities to daughters and sons.

Study 1

As previously mentioned, parents may believe that science is a more appropriate endeavour for boys than for girls. Indeed, in the US, men are almost three times more likely to be employed in the science workforce than are women (National Science Foundation, 2004). Similarly, in the UK, more males than females study science and engineering (Smith, 2011). Moreover, scientists are viewed as logical, intelligent, determined and objective, traits stereotyped as masculine (Kahle, 1988). A combination of gender differences in laboural participation and gender stereotypes may influence parents to encourage sons more than daughters to pursue scientific interest.

Reflecting such gender differences, research suggests that parents hold gendered beliefs about children's competencies in mathematics and science.

Beginning in fourth grade, parents of sons rated their children as having more science ability than did parents of daughters (Andre et al., 1999). Additionally, parents also reported science as being more important for sons than daughters. This bias continues into the eighth grade with parents continuing to rate sons as better at science and more interested in science than daughters (Tenenbaum & Leaper, 2003).

Such beliefs may be implicit, but are frequently communicated in everyday conversations. Indeed, parents do not engage sons and daughters similarly in explanatory conversations about science. For example, while visiting science and technology exhibits in a children's museum parents explained to boys in 29 per cent of their interactions, whereas parents explained to girls in 9 per cent of their interactions (Crowley et al., 2001). This effect was more pronounced among fathers than among mothers. Contrary to the explanation that parents simply follow boys' greater interest in science, parents did not explain to boys more than girls because boys asked more questions. Before given an explanation, 15 per cent of boys and 13 per cent of girls asked a question. This difference was not statistically significant. Moreover, there was no difference in the degree of involvement girls and boys displayed at the exhibits as measured by approaching or manipulating the exhibit, or the amount of time children interacted with exhibits.

Additional support for differential parental socialization was found in two additional studies. Tenenbaum and colleagues (Tenenbaum & Leaper, 2003; Tenenbaum et al., 2005) found that parents are especially likely to explain science more to daughters than to sons whilst engaged in physical science. Indeed, fathers used more explanation when explaining a physical task to sons than to daughters, but used a similar amount when engaging in a biological science task (Tenenbaum & Leaper, 2003). Playing with magnets with their 5- and 9-year-old children, low-income mothers provided scientific explanations to sons more than to daughters; such talk was related to science literacy at age 11. Thus, it seems that parents engage sons more than daughters in everyday, informal science.

Another way that parents' beliefs are conveyed is through gender-differentiated encouragement of course selections. In parent–child conversations, parent–son dyads select more science and mathematics than foreign language courses (Tenenbaum, 2009). In contrast, parent–daughter dyads select more mathematics and language arts than science or foreign language courses. Generally speaking, compared to other courses, science courses have a different level of importance for parents of daughters and sons. Importantly, as Eccles (1994) argues, course selections need to be examined in context because decisions to pursue certain courses come at the expense of other courses.

The present study examined whether parents believed that daughters and sons should take different courses when reaching high school. In addition, through interviews, parents' reasoning was examined qualitatively. Science was selected as a domain which is masculine-stereotyped. As a comparison, foreign languages were selected because they tend to be feminine-stereotyped. It was expected that parents would be more likely to suggest science courses when discussing course choices for their sons than their daughters. Conversely, it was expected that parents would be more likely to suggest foreign language courses when discussing course selections for their daughters than their sons.

Method

Participants

CHILDREN

The sample consisted of mothers and fathers of 20 daughters ($M = 11$; 6 months, $SD = 1.40$) and 21 sons (11; 7 months, $SD = 1.39$). Families were recruited from schools, after-school activities, and summer camps from three metropolitan areas in the US (Boston, New York and San Francisco).

MOTHERS

Mothers ranged from 32 to 58 years ($M = 45.49$ years, $SD = 5.23$). The majority of mothers were of European-American descent. Mothers' education ranged from having completed the eleventh grade to professional school degrees.

FATHERS

Fathers ranged from 32 to 62 years ($M = 48.00$ years, $SD = 6.08$). The majority of fathers were of European-American descent. Fathers' educational background ranged from having completed high school to graduate and professional school.

Procedure

Two researchers visited families in their homes. Families were told that the researchers were interested in how 'parents contribute to children's course selections'. Mothers and fathers participated separately. Parents and children completed course selection forms and discussed them; these data have been reported elsewhere (Tenenbaum, 2009) and are not the focus of the present investigation. A subset of parents from the total sample was interviewed separately about their course selections. The questionnaires asked parents to report children's school grades. Letter grades were converted to a 12-point scale with an A scored as 12, an A- scored as 11, etc., ending with an F scored as a 0. In this repeated-measures design, the task was repeated for the other parent–child dyad during the same session. Children received a US$10 voucher to thank them for participation.

Transcription and coding

The interviews with parents were transcribed and verified. For the quantitative study, the question, 'were there any courses that you thought your child should take?' was coded. Parents' answers to the courses that children should take were coded as science (e.g. 'biology', 'physics', 'science'), foreign language (e.g. 'Spanish', 'French') or other (e.g. 'maths', 'design'). A second coder coded ten transcripts (12 per cent of the transcripts) and perfect reliability was achieved ($\kappa = 1.00$).

Results

Analysis plan

Quantitative and qualitative data are provided below. The qualitative data is provided to give a more developed sense of parents' reasoning. For the quantitative analyses, whether science or a foreign language was mentioned in each interview was coded as occurring or not because the data were highly skewed. Thus, if a parent offered three types of science courses that he or she wanted a child to take, it was coded as present. Parents were also asked if there were any courses that their children should not take. The answers to both these questions was analysed in the qualitative analysis to explain parents' reasoning about their course preferences for their children.

Preliminary analyses

Preliminary analyses indicated no gender differences in science marks, $F (1, 39) = 1.08, p = .38$.

Contrary to the hypothesis, fathers did not differentiate between sons and daughters when asked to make course selections (both $\chi^2 (1) < 1$). In fact, fourteen fathers of sons and fourteen fathers of daughters mentioned that their children should take science.

Similarly, mothers mentioned foreign languages for girls thirteen times and for boys twelve times. There was, however, a significant difference in the amount of times that science courses were mentioned for girls and boys. Mothers mentioned taking science courses for girls (twelve interactions) less frequently than for boys (nineteen times), Fisher exact test, $\chi^2 (1) = 5.16, p = .03$.

Using grounded theory (Glaser & Strauss, 1967), transcripts of the interviews were read over until key themes emerged. In the majority of cases, mothers simply did not mention science for their daughters. However, in the cases where they mentioned girls should not take science, mothers tended to use two key reasons why girls should not take science. The first one was that it would not be useful to them. An interview with a mother of an 11-year-old daughter illustrates this theme. When asked if there were courses her daughter should not take, she replied,

> Well I certainly thought about classes that I took that I never used like calculus. Or chemistry. There are some things that looking back on high school I thought what a waste of time so I guess is obvious as a parent if I've never used it in my lifetime why should this child have to go through it.

As can be seen in this example, the mother argues that higher-level mathematics and science will not be useful for her daughter's future.

The second theme to emerge was many mothers believed that daughters were not good at science. One mother noted, 'I didn't put any kind of science because she's not good at science so I don't think she'd grasp it later on.' Consider, however, that there were no gender differences in children's science marks.

Transcripts of interviews from mothers of sons were also read to look at mothers' reasoning. Three main themes emerged from these interviews. The first was that mothers believed that sons would find such classes fun or interesting. For example, a mother of an 11-year-old boy remarked, 'I think we added a couple of classes he seemed he would think they were fun if they were actually available. Like aviation I think would be a lot of fun for him, he checked that.'

Many mothers of boys also commented that they believed that science was part of basic courses or necessary for a broad education. One mother of a 12-year-boy responded, '[he should take] science and some writing or reading classes I mean I think the basic stuff he should take.' Similarly, a mother of a 10-year-old son added,

> I, I think um I mean I would at least like him to do uh you know to do a lab science course every year in high school but it might be that he would choose to um you know do one of the I mean everybody pretty much in his track would have to take it I mean he's taking biology next year and will probably take chemistry as a sophomore and physics as a junior so yeah I think I think you know I'd like to see him broadly educated even if that's not his thing.

The final reason was that mothers believed that science courses would be useful for their sons in the future. One mother responded to why her son should take science with 'because it could serve him well for in the future'. Another similarly replied, 'Um I think the kind of science he said he likes chemistry so I said fine because again you can if he were to like it he could also wind up doing something in the field so I said fine.'

Discussion

The present study found partial support for the hypothesis; as expected, mothers of daughters selected fewer science courses than did mothers of sons. However, mothers of sons and daughters were equally likely to select foreign language courses for daughters and sons. Moreover, fathers did not differentiate their children's course selections based on gender.

Through interviews, a more nuanced understanding of mothers' beliefs about children's science competencies was obtained. For daughters, mothers believed that science was not useful or, in a few cases, was too difficult for daughters. In contrast, mothers tended to report that science was a basic course for sons, or was fun, or useful. These underlying beliefs suggest mothers' interpretations of the importance of science may differ for girls and boys. The reasons that mothers provided give insight into how people may interpret the gendered division of labour in science. Moreover, if mothers communicate to sons that science is a basic course, sons may be more likely to pursue this option. Parents' beliefs may help explain why changing the numbers of women and men in science continues to be slow (National Science Foundation, 2004; Smith, 2011).

Eccles (1994) argues that children's decisions are based on self-perceptions. Children value those areas that are consistent with their self-image and gender roles. For example, if a child wishes to help others, she is more likely to want to enter professions that are consistent with this image (e.g. social worker) rather than enter an inconsistent occupation (e.g. computer programmer). This component is especially pertinent to how science may be perceived by students and especially girls. Given that much of the emphasis placed on girls to become more orientated toward others (Belenky et al., 1986; Cross & Markus, 1993), science may not be seen as fulfilling these goals. That the mothers thought that their sons would enjoy science suggests that the mothers perceive sons to enjoy doing something rational and orderly, as science is perceived (Kahle, 1988). Through encouraging children to pursue different academic domains, mothers create opportunities for sons and daughters to develop skills important for their future gendered selves.

Another way that parents may help children to develop different competencies and behaviours would be the opportunities that they provide children on a daily basis. As mentioned, girls are traditionally expected to become supportive and connected, whereas boys are expected to become autonomous and assertive (Cross & Markus, 1993). If parents were to engage children differently during everyday conversations, they would provide their children ways of enacting these gender behaviours. The next study examined whether parents engage preadolescent girls and boys differently in conversations about socio-emotional content. Given that connectedness is considered important for girls to achieve, it was expected that parents would engage daughters with more connected types of talk than they would with their sons. Conversely, parents would be expected to encourage autonomy in sons to help them become orderly and rational.

Study 2

Achieving autonomy as well as retaining a sense of connectedness remain important developmental tasks of adolescence (Grotevant & Cooper, 1985). Parents' encouragement of autonomy as well as connectedness is related to their adolescents' exploration (Grotevant & Cooper, 1985), ego development (Allen et al., 1994), school grades (Grolnick & Ryan, 1989) and educational decisions (Tenenbaum et al., 2006). Despite the importance of autonomy and connectedness for adolescents, there is evidence that parents encourage autonomy more in sons than daughters and connectedness more in daughters than sons (Leaper & Friedman, 2007). The present study had two primary aims. The first aim was to examine whether conversational patterns about an interpersonal negotiation situation varied with child and parent gender and whether the previous findings of gender differences in interpersonal negotiation skills (INS) would extend to parent–child dyads. The second aim was to determine whether these kinds of conversational patterns are related to adolescents' INS.

Gender differences have been found in solving dilemmas, with girls better able to negotiate a solution than boys (Selman et al., 1986). Gender differences in interpersonal skills may stem from differences in peer structure between girls and boys. Whereas boys are likely to cluster in large groups, girls tend to group themselves in dyads (Benenson et al., 1998). Dyadic groupings may provide more opportunities to resolve interpersonal conflicts (Leaper, 1994).

Conversations in this study were focused on an interpersonal task involving a peer and parent dilemma. Socio-emotional skills are more stereotyped as feminine than masculine (Brody, 1985). Moreover, being able to solve such problems whilst remaining connected to important others would be considered an important task for daughters. Parents might model as well as involve girls and boys in different types of conversations based on gender. More specifically, we would expect fathers to model autonomy more than mothers and we would expect mothers to model connectedness more than fathers. Finally, we would expect parents to remain more connected to daughters than to sons, and more separate from sons than daughters.

Findings from past research have provided some support for gender differences in the types of speech mothers and fathers model. For example, Grotevant and Cooper (1985) found that fathers used more relevant speech, indirect suggestions, and answers to requests for information, all of which were classified as connectedness than did mothers. Fathers also used more requests for action, classified as separateness, than did mothers. In contrast, mothers used more compliance, classified as forms of connectedness, than did fathers. In accordance with Grotevant and Cooper (1985), a comprehensive meta-analysis revealed that fathers tend to be more directive than mothers (Leaper et al., 1998). Unfortunately, however, there were too few studies including fathers to examine whether fathers as well as mothers talk differently to sons and daughters in the Leaper et al. (1998) meta-analysis. Importantly, in a comprehensive narrative review, Siegal (1987) argues that fathers are more likely than mothers to treat daughters and sons differently. Moreover, parents might speak differently to sons and daughters while solving an interpersonal dilemma, a task more feminine than masculine-stereotyped.

Given that prior research has suggested that parents view girls more than boys as nurturing and better able to negotiate peer relationships (Leaper, 1994), parents may believe that daughters will be more skilled at an interpersonal negotiation task than sons. In the Leaper et al. (1998) meta-analysis, mothers of daughters used more supportive speech with their children than did mothers of sons. Fagot (1998) found that mothers use more directives and instructions when speaking with their daughters than with their sons. Directives may limit the child's active problem solving abilities (Leaper, 2002).

When examining parent–child conversations, parent gender effects take place within a dyadic context. Thus, differences in children's behaviours need to be considered as well. When young children interact with their parents, children are more assertive than mothers, but less assertive than their fathers (Leaper, 2000). Thus, children may seek more autonomy when interacting with mothers than with fathers. Differences have also been discovered in the conversational patterns of boys and girls with girls found to be slightly more talkative than boys (Leaper & Smith, 2004). Given these findings, we expected that girls would build more on parents' remarks than would boys.

In this study, four types of conversational talk were designed around autonomy and connectedness in making decisions about an interpersonal negotiation task (Selman, 1981). Connectedness speech acts included two types of talk that would facilitate a mutuality of the relationship, i.e. agreement and building on others' ideas. In contrast, autonomy speech acts included talk that would encourage independence, i.e. disagreement and requesting information from the other person.

In sum, this study examined how mothers and fathers solve interpersonal dilemmas with their early adolescent sons and daughters. It also assessed the degree to which the types of talk varied with child and parent gender. Moreover, this study examined which types of talk would most successfully facilitate children's interpersonal negotiation strategies. Thus, this study examined four hypotheses and one research question: first, based on Grotevant and Cooper (1985) and Leaper et al. (1998), whereas mothers were expected to use more connected talk than were fathers (positive reinforcements), fathers were expected to use more autonomy talk than would mothers (question-asking behaviours). Second, it was hypothesized that parents would use more connected talk with daughters than with sons and more autonomy talk with sons than with daughters according to the findings of Leaper et al. (1998). Third, because girls tend to have better interpersonal negotiating skills (Selman et al., 1986) and are slightly more talkative than boys (Leaper & Smith, 2004), daughters were expected to use more connected talk than would sons, and sons were expected to use more autonomy talk than would daughters. Fourth, based on the findings of Selman et al. (1986), parent–daughter dyads were hypothesized to score higher on dilemmas than would parent–son dyads. Finally, parents' talk was explored as related to the level of interpersonal skill achieved by the parent–child dyad.

Method

Participants

CHILDREN

There were 25 girls (*M* age = 12.5 years, *SD* = 11.85 months) and 25 boys (*M* age = 12.4 years, *SD* = 10.19 months) in the sixth and eighth grades (sixth grade: *M* age = 11.8 years, *SD* = 7.8 months; eighth grade: *M* age = 13.1 years, *SD* = 6.18 months) and their mothers and fathers. Families lived in the San Francisco and central coast areas of California. Families were recruited from public schools, summer camps, and after-school activities. There was no significant age difference between girls and boys in either age group, $F(1, 48) < 1$.

PARENTS

The mean age of mothers was 43.1 years (*SD* = 4.8), ranging from 32 to 53 years. The majority of mothers identified themselves as European-American (83 per cent) and the remaining identified themselves as Latina or Asian descent. The mean age of fathers was 46 years (*SD* = 4.8), and their ages ranged from 34 to 59 years. Seventy-five per cent of fathers identified themselves as European-American; the rest identified themselves as Latino, Asian, or African American descent.

Procedure

Two researchers visited families in their homes and explained to participants that the researchers were interested in how 'parents contribute to children's learning in everyday situations'. Following a full description of the study and informed consent procedures, parent participants provided written informed consent and children/adolescent participants provided verbal assent. Families were then told that they would be asked to complete four tasks. Three tasks involved science activities and were not used in the present study. The fourth task was the interpersonal dilemma, which was used for this study. For more information about the tasks and other questionnaires administered that were not used as part of the current study, see Tenenbaum and Leaper (2003). Mothers and fathers were visited separately, with the order of the parent visits counterbalanced.

INTERPERSONAL REASONING TASKS

Participants received a set of cards with printed dilemmas and questions. Parents and children read two different interpersonal dilemmas, which were adapted from Selman et al. (1986). Each set of two dilemmas included a conflict between the main character and an authority figure. For example:

> The main character is Patty. Patty is looking forward to recess because she and her friends are going to practise for the school competition in soccer. They have a game later in the week. During class, Patty's teacher suggests that Patty stay in at recess to get help in her math. Patty is behind in math and there is a test later in the week.

The second dilemma in each set concerned a conflict between peers, such as:

> The main character is Mary. Mary and Sue are friends. They have been assigned to work together on a science project in school and only have two days to finish the project. They meet after school and Mary says she wants to start working on the project right away, but Sue wants to play softball first.

The names of the characters in the stories matched the gender of the child participant. Whether peer or adult conflicts went first was counterbalanced across participants. Parents and children then answered a series of five questions after reading the dilemmas. Specifically, these five questions included: 1) 'What is the problem here and why is that a problem?', 2) 'How does the main character feel and why?', 3) 'What can the main character do to solve this problem?', 4) 'What could go wrong with this solution?', and 5) 'How would the main character know if the problem had been resolved?'

All videotapes were transcribed verbatim. Only the first ten minutes of the conversations were transcribed. The majority of the conversations were less than ten minutes. The transcripts were then coded for supportive measures used by parents as well as question asking behaviours in both parents and children. Mutually exclusive codes were assigned to each utterance.

Coding

Transcripts were coded for connectedness codes, which included building and agreement. Building codes were assigned for any follow-up statements after an initial answer. These statements gave support to the previous answer by adding additional thoughts (e.g. 'The main character could also feel confused.'). Codes of agreement were given when interlocutors agreed with the preceding statement (e.g. 'Right.', 'Yeah.', or 'That was a good idea.'). Transcripts were also coded for two autonomy codes. Codes of disagreement were given when participants disagreed with the previous statement (e.g. 'I don't think that would solve the problem.' or 'No, that's not what the question is asking.'). Questions that were generated by the participants themselves were given a code of curiosity questions. These questions allowed the participants to think about the dilemmas in new ways. For example, 'What would you do if you were in that situation?' or 'Do you think there is another way to handle the problem?' The number of times each participant used each code was tallied.

INS

To gain a sense of the dyad's reasoning strategies the coder first read through the entire dilemma. Using a scoring sheet adapted from the interpersonal negotiation strategies interview manual (Schultz, Yeates, & Selman, 1989), a score was then given to how the participants answered each question. The parent–child dyad was given the highest score used to answer the specific question. Because the parents and children discussed the stories together and were not independent, each dyad received a score for each of the dilemmas by computing the mean of their answers to the five questions. According to Schultz et al. (1989), a level of 0 relies on physical action to achieve one's aims or no understanding. More specifically, in relation to the first question, a level of 0 for the first question was coded when the problem was not understood or not understood beyond what the character would do (e.g. 'It's none of the teacher's business.'). A level of 1 focused on one of the participants having their needs met. For example, the dyad might say, 'Because Mary may not like that.' A level of 2 relied upon trying to meet both participants' needs separately. A dyad who replied, 'It's a problem for Mary because she'll get worried about the project, and it's a problem for Sue because she may need to unwind first' would receive a score of 2. Finally, a level of 3 focused on collaborating for mutual goals. For example, a dyad replying, 'Yeah, I think they're in conflict about how to accomplish their task. What works for one of them doesn't seem to be appropriate for the other character' captures the mutuality of the conflict and would receive a 3.

Reliability

Reliability for speech codes was reached by the first and third authors coding 20 of the 100 transcripts. A mean kappa coefficient of .73 was obtained. Disagreements were resolved through discussion and the second author coded the remainder of the transcripts.

For the moral dilemmas the first author and a research assistant individually coded twenty-six transcripts (26 per cent of the transcripts). Kappa coefficients were used in order to calculate the reliability statistics, with individual kappa coefficients being: question 1, $\kappa = .68$; question 2, $\kappa = .78$; question 3, $\kappa = .79$; question 4, $\kappa = .70$; and question 5, $\kappa = .75$, all of which reflect good agreement (Cohen, 1988). After reliability was achieved the remaining transcripts were coded by the first author.

Results

Descriptive statistics

Means and standard deviations were calculated for each coding variable. The means of selected variables are presented in Table 1.1. Mother–child scores on

Table 1.1 Speech code means and standard deviations

	Talk				
	Build	*Agree*	*Curiosity*	*Disagree*	*Direction*
	Mothers				
With daughters	14.9 (10.4)	12.4 (9.3)	7.5 (6.9)	.52 (1.2)	1.4 (1.7)
With sons	12.1 (7.2)	7.2 (4.4)	11.9 (13.3)	1.3 (1.8)	1.6 (2.1)
	Fathers				
With daughters	16.0 (10.8)	8.9 (6.4)	9.8 (6.7)	.48 (.91)	1.6 (1.5)
With sons	13.0 (7.4)	7.2 (5.7)	6.4 (6.5)	1.1 (1.4)	1.6 (1.8)
	Daughters				
With mothers	12.8 (9.7)	7.2 (5.2)	1.2 (1.8)	.88 (1.9)	.96 (1.2)
With fathers	16.1 (12.4)	8.2 (6.4)	1.0 (1.7)	.56 (1.0)	1.2 (2.2)
	Sons				
With mothers	10.9 (7.9)	7.7 (6.4)	.48 (.92)	1.1 (1.4)	.52 (.71)
With fathers	8.6 (5.5)	6.8 (5.3)	.48 (.71)	.64 (1.1)	.80 (1.2)

Note. Standard deviations appear in parentheses.

Table 1.2 Mean dilemma scores by dilemma type, parent gender and child gender

	Sixth grade	
	Peer	*Adult*
	Mothers	
Daughters	1.61 (.43)	1.44 (.26)
Sons	1.73 (.42)	1.38 (.38)
	Fathers	
Daughters	1.91 (.44)	1.45 (.33)
Sons	1.63 (.45)	1.33 (.40)

Note. Standard deviations appear in parentheses.

the peer dilemmas were significantly correlated with scores on the adult dilemma, r (48) = .39, p = .01. In contrast, father–child scores on the peer and adult dilemmas were not correlated, r (48) = .14. Table 1.2 presents mean scores by child gender and parent gender.

Parents' talk

CONNECTEDNESS MEASURES

Separate repeated measures analysis of variance (ANOVAs) were conducted for the two connectedness speech variables (i.e. building and agreement). Child gender was a between participants factor and parent gender was a repeated participants factor. There were no significant findings in building behaviours. There were no differences in the agreement behaviour of mothers and fathers, F (1, 48) = 2.85, p = .10 or parent gender × child interaction effects, F (1, 48) = 2.72, p = .11. However, both mothers and fathers used more agreement terms with daughters than they did with their sons, F (1, 48) = 4.71, p = .035, partial η^2 = .09.

AUTONOMY MEASURES

Separate repeated measures ANOVAs were conducted for the two autonomy speech variables (i.e. disagreement and questions). Child gender was a between participants factor and parent gender was a repeated participants factor. There were no differences in the disagreement behaviour between mothers and fathers, F (1, 48) < 1 nor was there a significant parent gender × child interaction effect, F (1, 48) < 1. However, parents used significantly more disagreement terms with their sons than daughters, F (1, 48) = 5.25, p = .026, partial η^2 = .09.

With regards to curiosity questions, there were no differences in the behaviour of mothers and fathers, F (1, 48) = 1.16, p = .28, or toward sons and daughters, F (1, 48) < 1. There was, however, a significant parent gender × child gender interaction effect, F (1, 48) = 5.25, p = .026, partial η^2 = .12. Mothers were more likely to ask their sons curiosity questions than were fathers, F (1, 24) = 5.37, p = .029, partial η^2 = .18. When looking at daughters, there were no differences in the amount of curiosity questions asked by the mothers and the fathers, F (1, 24) = 1.49, p = .23.

Children's talk

CONNECTEDNESS MEASURES

There were differences in building behaviours between boys and girls, with girls building more than boys, F (1, 48) = 4.58, p = .038, partial η^2 = .09. There were no differences in whether children were more likely to use building with mothers or fathers, F (1, 48) < 1. There was a marginally significant parent gender × child interaction effect, F (1, 48) = 3.91, p = .05, partial η^2 = .08, but no significant effects from the follow-up tests. There were no differences in the agreement behaviours between daughters and sons either on their own or with mothers and fathers.

AUTONOMY MEASURES

There were no significant parent gender effects, F (1, 48) <1, or parent gender × child interaction effects, F (1, 48) <1. There was a marginally significant child gender interaction effect, F (1, 48) = 3.86, p = .06, partial η^2 = .07, with daughters more likely to ask questions than were sons. Finally, there were no significant findings for children's disagreements.

Gender effects on INS scores

To test whether daughters scored higher on INS dilemmas than sons, a 2 (mother, father) × 2 (peer dilemma, adult dilemma) × 2 (son, daughter) mixed-design ANOVA was conducted on the mean of the parent–child moral dilemma score. Parent gender and type of dilemma were repeated participant factors while child gender was between participant factors. There was a main effect of type of dilemma, F (1, 48) = 43.75, p = .0001, η^2 = .49. Scores were higher on peer (M = 1.74, SD = .31) than on adult (M = 1.40, SD = .28) dilemmas. The main effects of parent gender, F (1, 48) = 1.25, p = .27 and child gender, F (1, 48) < 1 were non-significant as were all two-way interactions and the three-way interaction effect.

RELATIONS BETWEEN SCORES AND CORRELATIONS

Correlations were conducted between parents' speech codes and the scores the dyads received on the dilemmas. The more that fathers agreed, the higher the scores on the peer dilemma, r (48) = .36, p = .01. Similarly, the more that fathers questioned, the higher the scores on the peer dilemma, r (48) = .34, p = .01. No other relations were significant.

Discussion

The present study found that child–parent dyads received higher INS scores when discussing conflicts about peers than about adults. Contrary to the hypothesis, there was no effect of child gender on children's scores on INS. As expected, parents used more autonomy-type speech codes with sons, and more supportive speech codes with daughters. Finally, fathers' use of agreement and questions was related to the dyad's higher INS scores.

As hypothesized, gender differences in parents' talk were found with parents using more supportive codes (i.e. agreement) with daughters than sons and using more autonomous speech (i.e. disagreement) with sons than with daughters. Both autonomy and support are necessary as children negotiate the transition into adolescence (Allen et al., 1994). Emotional support may help children develop socio-emotional skills. Emotionally enabling speech contributes to the development of children's self-esteem and ego development (Allen et al., 1994). Autonomous decision making also may contribute to children's academic decisions. Achieving some measure of independence is a critical task facing adolescents (Grotevant & Cooper, 1985).

As expected, daughters supplied more supplementary solutions to the dilemmas (connected speech). It is possible that girls felt more comfortable in completing the task and were happier and more eager to participate (Selman et al., 1986). However, we did not find that sons asked more questions than did daughters.

The expected gender difference in INS scores was not found. Some research has been more equivocal. Smetana et al. (1991) did not find gender differences in children's reasoning about interpersonal conflicts. One limitation of the present study is the small sample size. Work with a larger sample could examine whether the lack of a gender difference in parent–child dyads is attributable to a small sample. However, the effect size associated with the dyad's scores suggests that gender effects, even if apparent, would be negligible in parent–child dyads.

Finally, fathers' but not mothers' speech was found to be related to the score that the dyad received on the INS dilemma. Specifically, fathers' use of questions and agreement predicted higher scores. Questions have been linked to increased conceptual development (Sigel et al., 1991) because they force the responder to distance himself or herself from the situation. Moreover, that both autonomy and supportiveness were both related to higher reasoning reinforces the view that autonomy and supportiveness both contribute to development.

The different types of speech may also contribute to different developmental trajectories for children. For instance, daughters are more connected traditionally to the family than are sons (Fagot, 1995). Perhaps the greater use of supportive speech contributes to connection within the family. Future research should examine whether there are relations between parents' supportive speech and children's reported connectedness.

The current study focused on answers deemed to provide support and autonomy. Future studies may consider the content of answers that are given by both parents and children as well as who controlled the conversation. Parents who used more controlling speech during a homework task had children who produced less creative answers to homework problems, were less socially competent, and had more depressive symptoms (Grolnick et al., 2002; McDowell et al., 2003). Future work should examine longitudinal relations between parents' talk and children's future INS.

The findings of this study, in sum, indicate that parents engage daughters and sons differently when engaging in interpersonal tasks. Parents tended to agree more with daughters than with sons, whereas they disagreed more with sons than with daughters. Although these patterns are not the same patterns one might find in adult conversations, they mirror expected cultural stereotypes. When talking with peers, girls tend to be more supportive than are boys (Leaper & Smith, 2004). By agreeing with daughters, parents are engaging daughters more than sons in conversations that are supportive. Such conversations become part of daughters' conversational repertoire and become crystallized.

General discussion

These studies both indicate that parents may provide different opportunities for children to learn gender-typed skills and competencies. In a comprehensive meta-analysis, Lytton and Romney (1991) reported that parents encouraged gender appropriate activities for their children. Another meta-analysis of gender differences in speech found that mothers used more affiliative speech with daughters than with sons (Leaper et al., 1998). Activities as well as conversations constitute means through which children may learn about their parents' expectations.

In two very different contexts, parents encouraged daughters and sons very differently. When discussing future science options, mothers were more encouraging of sons than of daughters. Interestingly, science is considered an orderly and rational domain (Kahle, 1988) with a stereotyped image of a lone scientist who works individually. When discussing interpersonal dilemmas, parents used more connected speech with daughters and more autonomous speech with sons. In two different contexts involving different domains, sons are being given messages that suggest autonomy is valued.

Parent–child interactions need to be considered as both a reflection of societal practices and a contributor to future practices. For instance, the macrosystem of a gender disparity in science participation (National Science Foundation, 2004) may influence the microsystem of parent–child interactions as seen in parents' beliefs about children's competencies, the types of conversations parents may hold with children, and the specific activities that parents encourage children to pursue. Parent–child interactions then contribute to future gender disparities (or not) in the macrosystem. In other words, parent–child interactions cannot be separated from the cultural context in which they take place.

Of course many of parents' beliefs and expectations are not expressed explicitly. Indeed, parents may not be fully aware of their beliefs and attitudes about gender. However, there is a relation between parents' and children's gender beliefs (Tenenbaum & Leaper, 2003). It is through everyday interactions, such as those examined in this chapter, that enable children to appropriate cultural messages about gender.

References

Allen, J. P., Hauser, S. T., Bell, K. L., & O'Connor, T. G. (1994). Longitudinal assessment of autonomy and relatedness in adolescent–family interactions as predictions of adolescent ego development and self-esteem. *Child Development, 65*, 179–194.

Andre, T., Whigham, M., Hendrickson, A., & Chambers, S. (1999). Competency beliefs, positive affect, and gender stereotypes of elementary students and their parents about science versus other school subjects. *Journal of Research in Science Teaching, 36*, 719–747.

Belenky, M. F., Clinchy, B. M., Goldberger, N. R., & Tarule, J. M. (1986). *Women's ways of knowing: the development of self, voice, and mind.* New York: Basic Books, Inc.

Benenson, J., Apostoleris, N., & Parnass, J. (1998). The organization of children's same-sex peer relationships. In Bukowski, W. M., & Cillessen, A. H. (Eds) & Damon, W. (Series Ed.), *New directions for child development: vol. 80. Sociometry then and now: building on six decades of measuring children's experiences with the peer group* (pp. 5–23). San Francisco, CA: Jossey-Bass.

Berenbaum, S. A., Martin, C. L., & Ruble, D. N. (2008). Gender development. In Damon, W. & Lerner, R. (Eds), *Advanced child and adolescent development* (pp. 647–696). New York: Wiley.

Brody, L. R. (1985). Gender differences in emotional development: A review of theories and research. *Journal of Personality, 53*, 102–131.

Cohen, J. (1988). *Statistical power analysis for the behavioral sciences* (2nd ed.). Hillsdale, NJ: Lawrence Erlbaum Associates.

Cross, S. E., & Markus, H. R. (1993). Gender in thought, belief, and action: a cognitive approach. In Beall, A. E. & Sternberg, R. J. (Eds), *The psychology of gender* (pp. 55–98). New York: Guilford Press.

Crowley, K., Callanan, M. A., Tenenbaum, H. R., & Allen, E. (2001). Parents explain more often to boys than to girls during shared scientific thinking. *Psychological Science, 12*, 258–261.

Eccles, J. S. (1994). Understanding women's educational and occupational choices: applying the Eccles et al. model of achievement-related choices. *Psychology of Women Quarterly, 18*, 585–609.

Fabes, R. A., Martin, C. L., & Hanish, L. D. (2003). Young children's play qualities in same-, other-, and mixed-sex peer groups. *Child Development, 74*, 921–932.

Fagot, B. I. (1995). Parenting boys and girls. In Bornstein, M. H. (Ed.), *Handbook of parenting* (Vol. 1) (pp. 91–118). Mahwah, NJ: Lawrence Erlbaum Associates.

Fagot, B. I. (1998). Social problem solving: effect of context and parent sex. *International Journal of Behavioral Development, 22*, 389–401.

Glaser, B. G., & Strauss, A. L. (1967). *The discovery of grounded theory: strategies for qualitative research.* Chicago, IL: Aldine Publishing Company.

Grolnick, W. S., & Ryan, R. M. (1989). Parent styles associated with children's self-regulation and competence in school. *Journal of Educational Psychology, 81*, 143–154.

Grolnick, W. S., Gurland, S. T., & DeCourcey, W. (2002). Antecedents and consequences of mothers' autonomy support: an experimental investigation. *Developmental Psychology, 38*, 143–155.

Grotevant, H., & Cooper, C. (1985). Patterns of interaction in family relationships and the development of identity exploration in adolescence. *Child Development, 56*, 415–428.

Kahle, J. B. (1988). Gender and science education II. In Fenshem, P. (Ed.), *Development and dilemmas in science education* (pp. 249–266). London: Falmer Press.

Karmiloff-Smith, A. (1995). *Beyond modularity: a developmental perspective on cognitive science.* Cambridge, MA: MIT Press.

Leaper, C. (1994). Consequences of gender segregation on social relationships. In Leaper, C. (Ed.) & Damon, W. (Series Ed.), *New directions for child development: vol. 65. Childhood gender segregation: causes and consequences* (pp. 67–86). San Francisco, CA: Jossey-Bass.

Leaper, C. (2000). Gender, affiliation, assertion, and the interactive context of parent-child play. *Developmental Psychology, 36*, 381–393.

Leaper, C. (2002). Parenting girls and boys. In Bornstein, M. H. (Ed.), *Handbook of parenting, volume 1: children and parenting* (2nd ed.) (pp. 189–225). Mahwah, NJ: Lawrence Erlbaum.

Leaper, C., & Friedman, C.K. (2007). The socialization of gender. In J. Grusec & P. Hastings (Eds), *Handbook of socialization: Theory and research* (pp. 561–587). New York: Guilford.

Leaper, C., & Smith, T. (2004). A meta-analytic review of gender variations in children's language use: talkativeness, affiliative speech and assertive speech. *Developmental Psychology, 40*, 993–1027.

Leaper, C., Anderson, K. J., & Sanders, P. (1998). Moderators of gender effects on parents' talk to their children: a meta-analysis. *Developmental Psychology, 34*, 3–27.

Leman, P. J., & Tenenbaum, H. R. (2011). Practising gender: children's relationships and the development of gendered behaviour and beliefs. *British Journal of Developmental Psychology, 29*, 153–157.

Lytton, H., & Romney, D. M. (1991). Parents' differential socialization of boys and girls: a meta-analysis. *Psychological Bulletin, 109*, 267–296.

McDowell, D. J., Parke, R. D., & Wang, S. J. (2003). Differences between mothers' and fathers' advice-giving style and content: relations with social competence and psychological functioning in middle childhood. *Merrill-Palmer Quarterly, 49*, 55–76.

National Science Foundation. (2004). *Women, minorities, and persons with disabilities in science and engineering: 2004.* Arlington, VA: Author. Retrieved on 30 December 2004 from http://www.nsf.gov/sbe/srs/wmpd/start.htm.

Ogbu, J. U. (1981). Origins of human competence: a cultural-ecological perspective. *Child Development, 52*(2), 413–429. doi:10.2307/1129158

Rogoff, B. (2003). *The cultural nature of human development.* New York: Oxford University Press.

Schultz, L. H., Yeates, K. O., & Selman, R. L. (1989). *The interpersonal negotiation strategies interview manual.* Unpublished coding manual, Harvard University.

Selman, R. (1981). The development of interpersonal competence: the role of understanding in conduct. *Developmental Review, 1*, 401–422.

Selman, R. L., Beardslee, W., Schultz, L. H., Krupa, M., & Podorefsky, D. (1986). Assessing adolescent interpersonal negotiation strategies: toward the integration of structural and functional models. *Developmental Psychology, 22*, 450–459.

Siegal, M. (1987). Are sons and daughters treated more differently by fathers than by mothers? *Developmental Review, 7*, 183–209.

Sigel, I. E., Stinson, E. T., & Flaugher, J. (1991). Socialization of representational competence in the family. In Okagaki, L. & Sternberg, R. J. (Eds), *Directors of development* (pp. 121–141). Hillsdale, NJ: Lawrence Earlbaum Associates.

Sjøberg, S., & Imsen, G. (1988). Gender and science education I. In Fenshem, P. (Ed.), *Development and dilemmas in science education* (pp. 218–248). London: Falmer Press.

Smetana, J. G., Killen, M., & Turiel, E. (1991). Children's reasoning about interpersonal and moral conflicts. *Child Development, 62*, 629–644.

Smith, E. (2011). Women into science and engineering? Gendered participation in higher education STEM subjects. *British Educational Research Journal, 37*, 993–1014.

Tenenbaum, H. R. (2009). 'You'd be good at that': gender patterns in parent-child talk about courses. *Social Development, 18*, 447–463.

Tenenbaum, H. R., & Leaper, C. (2003). Parent–child conversations about science: socialization of gender inequities. *Developmental Psychology, 39*, 34–47.

Tenenbaum, H. R., Ford, S., & Alkhedairy, B. (2011). Telling stories: gender differences in peers' emotion talk and communication style. *British Journal of Developmental Psychology, 29*, 707–721.

Tenenbaum, H. R., Porche, M. V., Snow, C. E., Tabors, P., & Ross, S. (2007). Maternal and child predictors of low-income children's educational attainment, *Journal of Applied Developmental Psychology, 28*, 227–238.

Tenenbaum, H. R., Snow, C. E., Roach, K., & Kurland, B. (2005). Talking and reading science: longitudinal data on sex differences in mother-child conversations in low-income families. *Journal of Applied Developmental Psychology, 26*, 1–19.

2 Gendered interactions and their consequences

A dynamical perspective

Matthew D. DiDonato, Carol Lynn Martin and Dawn England

Throughout the lifespan, females and males prefer the company of same-sex peers (Maccoby, 1990, 1998; Mehta & Strough, 2009, 2010). Thus, boys and girls are thought to be socialized within separate cultures, where girls learn how to behave and interact from other girls, and boys from other boys (Leaper, 1994; Maccoby, 1998). A consequence of this gender segregation is the magnification of differences in the characteristics of boys' and girls' social interactions (Maccoby, 1990). Boys are exposed to and learn about being assertive, forceful and competitive, whereas girls are exposed to and learn about being affiliative, relational and obliging (Fabes et al., 2003; Leaper & Smith, 2004).

Gender segregation and same-sex affiliation become self-fulfilling strategies. As the styles of one's own gender group are learned, it becomes easier to spend time with same-sex peers and progressively more difficult to engage in interactions with members of the other sex – a repeating cycle of segregation. Based on existing theory and research (e.g. Leaper, 1994; Maccoby, 1998; Martin & Fabes, 2001), we recently proposed a heuristic model to guide the conceptualization of gender segregation and its perpetuation over time, called the Gender Segregation Cycle (GSC; Martin et al., 2012). In this transactional model, time spent with same-sex peers contributes to increased gender-stereotypic thinking, to fewer positive and more negative attitudes toward other-sex peers, and to decreased feelings of efficacy about relating to other-gender peers. The cycle is perpetuated as these outcomes then facilitate more gender segregation as children seek out same-sex interaction partners and avoid other-sex peers. By discouraging other-sex interactions, GSC processes limit exactly the sorts of behaviours known to improve intergroup relationships as demonstrated by a wide variety of studies on the importance of promoting positive relationships through intergroup contact (Pettigrew, 1998; Pettigrew & Tropp, 2006).

Because the GSC magnifies differences in socialization histories and limits intergroup contact, one would expect to find that boys and girls often have difficulty in their interactions with each other. Prior research substantiates this hypothesis. When interacting with other-sex peers, children and adolescents often communicate poorly and experience poor performance in collaborative activities (Harskamp et al., 2008; Holmes-Lonergan, 2003; Leaper & Smith, 2004; Leman et al., 2005; Underwood et al., 2000). These findings highlight the importance of discovering why boys and girls suffer challenges in mixed-sex interactions and determining what can be done to alleviate them.

Most studies examining same- and mixed-sex interactions have focused on aggregate measures to characterize behaviour. However, research is beginning to show that behaviour may be variable, even across relatively short time periods, and that behavioural variability is related to important social and behavioural outcomes (DiDonato et al., 2012; Martin et al., 2005; Martin & Ruble, 2009). For example, when measured many times daily throughout a semester, preschool children's peer and activity play varies considerably in its degree of gender typing. At one measurement occasion a girl may play dress up with a group of female peers, and at the next she may throw a ball with a boy. DiDonato and colleagues (2012) found that when a girl adapted her gendered behaviour over time, that is, she altered her behaviour to suit her changing individual predispositions (e.g. fondness for particular peers and toys) and environmental characteristics (e.g. which toys and peers were available for play), she also reported positive psychological adjustment. Alternatively, random behaviour was related to poor adjustment.

Such variability raises several questions for social and developmental scientists: What does such variability mean? Does it carry information about development or behaviour? If so, how might that variability be quantified? Unfortunately, conventional statistical procedures are unable to reach the heart of these questions. Dynamical systems techniques, however, highlight variability as the prime indicator of behaviour and change. Thus, we advocate taking a dynamical approach to studying boys' and girls' same- and mixed-sex social interactions.

In this chapter, we first outline the early socialization histories of young children, highlighting the development of sex segregation, how it leads to divergence in boys' and girls' socialization experiences, and the difficulties that girls and boys experience when working together. We then propose a new approach to conducting research on mixed-sex interactions that focuses on methodological and analytical techniques from dynamical systems theory. As an illustration, we provide a detailed example of a study of young adolescents involved in either mixed-sex or same-sex interactions as they engage in a cooperative task. Finally, we conclude with a discussion of our findings, their implications for improving the quality of mixed-sex interactions, and how dynamics can advance the study of peer social relationships in the future.

Gendered social interactions: early socialization histories and mixed-sex interactions

As early as age three, girls and boys begin to show preferences for interacting with same-sex peers (LaFreniere et al., 1984; Maccoby & Jacklin, 1987; Serbin et al., 1994). In preschool and early childhood, these patterns become well-established and even strengthen, such that children spend much more of their time in social interactions in same-sex than in other-sex or mixed-sex groups (Maccoby & Jacklin, 1987; Martin & Fabes, 2001). Interest in other-sex peers increases in early adolescence, but the time spent with same-sex peers remains high (Mehta & Strough, 2010; Vaughn, 2001).

A consequence of this sex segregation is that differences in the styles of interaction between boys and girls become magnified over time. For example, male and female preschoolers who spend more time with same-sex peers during the fall term of preschool show more sex-typed behaviour and interaction patterns in the spring (Martin & Fabes, 2001). As same-sex peer play increased, girls more frequently played near adults, and boys became more aggressive, engaged in more rough-and-tumble play, and played less frequently near adults. This 'social dosage' effect suggests that same-sex peers effectively socialize children into the norms, styles and behaviours associated with their own gender group and that this occurs more for children who spend more time in these groups (Martin et al., 2012).

The GSC reflects the tendency of interactions with same-sex peers to lead to a variety of sex-differentiated outcomes, which then have the potential to negatively influence mixed-sex interactions. Gender segregated playgroups allow children many opportunities to directly communicate group norms, to learn through modelling, and to practise the skills and behaviours typical of their own gender group while reducing many opportunities to learn to communicate effectively with other-sex children. Problems may arise when girls and boys come together to work or learn, as members of each sex have practised a different set of interaction skills with their peers. Preschool children use more negative and controlling verbal and non-verbal behaviour when working in mixed-sex dyads compared to same-sex dyads (Holmes-Lonergan, 2003; Leaper & Smith, 2004; Leman et al., 2005), and school-age children working in mixed-sex pairs cooperate less than those working in same-sex dyads, even when explicitly instructed to do so (Underwood et al., 1994). Girls also forfeit more resources when working unsupervised with boys, though this effect was neutralized when an adult instructed the children to cooperate (Powlishta & Maccoby, 1990). Although some studies show that difficulties in mixed-sex interactions disappear in older children (e.g. approximately 9 years old; Leman & Björnberg, 2010), others show that older students in mixed-sex dyads perform more poorly on cooperative academic tasks and exhibit a less balanced interactive style (e.g. females in mixed-sex dyads asked more questions and offered less directions) than those working in same-sex dyads (Harskamp et al., 2008) and have lower levels of verbal interaction and cooperative sharing behaviours (Underwood et al., 2000).

The dynamics of peer interactions

Much of the research on peer interactions has been aimed at examining aggregate levels of behaviour. For example, researchers interested in peer affiliation may tally or average the number of affiliative behaviours for each interaction partner. Much has been learned from research conducted from within this framework. However, some research, most of it conducted outside the field of peer interactions, shows that behavioural variability characterizes many important interaction processes (see Hollenstein 2011 for a brief review; also Dale & Spivey, 2006; Gorman et al., & Cooke, 2010; Marsh et al., 2006, 2009; Richardson et al., 2007; Schmidt et al., 1990; Shockley et al., 2003). For example, studies of postural sway show that people are not perfectly stationary when standing, but sway slightly around their centre of mass. This displacement can be measured over time and plotted as a time series, the values of which often display considerable variability. When two people interact, the patterns of variability in their postural sway become more similar over time, that is, they start swaying together (Shockley et al., 2003). Thus, variability in postural sway can be studied to examine behavioural coordination in interacting individuals. Dynamical systems theory provides a toolkit for quantifying and interpreting such behavioural variability. Much like correlations and *t*-tests can be used to characterize different aspects of psychological phenomena (i.e. relations between variables and mean differences, respectively), dynamics allows researchers to examine aspects of peer interactions related to temporal variation rather than aggregate behaviour. We believe that something may be learned from studying variability in peer interactions and that dynamics can provide the tools necessary to do so.

A dynamic system is a system of elements that changes over time (Thelen & Smith, 2006). A boy and a girl working together to solve a maths problem or a group of children on a playground each comprise a system. As their interactions become coordinated, global patterns of behaviour emerge, such as successful problem solving or forming a game of tag. These interactions evolve over time in response to changing circumstances, generating new forms of behaviour. If several children leave the game of tag, those that remain may form a new game more suitable for fewer players. The dynamics of the system are ever changing and reorganizing to form novel patterns of behaviour.

Many studies show that dynamical systems theory is a useful paradigm from which to examine dyad- and group-level social interaction. Researchers have most commonly studied interpersonal coordination, or how well interaction partners organize their disparate individual interaction styles into a harmonious interpersonal exchange. Studies show that such harmony is evident when interaction partners' behaviour becomes more similar over time. For example, two adults who are interacting while sitting in separate rocking chairs will eventually match rocking frequency, moving back and forth at the same time, even without being expressly told to do so (Marsh et al., 2009; Richardson et al., 2007). Other behaviours that converge over time include aspects of verbal communication such as speaking rate, intensity and activity (McGarva & Warner, 2003; Natale, 1975), pausing frequency (Cappella & Planalp, 1981), accent (Giles, Coupland, & Coupland, 1991), and syntactic usage (Dale & Spivey, 2006), non-verbal communication such as postural sway (Shockley et al., 2003) and leg swinging (Schmidt et al., 1990), and even biological processes such as heart rate variability (Watanabe et al., 1996). This convergence reflects behavioural coordination. Such coordination facilitates a smooth exchange of information (Watanabe et al., 1996), and greater coordination is related to greater reported rapport, camaraderie and comfort between interaction partners (Chartrand & Jeffries,

2003; Lakin & Chartrand, 2003; Marsh et al., 2009; Matarazzo et al., 1968; Richardson et al., 2007).

Importantly, interactions need not be equal or symmetric to display coordination. For example, expert–novice interactions may still be harmonious despite the fact that one partner is clearly more knowledgeable or assumes a leadership position more than the other. In fact, some research shows that interactions between unequal partners are characterized by more coordination than those between equal partners (Schmidt et al., 1994). Thus, as long as interaction partners are similar in their interaction styles, coordination should be evident regardless of the distribution of knowledge or power in the relationship. However, because prior research shows that boys and girls exhibit markedly different interaction styles, we expect that they will have difficulty achieving and maintaining coordination.

Given that dynamics has been successfully applied to the study of interpersonal coordination, we believe that it may also be useful for the study of gendered social interactions. To illustrate, we next provide a detailed example of a dynamical study of young adolescents involved in either mixed-sex or same-sex interactions.

Exploring coordination in dyads using dynamics

Prior work shows that boys and girls often experience difficulty in their interactions with each other. Research applying dynamics to the study of interpersonal coordination suggests that this may be due to a lack of coordination. Similarity or disparity in communication style may serve to facilitate or hinder coordination between interaction partners. For example, when two individuals sit in rocking chairs that are of the same size, they easily coordinate their rocking frequency, even without being expressly instructed to do so. If the rocking chairs differ dramatically in size, however, coordination of rocking frequency becomes difficult to achieve and maintain (for a similar example see Richardson et al., 2007). The same pattern may also describe same- and mixed-sex interactions. In a same-sex interaction, the partners may be 'rocking in chairs of the same size'. They communicate in similar ways and thus find it easy to establish and sustain coordination. Alternatively, when boys and girls work together they may find that the ways in which they communicate are different enough that it is difficult for them to establish much rapport. Coordination is not achieved, or perhaps only minimally, which may adversely affect their interactive experience.

We used dynamical methods and analyses to investigate gendered interpersonal coordination in pairs of young adolescents. Potential differences in coordination were assessed across dyad types (i.e. same-sex versus mixed-sex), and, like previous work (Chartrand & Jeffries, 2003; Lakin & Chartrand, 2003; Marsh et al., 2006, 2009; Matarazzo et al., 1968; Richardson et al., 2007), the relation of coordination to participants' perceptions of their interaction partner was examined. Fifth-grade boys and girls were paired with an unfamiliar same- or other-sex peer with whom they completed an academic exercise. Pairing adolescents with an unfamiliar peer enabled us to examine the formation of interaction patterns characteristic of each dyad instead of pre-existing styles participants may have had with an established peer.

Participants' vocalizations were recorded during the exercise, from which numerous repeated measures were extracted to create a time series of vocal activity for each adolescent. Speech is essential to many cooperative activities, especially those in which two or more people aim to achieve a common goal, as verbal communication fosters interpersonal coordination (Clark, 1996; Shockley et al., 2003). In addition, the length and patterning of utterances has been shown to be a good marker of interpersonal coordination (Matarazzo et al., 1968; McGarva & Warner, 2003; Street et al., 1983). For example, interaction styles may at first be disparate, where one interaction partner speaks quickly with few pauses whereas the other speaks slowly with long pauses. However, the interaction partners may after a time change their interaction patterns to accommodate their partner, thus increasing coordination.

Following the exercise, the adolescents were asked to report how much they liked working with their partner. As in other research (Chartrand & Jeffries, 2003; Lakin & Chartrand, 2003; Marsh et al., 2006, 2009; Richardson et al., 2007), this measure served to establish interpersonal coordination as a marker of rapport and harmony between interaction partners. Identifying it as such is the first step to distinguishing interpersonal coordination as an indicator of the success or failure of peer interactions and to determining how it may be influenced to improve mixed-sex interactions.

Overall, we expected to find a positive relation between coordination and positive perceptions of one's interaction partner. Because of the collaborative difficulties adolescents often experience when working with other-sex partners (Harskamp et al., 2008; Underwood et al., 2000), we also anticipated differences in coordination and partner liking between same-sex and mixed-sex dyads, with adolescents in same-sex dyads experiencing greater coordination and reporting more partner liking than those in mixed-sex dyads. Furthermore, we hypothesized that coordination would mediate the differences in partner liking across dyad types. That is, we expected the greater coordination of same-sex dyads to account for the dyad differences in partner liking.

Method

Data for the present analysis were part of a larger study of young adolescents' same- and mixed-sex dyadic interactions within a science-based academic setting, with the goal of determining peer interaction processes related to girls' interest and motivation for science. Interaction partners were asked to collaborate on a series of chemistry-based science tasks in which they constructed molecules using pieces from an organic chemistry molecule model building set. The molecule building pieces were small coloured spheres and connectors representing atoms and bonds, respectively, and a two-dimensional diagram to use as a guide to build the molecule. A total of ten molecules were assembled. A chemistry task was chosen because chemistry is a field in which women are particularly underrepresented compared to men (National Science Foundation, 2008), and because the successful completion of each molecule requires spatial reasoning, typically a skill of male proficiency (Ceci et al., 2009).

The participants for the study were fifth-grade students (*M* age = 11.11 years, *SD* = .45 years) recruited from public and charter elementary schools in the Phoenix metropolitan area of Arizona. Adolescents included in the present study were those with an available interaction partner (adolescents whose interaction partner was absent completed a subset of the pre- and post-interaction measures and were paired with a member of the research team for the exercise; these data were not used in the present study) and with complete audio data (technical difficulties during data collection led to the loss of audio data for some dyads). The final sample consisted of 64 same-sex (33 girl–girl, 31 boy–boy) and 33 mixed-sex dyads, resulting in a total of 194 participants (51 per cent girls). The majority of the sample consisted of Non-Hispanic White adolescents (67 per cent), with the remainder Hispanic (10 per cent), Asian American (6 per cent), Black (3 per cent), Native American (2 per cent), Pacific Islander (1 per cent), or Other (11 per cent). The families of most participants (70 per cent) reported a total income of US$60,000 or more.

To arrange dyads, participating adolescents were paired with an unfamiliar same- or other-sex peer (i.e. a peer from a different school) with whom they collaborated on the chemistry exercise. The exercise was conducted in a laboratory equipped with a table and two chairs. The adolescents were instructed to sit in the chairs, facing each other across the table. Each dyad member was asked to wear a headset microphone, used to record his or her vocalizations during the interaction.

To facilitate a naturalistic interaction between dyad members, the exercise was designed to progress with as little experimenter intervention as possible. Thus, before beginning, the rules of the exercise were thoroughly explained. The adolescents were each provided with ten folders, one per molecule, each containing half of the pieces required to build a molecule (to encourage collaboration between the dyad members). Adolescents were instructed to acquire the appropriate folder, use the pieces within to complete the molecule, and dispose of their materials and move on to the next molecule after completion.

After the exercise, the participants completed an eight-item measure of their experience with their partner (α = .82). Rated on a 7-point scale (1 = *not at all*; 7 = *a lot*), sample items included 'Would you like to work with the same kid again on similar tasks?' 'Overall, how much did you like your partner?' and 'How often did your partner listen to you?' Higher scores indicated a more positive interaction experience.

Dynamical analysis of dyadic peer interactions

Our goal was to dynamically analyse the adolescent's speech patterns to quantify coordination in dyadic interactions. To do this, we first collected data on each adolescent's vocalizations in the form of a time series. Adolescents' vocalizations were recorded through headset microphones onto a laptop computer equipped with an audio recording software package (Cubase LE4). Each participant's vocalizations were recorded independently, but in synchrony, into separate.wav files. Time series were generated by sampling each participant's .wav file four times per second (McGarva & Warner, 2003), where at each sampling a '1' was recorded if the adolescent spoke and a '0' if he or she did not (Warlaumont et al., 2010). This resulted in a dichotomous time series of 0s and 1s spanning the length of the interaction for each adolescent.

Because verbal communication is important for coordination (Clark, 1996; Shockley et al., 2003), and previous work shows that interaction partners coordinate various vocal characteristics (Matarazzo et al., 1968; McGarva & Warner, 2003; Street et al., 1983), we focused on adolescent's speech (the 1s), not silence (0s), for the dynamical analyses. To do this, we transformed the 0s in one adolescent's time series (within each dyad) into 2s. Thus, one adolescents' time series was composed of 0s and 1s, whereas the other's series was composed of 1s and 2s. The significance of this transformation for the analysis is described below.

Dyadic coordination of the adolescent's speech patterns was assessed with Cross Recurrence Quantification Analysis (CRQ; conducted with the Matlab CRP Toolbox (Marwan & Kurths, 2002)), a dynamical technique used for examining shared or recurrent behaviour between two systems (Zbilut et al., 1998). CRQ was employed because recurrent behaviour between two systems is indicative of coordination (Dale & Spivey, 2006; Shockley, 2005). CRQ involves plotting the time series of one adolescent along the horizontal axis and the other along the vertical axis, which generates a visual representation of the shared structure between the two time series, called a recurrence plot. The filled dots in Figure 2.1 illustrate how a recurrence plot is created. Because the only values that can recur between the time series are 1s (i.e. 1s are the only values that exist in both time series), a point is plotted within the recurrence plot at each point where both time series have a '1' (i.e. when each adolescent is speaking). Starting with the first '1' (i.e. the first instance of speech) in the time series on the horizontal axis, a point is plotted wherever the second time series also has a '1'. This process is continued for each value of '1' in the horizontal time series. Thus, behaviour across two series can recur contemporaneously or at different points in time. The adolescents may express similar vocal characteristics at approximately the same time, or a vocal pattern expressed by one adolescent early in the interaction may be repeated by the other adolescent several times throughout the entire interaction. Completed recurrence plots are shown in Figure 2.2.

In practice, CRQ is not typically conducted with raw time series, such as those in the preceding example, but with series that are reconstructed in the appropriate dimensional space.[1] Imagine looking at a group of football players on a field. When viewing them from a standing position, or a one-dimensional perspective, the players appear to be relatively close together (Figure 2.3A); however, if you instead take an aerial view, observing the field from a two-dimensional perspective, the players appear to be spread out (Figure 2.3B). The one-dimensional perspective distorted the available information, making the players seem close together when in reality they were not. The same is true for a time series. If projected in a dimension that is too low, information may be distorted and the time series may not be accurately represented. By projecting a time series into higher

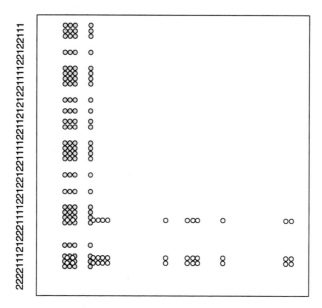

Figure 2.1 An incomplete recurrence plot, shown to illustrate how a recurrence plot
is created. The filled dots represent a recurrence plot with an embedding
dimension of 1, and the open dots represent a recurrence plot with an
embedding dimension of 2.

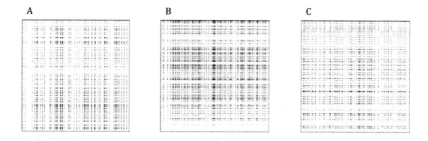

Figure 2.2 Examples of cross-recurrence plots. Cross-recurrence plots illustrate a boy–
boy dyad (Panel A), a girl–girl dyad (Panel B), and a mixed-sex dyad
(Panel C). Dark regions signify areas of recurrence or coordination between
dyad members. A greater number of points on the plot (i.e. the darker the
plot) the greater the coordination.

dimensions, one can eliminate distortions due to lower-dimensional projection
and perform a CRQ on the reconstructed series. Recurrent points are those that
have similar values in reconstructed space.

A.   B.

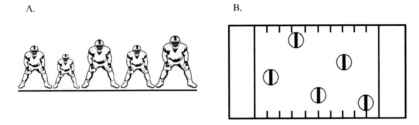

Figure 2.3 An illustration of one- (Panel A) and two- (Panel B) dimensional projection
on a football field

The appropriate embedding dimension is chosen with a false nearest neighbours' analysis. Consider Figure 2.3A again. When viewed in one dimension,
the two football players on the right appear to be neighbours, that is, they are
close together; however, when viewed in two dimensions (Figure 2.3B) they are
not. Thus, they were false neighbours; when viewed in a higher dimension they
are no longer close together. A false nearest neighbours' analysis calculates the
percentage of points in a time series (or two time series) that are false neighbours.
The appropriate embedding dimension is one in which the percentage of false
neighbours is zero (typically the percentage of false neighbours in subsequent
dimensions is also zero; thus, the lowest dimension is chosen). In the present
study, the percentage of false nearest neighbours reached zero at an embedding
dimension of two.

For CRQ with categorical data, such as those in the present study, the chosen
embedding dimension dictates how many values must be consecutively recurrent
across two time series to merit plotting a point on the recurrence plot. An example
is illustrated in Figure 2.1 with the horizontally ordered open dots. Because we
chose an embedding dimension of two, two consecutive 1s must be present in
both series for a point to be plotted. Starting with the first '11' on the time series
on the vertical axis, a point is plotted wherever the horizontal time series also has
'11'. This process is continued for each value of '11' in the horizontal time series.
The recurrence plots in Figure 2.2 were generated with an embedding dimension
of two.

A variety of measures can be calculated from a recurrence plot to assess various characteristics of systems under consideration. We calculated per cent recurrence (%REC), which is the ratio of the number of recurrent points on the plot
relative to the total number of possible recurrent points. For example, plotting two
500-point time series generates a recurrence plot with 250,000 potential points of
recurrence. If 2500 of those points are recurrent, %REC equals 1 per cent, which
indicates that for 1 per cent of the interaction the adolescents coordinated their
vocal communication patterns. %REC has been found to reflect behavioural similarity or coordination in dyadic interactions in previous research (Dale & Spivey,
2006; Shockley, 2005), and was used in the present study to examine differences
in coordination in adolescent dyads.

Results

Four hypotheses were tested in the present study: (a) adolescents in same-sex dyads would report more positive partner perceptions than those in mixed-sex dyads; (b) adolescents working in same-sex dyads would exhibit greater coordination than those in mixed-sex dyads; (c) coordination would positively predict partner perceptions; and (d) coordination would mediate differences across dyad types in levels of partner perceptions.

Means and standard deviations for coordination (%REC) and partner perceptions are presented in Table 2.1 separately by dyad type. Coordination was a dyad-level variable; thus, the mean and standard deviation were calculated across girl–girl, boy–boy, and girl–boy dyads. Partner perceptions were individual-level variables, and their respective descriptive statistics were calculated within dyad type.

Because adolescents' partner perceptions were measured at the individual level, but are nested within dyads (i.e. boy–boy, girl–girl or girl–boy), multi-level modeling (MLM) procedures were employed to address the first hypothesis. Using SAS 9.3, the following model was estimated to examine differences between adolescents in same- and mixed-sex dyads in their partner perceptions:

Level 1: $partner\ perception_{ij} = \beta_{0j} + r_{ij}$ $\qquad$ (1)

Level 2: $\beta_{0j} = \gamma_{00} + \gamma_{01}(boy\text{–}boy\ dyad) + \gamma_{02}(girl\text{–}girl\ dyad) + u_{0j}$ $\qquad$ (2)

Dyad type (boy–boy, girl–girl, girl–boy) was dummy coded, with mixed-sex dyads as the reference group. Thus, γ_{01} and γ_{02} compared all-boy and all-girl dyads, respectively, to mixed-sex dyads on their mean levels of partner perceptions. Significant positive coefficients for γ_{01} and γ_{02} would show that boys and girls in same-sex dyads reported greater partner perceptions than those in mixed-sex dyads. Consistent with our hypothesis, adolescents who worked in boy–boy ($\gamma_{01} = .33$, $p < .05$) and girl–girl dyads ($\gamma_{02} = .79$, $p < .01$) reported liking their partner more than boys and girls in mixed-sex dyads.

To address the second hypothesis, a multiple regression analysis was conducted to examine differences between same- and mixed-sex dyads in levels of coordination. Because both dyad type and coordination are group-level variables,

Table 2.1 Descriptive statistics for study 1 variables

Measure (absolute range; actual range)	Boy–boy dyads (n = 62)		Girl–girl dyads (n = 66)		Girl–boy dyads (n = 66)	
	M	SD	M	SD	M	SD
Coordination (%REC) (0 – 100%; .07 – 28.33%)	6.86	5.99	10.38	5.95	7.38	4.94
Partner perceptions (1 – 7; 3.63 – 7)	6.09	.74	6.56	.54	5.77	.93

Note. %REC is a measure of coordination. A value of 10 per cent indicates that the adolescents' vocal patterns were coordinated for 10 per cent of the interaction.

a MLM was not required. Again, dyad type was dummy coded, with mixed-sex dyads as the reference group. A significant positive regression coefficient would show that boy–boy or girl–girl dyads exhibited greater coordination than adolescents in mixed-sex dyads. The results partially supported our hypothesis. Adolescents in girl–girl dyads were better coordinated than those in mixed-sex dyads ($\beta = .25$, $p < .05$), but there were no differences between boy–boy and girl–boy dyads ($\beta = -.04$, *ns*).

Examining the third hypothesis necessitated the prediction of an individual-level variable from a group-level variable. Thus, a second MLM was estimated to examine the prediction of adolescents' partner perceptions from their dyadic coordination:

Level 1: *partner perception*$_{ij} = \beta_{0j} + r_{ij}$ (3)
Level 2: $\beta_{0j} = \gamma_{00} + \gamma_{01}$*(coordination)* $+ u_{0j}$ (4)

where γ_{01} estimated the effect of coordination on partner perceptions. The results confirmed our hypothesis ($\gamma_{01} = .03$, $p < .01$), showing that a 1 per cent increase in coordination predicted a .03-unit increase in adolescent-reported liking of their interaction partner.

A final MLM was estimated to examine the fourth hypothesis, that coordination would mediate the dyad-level differences in partner perceptions:

Level 1: *partner perception*$_{ij} = \beta_{0j} + r_{ij}$ (5)
Level 2: $\beta_{0j} = \gamma_{00} + \gamma_{01}$*(boy–boy dyad)* $+ \gamma_{02}$*(girl–girl dyad)* $+$ (6)
γ_{03}*(coordination)* $+ u_{0j}$

A significant mediating effect would show that differences in partner preferences between same- and mixed-sex dyads is at least partly due to dyad differences in coordination. Mediation was estimated by calculating the product of the effect of coordination on partner perceptions (γ_{03} in Equation 6) and the effect of dyad type (boy–boy or girl–girl) on coordination (estimated in the regression analysis; Sobel, 1982). Contrary to our hypotheses, the results showed that coordination was not a significant mediator of the differences in partner perceptions between mixed-sex and girl–girl ($z = 1.44$, $p = .15$) or boy–boy dyads ($z = .37$, $p = .71$).

Discussion

Scientists studying psychology or human relationships frequently apply dynamics to the study of dyadic social interaction and find that coordination predicts important outcomes related to interactive success or failure (Gorman et al., 2010; Richardson et. al., 2007). Many studying gender, however, have not yet embraced dynamics as a perspective or tool with which gendered social interactions can be examined. Here, we explored the potential of using this approach. By employing methodological and analytical techniques from dynamical systems theory, we captured young adolescents' dyadic coordination and examined it in relation to the self-reported quality of their interactions.

Although applying dynamics to the study of interpersonal coordination is not new in psychological research (e.g. Dale & Spivey, 2006; Schmidt et al., 1990; Shockley, 2005), the present study is the first to use dynamics to examine gendered social interactions. We measured coordination in young adolescents' interaction patterns using CRQ, with the goal of exploring differences in coordination between same-sex and mixed-sex dyads and examining the relation of that coordination to their post-interaction partner perceptions. The results suggest that CRQ is a useful method for assessing coordination. Many methodological challenges have arisen in assessing and defining coordination (Scholz & Kelso, 1990; Zanone & Kelso, 1997). For example, one issue involves the measurement of coordination, with many of the earlier studies relying on observers' reports of coordinated interactions (i.e. perceived synchrony) between members of a dyad. Some advances have been made to improve detection of coordination using raters, but this approach has difficulties defining the specific qualities that raters apply (e.g. Bernieri et al., 1988). CRQ is useful in that it does not require a reporter to observe and rate the quality of interactions, and instead uses precisely defined measures of coordination.

Previous research examining the characteristics of same- and mixed-sex interactions has shown that boys and girls often experience more difficulty working with each other than with same-sex peers. When working with a member of the other sex, children and young adolescents act more controlling and are less cooperative (Holmes-Lonergan, 2003; Leaper & Smith, 2004; Leman et al., 2005), more frequently disagree over resources (Powlishta & Maccoby, 1990), and struggle more on academic tasks (Harskamp et al., 2008; Underwood et al., 2000). Thus, in the present study, we expected boys and girls in same-sex dyads to report more positive partner perceptions than those working in mixed-sex dyads. The results confirmed our hypothesis. Boys and girls in same-sex dyads reported liking their partner more than those working with a member of the other sex.

Because previous work has shown that same-sex interactions are more harmonious than mixed-sex exchanges, we expected to find that all-boy and all-girl dyads would exhibit greater coordination than mixed-sex dyads. Our hypothesis was partially supported. Girl–girl dyads showed greater coordination than mixed-sex dyads; however, boy–boy dyads were not found to differ from girl–boy dyads.

The sex difference in patterns raises many interesting questions. Are girls simply more coordinated than boys? Or, are they more coordinated in a specific domain? For example, a significant difference for all-girl but not all-boy dyads may have resulted because patterns of vocal coordination better characterize social coordination in girls than in boys. Studies show that girls have a slight advantage in verbal ability compared to boys throughout childhood and adolescence (see studies cited in Hyde & Linn, 1988), that girls speak more than boys during social interactions (see studies cited in Leaper & Smith, 2004), and that girls' play more often involves discourse in small groups than does boys' play (Blatchford et al., 2003). Alternatively, boys' coordination may revolve more around non-verbal communication. Boys are generally more active than girls (Eaton & Enns, 1986; Ridgers et al., 2005) and their play often revolves more around physical activities, such as a game of baseball or tag, than verbal exchange (Blatchford et al., 2003; Ridgers et al., 2005, 2006).

A dynamical perspective on these questions suggests two broad hypotheses. First, children's prior experiences and individual qualities will be carried forward into future interactions. Dyadic coordination results from practice and socialization within a particular domain, thus we would expect girls to be more coordinated and practised in the verbal domain and boys more practised and coordinated in the physical domain. However, it is important to consider other prior experiences and potential biological predispositions: girls may be more coordinated than boys across multiple domains. In that case, studies of physical movements or those incorporating multiple indicators of coordination may show girls have a coordination advantage over boys. Second, a dynamical perspective would suggest adaptability of the coordinated system in the face of changing situations, such that both girls and boys should improve their coordination with partners over time. This ability for individuals to adapt over time implies that increasing contact with individuals and with groups should improve coordination.

Consistent with these ideas, future studies should examine coordination in other domains, such as in physical movements, to explore the possibility that boys are advantaged in this type of coordination. For instance, the distance between interactions, partners or their posture could be examined to determine if their movements become more synchronous or disparate. Such patterns may more accurately characterize boys' dyadic coordination than did the verbal coordination of the present study. Regardless of whether girls are more advantaged in certain domains than boys or more generally advantaged in coordination, sex differences in prior experiences may contribute to maintaining and sustaining the gender segregation cycle, which poses another challenge for researchers to address in attempting to improve mixed-sex relations.

Although we expected to find coordination to be higher in same-sex dyads, some researchers have suggested otherwise. Schmidt and colleagues (1994) offered the possibility that social coordination may require partners to exhibit either leadership/dominance or following/submission to promote optimal success, which, given sex differences in leadership, would suggest that mixed-sex dyads might be higher in coordination than same-sex dyads. Our finding that girl–girl dyads showed the highest coordination does not conform to this suggestion. However, further exploration of the role of leadership in coordination might provide interesting insights into same- and mixed-sex dynamics. For instance, in boy–boy dyads both children may be vying for leadership positions whereas two girls may not. However, the two boys may also be quite comfortable with leadership jockeying, and so still report liking each other. For girl–girl dyads, neither or both may adopt the leadership role, or they may more flexibly adjust leadership/follower roles, thereby allowing for both coordination and partner liking.

The context in which dyads work also may influence the dyadic interactions between girls and boys. In our study, children were asked to complete a physical science task involving the construction of molecules. The physical sciences continue to be strongly stereotyped as being for males (National Science Foundation, 2008), and these stereotypes may have been invoked during the study. Furthermore, the construction tasks we used involved spatial skills, and both of these contextual features placed girls in a setting that was likely uncomfortable. How the nature of the task influenced coordination, however, is unknown, since the study did not also include a task involving female-typical skills or even neutral tasks for comparison. Future explorations into interactional contexts should provide important insights into whether coordination is patterned similarly, disrupted or enhanced depending on the comfort of the individuals involved within particular interactional contexts.

The relation of coordination and positive interaction experiences is well documented: coordination is related to greater rapport and feelings of harmony and comfort (Chartrand & Jeffries, 2003; Lakin & Chartrand, 2003; Marsh et al., 2006, 2009; Matarazzo et al., 1968; Richardson et al., 2007). Thus, we expected to find a similar relation. Consistent with our hypothesis, greater coordination was predictive of more positive perceptions of one's interaction partner. The more similar adolescents were in their patterns of vocal activity, the more likely they were to report enjoying the interaction with their partner. Greater coordination likely facilitated a smoother and more efficient exchange of information (Watanabe et al., 1996), aiding communication and easing what was likely a somewhat stressful situation, making it more enjoyable to work together. The next step for future research is to identify factors that buttress interpersonal coordination and encourage adaptation. For example, if vocal communication is indeed an important determinant of girls' interpersonal coordination, encouraging boys to speak more when interacting with girls may improve mixed-sex interactions, alleviating some of the negative experiences between boys and girls. Alternatively, if physical coordination is important for boys, encouraging girls to be more active could lead to similarly improved mixed-sex interactions.

Last, to further explore the effect of coordination on adolescents' perceptions of their interaction partner, we examined coordination as a potential mediator of the dyad-level differences in partner perceptions. The results showed that it was not a significant mediator of the differences in partner perceptions between all-boy and mixed-sex dyads. This was expected, as these dyads did not significantly differ in how much they liked working with their partner. Coordination did, however, partly explain the difference in partner perceptions between girl–girl and girl–boy dyads, but not at a statistically significant level. It may be that coordination is just one of many characteristics of social interaction that contribute to girls' liking of their interaction partners.

Future directions for the dynamical study of gendered relationships

The application of dynamics to gendered interactions suggests a number of future directions that would be worth exploring. For example, in the present study, the majority of the participants were White adolescents, which may have had an effect on dyadic coordination, particularly for mixed-sex dyads. Research shows that there is ethnic variation in gendered attitudes. Hispanic and Black men often harbour more traditional gender role attitudes compared to their White counterparts (see studies cited in Kane, 2000) and it is possible that boys are exposed to traditional gender role attitudes from male authority figures, which may result in more heavily sex-segregated peer interactions as they may desire to conform to these gender roles. Race and gender have also been shown to influence children's conversation patterns, playmate preferences and peer collaborations in dyadic relationships (Leman & Lam, 2008; Leman et al., 2011). Based on the Gender Segregation Cycle and prior experiences affecting current and future interactions in dynamic systems, we would expect that a boy's lack of experience interacting with girls may result in poorer coordination than was found in mixed-sex dyads in the present study. Future research should examine not only the interaction of ethnicity and gender on same- and mixed-sex dyadic coordination, but also how experience with other-sex peers affects coordination in mixed-sex dyads and how that coordination affects young adolescents' partner perceptions.

Although we deliberately paired adolescents with an unfamiliar peer to examine the formation of novel interaction patterns, the quality of the relationship they have with an existing peer may influence the link between coordination and partner perceptions. Compared to play with an unfamiliar partner, play with a familiar peer is characterized by more task-relevant utterances, more cognitively engaging and complex behaviours, and more positively and negatively valenced expressions (Doyle et al., 1980; Furman, 1987; George & Krantz, 1981). Thus, a poor (or successful) interaction with a peer that an adolescent sees or interacts with frequently may have a greater effect on partner perceptions than an interaction with an unfamiliar peer. However, it is notable that we found a significant relation between coordination and partner perceptions with unfamiliar peers. Based on a dynamics perspective, we expect that familiar peers, with their longer history of interactions, would have more coordinated interactions to begin, and will show less change over time in their coordination than unfamiliar peers. Future work could explore the effects that familiar peers have on ease of coordination and on partner perceptions.

Dynamics is also useful for examining patterns of influence within social interactions. Many studies have been conducted to document the role that peers play in influencing children's and adolescents' behaviour (e.g. Altermatt & Pomerantz, 2003; Berndt et al., 1990; Crosnoe et al., 2003; Dishion et al., 1999; Gardner & Steinberg, 2005; Kindermann, 1993; Mounts & Steinberg, 1995; Powlishta & Maccoby, 1990; Ryan, 2001; Urdan, 1997); however, many of these studies involved methodological or analytical techniques that obscured the underlying peer interaction processes. From these studies we recognize that friends' risky behaviours and academic habits converge over time, but how? Influence may be mutual, where neither person takes a leadership position, or the influence may be unidirectional, where one peer guides the behaviour of the others (Clark, 1996). Dale and Spivey (2006) showed that dynamics could be used to examine different forms of influence. Although they could not examine group or individual differences (they only examined three dyads), the authors found variation in the degree to which parents and children influenced their interactions; in some dyads the child led the interaction and in others the parent led the interaction. Similar techniques may be used to examine influence in same- and mixed-sex interactions. For instance, research shows that girls often forfeit more resources when working with boys than with girls (Powlishta & Maccoby, 1990). This lack of influence over boys may contribute to the differences in liking across girl–girl and girl–boy dyads. Because they feel they have no control over boys, girls may prefer working with a girl with whom they have a more egalitarian interaction experience. Future work should explore influence, as well as other factors, that are potentially related to social coordination.

The stability of an interaction may also be explored through dynamics. A system is stable to the extent to which it is robust to internal and external disturbances, or perturbations, that may disrupt behaviour (Morrison, 1991). Perturbations may arise naturally through the course of interaction, but they may also be experimentally applied. Gorman and colleagues (2010) studied the effect of an experimental perturbation on three-person unmanned aerial vehicle teams. Interestingly, they found that teams whose members were unfamiliar, that is, they had never worked with one another before, were more successful in overcoming the perturbation than teams whose members had extensive experience working together. Considering that boys and girls are less familiar with each other than with same-sex peers, an interesting and unexpected prediction would be that mixed-sex peer groups might overcome perturbations more quickly than groups of same-sex peers. Thus, each type of group may offer certain advantages and disadvantages. Specifically, same-sex groups might be more comfortable and appealing because interactions are more easily coordinated, but they could also be less flexible and more rigidly set in their patterns. Research by Benenson and Christakos (2003) provides some support for this hypothesis. Girls' same-sex best friendships were found to be fragile compared to boys'. This fragility might be a consequence of high levels of coordination, and thus high rigidity, which may result in relationship dissolution after a serious conflict. In contrast, mixed-sex groups might be disadvantaged because they are less comfortable and less coordinated, but they may be more flexible when perturbations arise. If future research confirms these patterns, it becomes even more important to encourage individuals to spend time in mixed-sex groups to allow for flexibility in problem solving.

That we found evidence of coordination in the length and patterning of utterances, without regard to the content of their speech, suggests that information is carried not only in the words that are communicated but how and when they are spoken. This has implications for future work aimed at studying dyadic coordination. For instance, it may not be necessary to rely on time-intensive methods of extracting interaction data (e.g. transcription). Rather, measurements of non-content speech variables can be collected rapidly and immediately with the methods described in the present research. Such methods also present the opportunity for real-time analyses, which may be valuable for instantly examining the effect of intervention efforts.

A dynamical approach to improving gender relationships

A dynamical approach to human behaviour would suggest that coordination is malleable and that it changes with exposure to differing circumstances. Increased contact with a peer should improve dyadic coordination between any two children. Importantly, dynamics also suggests that gender relationships should improve if girls and boys can learn to behave in coordinated ways with other-sex peers, perhaps through exposure to members of the other sex. Mere contact with other group members can improve intergroup liking (e.g. see Pettigrew 1998 for a review); one possible mechanism accounting for improving group relations is the increased coordination likely to result from increased contact with other group members. Relatedly, we have argued that efforts should be expanded to increase the exposure that girls and boys have with one another with the goal of improving coordination and enhancing intergroup liking, particularly within academic settings. Unfortunately, strong proponents of separating the sexes have been very influential in reducing contact instead of enhancing it. More public schools in the United States are beginning to offer same-sex schooling options, such as all male or female classrooms or a complete same-sex school structure (NASSPE, 2012). However, given that boys and girls must often interact with each other outside of their primary and secondary school classrooms, same-sex schooling does not appear to be the answer to lifelong academic or social success. Instead, researchers must determine why boys and girls suffer poor other-sex interactions and establish what can be done to improve them.

In keeping with the dynamics approach and studies of intergroup contact, we have proposed a transactional Gender Integration Cycle to describe how increasing contact between the sexes can expand the repertoire of skills and behaviours that each sex has, which should lead to overall improvements in the work and school lives of both girls and boys (Martin et al., 2012). Specifically, when girls and boys come together in positive circumstances (intergroup contact), they gain experience in adjusting their own behaviour to their partner's behaviour, which may be different from the behaviour to which they are accustomed from exposure to same-sex peers. Over time, these mixed-sex encounters should become increasingly more coordinated, and this coordination should occur more quickly. In essence, their rocking chairs gradually achieve a similar size, thereby allowing for greater coordination. As a result, these interactions become more enjoyable and are less likely to be avoided because of disinterest or discomfort with other-sex peers. A positive feedback loop is initiated, one in which increased contact leads to increased coordination and liking, which then promotes additional contact, and the likelihood of maintaining this cycle is enhanced.

The present study was the first to explore gendered dyadic interactions from a dynamical perspective, and in doing so found that interpersonal coordination was related to interactive success or failure in gendered social interactions. Greater coordination was related to more positive partner perceptions across dyad types, and it partly accounted for the more positive partner perceptions reported by girls in same-sex dyads compared to those in mixed-sex dyads. These results suggest that by finding ways to increase coordination between boys and girls, researchers and educators can facilitate more harmonious mixed-sex interactions, setting the stage for improved inter-gender relations.

Together with prior work (DiDonato et al., 2012; Martin et al., 2005), the present research demonstrates that dynamics can be applied to the study of gender and that doing so may provide a fuller, more nuanced understanding of gendered phenomena. For example, consistent with previous research, DiDonato et al. (2012) found that an aggregate measure of gender typicality was positively related to psychological adjustment; however, when the same data were examined dynamically, overall gender typicality was no longer important. Instead, it was a child's ability to adaptively change their gendered behaviour over time that predicted positive adjustment. Similarly, in the present research, we focused on the dynamics of young adolescents' speech patterns rather than an aggregate measure. Creating an aggregate score by collapsing across the interaction would have eliminated dynamical variability and the ability to examine how vocal patterns are coordinated both contemporaneously (coordination at the same point in time for both dyad members) and at different points in time (how speech patterns for one adolescent affect later speech patterns for the other) during the interaction. By rapidly measuring their vocalizations, we were able to examine fluctuations in their vocal patterns throughout an interaction and examine how the coordination of those vocal patterns was related to their interaction experience.

It is our hope that the present research, in conjunction with other studies of the dynamics of gender, inspires other scientists to examine gendered phenomena from a dynamical perspective. By examining both aggregate levels of behaviour and the dynamics of variability, we can gain a fuller understanding of gendered relationships and the development of these relationships over time.

Note

1   Other parameters must also be chosen to conduct CRQ. For a detailed description of these parameters and how they are chosen please see Shockley, 2005.

References

Altermatt, E. R., & Pomerantz, E. M. (2003). The development of competence-related and motivational beliefs: an investigation of similarity and influence among friends. *Journal of Educational Psychology, 95*, 111–123.

Benenson, J. F., & Christakos, A. (2003). The fragility of females' versus males' closest same-sex friendships. *Child Development, 74*, 1123–1129.

Berndt, T. J., Laychak, A. E., & Park, K. (1990). Friends' influence on adolescents' academic achievement motivation: an experimental study. *Journal of Educational Psychology, 82*, 664–670.

Bernieri, F. J., Reznick, J. S., & Rosenthal, R. (1988). Synchrony, pseudosynchrony, and dissynchrony: measuring the entrainment process in mother-infant interactions. *Journal of Personality and Social Psychology, 54*, 243–253.

Blatchford, P., Baines, E. & Pellegrini, A. (2003). The social context of school playground games: sex and ethnic differences, and changes over time after entry to junior school. *British Journal of Developmental Psychology, 21*, 481–505.

Cappella, J., & Planalp, S. (1981). Talk and silence sequences in informal conversations: III. interspeaker influence. *Human Communication Research, 7*, 117–132.

Ceci, S. J., Williams, W. M., & Barnett, S. M. (2009). Women's underrepresentation in science: sociocultural and biological considerations. *Psychological Bulletin, 135*, 218–261.

Chartrand, T. L., & Jeffries, V. (2003). Consequences of automatic goal pursuit and the case of nonconsious mimicry. In J. P. Forgas, K. D. Williams, & W. von Hippel (Eds), *Responding to the social world: implicit and explicit processes in social judgments and decisions* (pp. 290–305). New York: Psychology Press.

Clark, H. H. (1996). *Using language.* New York: Cambridge University Press.

Crosnoe, R., Cavanagh, S., & Elder, Jr. G. H. (2003). Adolescent friendships as academic resources: the intersection of friendship, race, and school disadvantage. *Sociological Perspectives, 46*, 331–352.

Dale, R., & Spivey, M. J. (2006). Unraveling the dyad: using recurrence analysis to explore patterns of syntactic coordination between children and caregivers in conversation. *Language and Learning, 56*, 391–430.

DiDonato, M. D., Martin, C. L., Hessler, E. E., Amazeen, P. G., Hanish, L. D., & Fabes, R. A. (2012). Dynamical patterns of children's gendered behaviour. *Nonlinear Dynamics, Psychology, and Life Sciences, 16*, 159–184.

Dishion, T. J., McCord, J., & Poulin, F. (1999). When interventions harm: peer groups and problem behaviour. *American Psychologist, 54*, 755–764.

Doyle, A.-B., Connolly, J. & Rivest, L.-P. (1980). The effect of playmate familiarity on the social interactions of young children. *Child Development, 51*, 217–223.

Eaton, W. O., & Enns, L. R. (1986). Sex differences in human motor activity level. *Psychological Bulletin, 100*, 19–28.

Fabes, R. A., Martin, C. L., & Hanish, L. D. (2003). Young children's play qualities in same-, other-, and mixed-sex peer groups. *Child Development, 74*, 921–932.

Furman, W. (1987). Acquaintanceship in middle childhood. *Developmental Psychology, 23*, 563–570.

Gardner, M., & Steinberg, L. (2005). Peer influence on risk-taking, risk preference, and risky decision-making in adolescence and adulthood: an experimental study. *Developmental Psychology, 4*, 625–635.

George, S. W., & Krantz, M. (1981). The effects of preferred play partnership on communication adequacy. *The Journal of Psychology: Interdisciplinary and Applied, 109*, 245–253.

Giles, H., Coupland, N., & Coupland, J. (1991). Accommodation theory: communication, context, and consequences. In Giles, H., Coupland, J., & Coupland, N. (Eds), *Contexts of accommodation: developments in applied sociolinguistics* (pp. 1–68). New York: Cambridge University Press.

Gorman, J. C., Amazeen, P. G., & Cooke, N. J. (2010). Team coordination dynamics. *Nonlinear Dynamics, Psychology, and Life Sciences, 14*, 265–289.

Harskamp, E., Ding, N., & Suhre, C. (2008). Group composition and its effects on female and male problem-solving in science education. *Educational Research, 50*, 307–318.

Hollenstein, T. (2011). Twenty years of dynamic systems approaches to development: significant contributions, challenges, and future directions. *Child Development Perspectives, 5*, 256–259. doi: 10.1111/j.1750-8606.2011.00210.x

Holmes-Lonergan, H. A. (2003). Preschool children's collaborative problem-solving interactions: the role of gender, pair type, and task. *Sex Roles, 48*, 505–517.

Hyde, J., & Linn, M. (1988). Gender differences in verbal ability: a meta-analysis. *Psychological Bulletin, 104*, 53–69.

Kane, E. W. (2000). Racial and ethnic variations in gender-related attitudes. *Annual Review of Sociology, 26*, 419–439.

Kindermann, T. A. (1993). Natural peer groups as contexts for individual development: the case of children's motivation in school. *Developmental Psychology, 29*, 970–977.

LaFreniere, P., Strayer, F. F., & Gauthier, R. (1984). The emergence of same-sex affiliative preferences among preschool peers: a developmental/ethological perspective. *Child Development, 55*, 1958–1965.

Lakin, J., & Chartrand, T. L. (2003). Using nonconscious behavioural mimicry to create affiliation and rapport. *Psychological Science, 14*, 334–339.

Leaper, C. (1994). Exploring the consequences of gender segregation on social relationships. In Leaper, C. (Ed.), *Childhood gender segregation: causes and consequences* (pp. 67–86). San Francisco, CA: Jossey-Bass.

Leaper, C., & Smith, T. E. (2004). A meta-analytic review of gender variation in children's language use: talkativeness, affiliative speech, and assertive speech. *Developmental Psychology, 6*, 993–1027.

Leman, P. J., & Lam, V. L. (2008). The influence of race and gender on children's conversations and playmate choices. *Child Development, 79*(5), 1329–1343. doi: http://dx.doi.org/10.1111/j.1467-8624.2008.01191.x

Leman, P. J., & Björnberg, M. (2010). Conversation, development, and gender: a study of changes in children's concepts of punishment. *Child Development, 81*, 958–971.

Leman, P. J., Ahmed, S., & Ozarow, L. (2005). Gender, gender relations, and the social dynamics of children's conversations. *Developmental Psychology, 41*, 64–74.

Leman, P. J., Macedo, A. P., Bluschke, A., Hudson, L., Rawling, C., & Wright, H. (2011). The influence of gender and ethnicity on children's peer collaborations. *British Journal of Developmental Psychology, 29*(1), 131–137. doi: http://dx.doi.org/10.1348/026151010X526344

Maccoby, E. E. (1990). Gender and relationships: a developmental account. *American Psychologist, 45*(4), 513–520.

Maccoby, E. E. (1998). *The two sexes: growing up apart, coming together.* Cambridge, MA: Belknap Press.

Maccoby, E. E., & Jacklin, C. N. (1987). Gender segregation in childhood. In Hayne, W. R. (Ed.), *Advances in child development and behaviour* (Vol. 20) (pp. 239–287). Orlando, FL: Academic Press, Inc.

Marsh, K. L., Richardson, M. J., Baron, R. M., & Schmidt, R. C. (2006). Contrasting approaches to perceiving and acting with others. *Ecological Psychology, 18*, 1–38.

Marsh, K. L., Richardson, M. J., & Schmidt, R. C. (2009). Social connection through joint action and interpersonal coordination. *Topics in Cognitive Science, 1*, 320–339.

Martin, C. L., & Fabes, R. A. (2001). The stability and consequences of young children's same-sex peer interactions. *Developmental Psychology, 37*, 431–446.

Martin, C. L., & Ruble, D. N. (2009). Patterns of gender development. *Annual Review of Psychology, 61*, 353–381.

Martin, C. L., Fabes, R. A., Hanish, L. D., & Hollenstein, T. (2005). Social dynamics in the preschool. *Developmental Review, 25*, 299–327. doi: 10.1016/j.dr.2005.10.001.

Martin, C. L., Fabes, R. A., Hanish, L., Updegraff, K., Miller, C., Gaertner, B., Kochel, K., & Foster, S. (April, 2012). The Sanford Harmony Program: program description and preliminary findings. Invited address presented at the Gender Development Research Conference, San Francisco, CA.

Marwan, N., & Kurths, J. (2002). Nonlinear analysis of bivariate data with cross recurrence plots. *Physics Letters A, 302*, 299–307.

Matarazzo, J. D., Wiens, A. N., Matarazzo, R. G., & Saslow, G. (1968). Speech and silence behaviour in clinical psychotherapy and its laboratory correlates. In Shlien, J. M. (Ed.), *Research in psychotherapy*. Washington, DC: American Psychological Association.

McGarva, A. R., & Warner, R. M. (2003). Attraction and social coordination: mutual entrainment of vocal activity rhythms. *Journal of Psycholinguistic Research, 32*, 335–354.

Mehta, C. M., & Strough, J. (2009). Sex segregation in friendships and normative contexts across the life span. *Developmental Review, 29*, 201–220.

Mehta, C. M., & Strough, J. (2010). Gender segregation and gender-typing in adolescence. *Sex Roles, 63*, 251–263.

Morrison, F. (1991). *The art of modeling dynamic systems: forecasting for chaos, randomness, and determinism*. New York: John Wiley and Sons.

Mounts, N. S., & Steinberg, L. (1995). An ecological analysis of peer influence on adolescent grade-point-average and drug use. *Developmental Psychology, 31*, 915–922.

NASSPE. (2012). Single-sex schools, schools with single-sex classrooms, what's the difference? Retrieved on 7 February 2012 from http://www.singlesexschools.org/schools-schools.htm.

Natale, M. (1975). Social desirability as related to convergence of temporal speech patterns. *Perceptual and Motor Skills, 40*, 827–830.

National Science Foundation. (2008). Science and engineering indicators 2008. Retrieved on 1 November 2009 from: http://www.nsf.gov/statistics/seind08.

Pettigrew, T. F. (1998). Intergroup contact theory. *Annual Review of Psychology, 49*, 65–85.

Pettigrew, T. F., & Tropp, L. R. (2006). A meta-analytic test of intergroup contact theory. *Journal of Personality and Social Psychology, 90*, 751–783.

Powlishta, K. K., & Maccoby, E. E. (1990). Resource utilization in mixed-sex dyads: the influence of adult presence and task type. *Sex Roles, 23*, 223–240.

Richardson, M. J., Marsh, K. L., Isenhower, R. W., Goodman, J. R. L., & Schmidt, R. C. (2007). Rocking together: dynamics of unintentional and intentional interpersonal coordination. *Human Movement Science, 26*, 867–891.

Ridgers, N. D., Stratton, G., & Fairclough, S. J. (2005). Assessing physical activity during recess using accelerometry. *Preventive Medicine, 41*, 102–107.

Ridgers, N. D., Stratton, G., & Fairclough, S. J. (2006). Physical activity levels of children during school playtime. *Sports Medicine, 36*, 359–371.

Ryan, A. M. (2001). The peer group as a context for the development of young adolescent motivation and achievement. *Child Development, 72*, 1135–1150.

Schmidt, R. C., Carello, C., & Turvey, M. T. (1990). Phase transitions and critical fluctuations in the visual coordination of rhythmic movements between people. *Journal of Experimental Psychology: Human Perception and Performance, 16*, 227–247.

Schmidt, R. C., Christianson, N., Carello, C., & Baron, R. (1994). Effects of social and physical variables on between-person visual coordination. *Ecological Psychology, 6*, 159–183.

Scholz, J. P., & Kelso, J. A. (1990). Intentional switching between patterns of bimanual coordination depends on the intrinsic dynamics of the patterns. *Journal of Motor Behaviour, 22*(1), 98–124.

Serbin, L. A., Moller, L. C., Gulko, J., Powlishta, K. K., & Colburne, K. A. (1994). The emergence of gender segregation in toddler playgroups. In Leaper, C. (Ed.), *Childhood gender segregation: causes and consequences. New directions for child development, No. 65* (pp. 7–17). San Francisco, CA: Jossey-Bass.

Shockley, K. (2005). Cross recurrence quantification of interpersonal postural activity. In Riley, M. A., & Van Orden, G. C. (Eds), *Tutorials in contemporary nonlinear methods for the behavioural sciences* (pp. 142–177). Retrieved 8 February 2009 from http://www.nsf.gov/sbe/bcs/pac/nmbs/nmbs.jsp.

Shockley, K., Santana, M., & Fowler, C. A. (2003). Mutual interpersonal postural constraints are involved in cooperative conversation. *Journal of Experimental Psychology: Human Perception and Performance, 29*, 326–332.

Sobel, M. E. (1982). Asymptotic intervals for indirect effects in structural equation models. In Leinhart, S. (Ed.), *Sociological methodology* (pp. 290–312). San Francisco, CA: Jossey-Bass.

Street, R. L., Jr., Street, N., & van Kleeck, A. (1983). Speech convergence among talkative and reticent three-year olds. *Language Sciences, 5*, 79–96.

Thelen, E., & Smith, L. B. (2006). Dynamic systems theories. In Lerner, R. M., & Damon, W. (Eds) *Handbook of child psychology* (6th ed.) (pp. 258–312). Hoboken, NJ: John Wiley & Sons Inc.

Underwood, G., Jindal, N., & Underwood, J. (1994). Gender differences and effects of co-operation in a computer-based language task. *Educational Research, 36*, 63–74.

Underwood, J., Underwood, G., & Wood, D. (2000). When does gender matter? Interactions during computer-based problem solving. *Learning and Instruction, 10*, 447–462.

Urdan, T. C. (1997). Examining the relations among early adolescent students' goals and friends' orientation toward effort and achievement in school. *Contemporary Educational Psychology, 22*, 165–191.

Vaughn, L. M. (2001). Teaching and learning in the primary care setting. In Baker, R. (Ed.), *Handbook of pediatric primary care* (2nd ed.) Philadelphia, PA: Lippincott, Williams, and Wilkins.

Warlaumont, A. S., Oller, D. K., Dale, R., Richards, J. A., Gilkerson, J., & Xu, D. (August, 2010). Vocal interaction dynamics of children with and without autism. In Ohlsson, S., & Catrambone, R. (Eds), *Proceedings of the 32nd Annual Conference of the Cognitive Science Society*. Austin, TX: Cognitive Science Society, 121–126.

Watanabe, T., Okubo, M., & Kuroda, T. (1996). Analysis of entrainment in face-to-face interaction using heart rate variability. *Proceedings of IEEE International Workshop on Robot and Human Communication*, 141–145.

Zanone, P. G., & Kelso, J. A. S. (1997). Coordination dynamics of learning and transfer: collective and component levels. *Journal of Experimental Psychology: Human Perception and Performance, 23*(5). doi: 10.1037/0096-1523.23.5.1454.

Zbilut, J. P., Giuliani, A., & Webber, C. L., Jr. (1998). Detecting deterministic signals in exceptionally noise environments using cross-recurrence quantification. *Physics Letters A, 246*, 122–128.

3 Teasing, threats and texts

Gender and the 'dark-side' of cyber-communication

Angela Ittel, Margarita Azmitia, Jan S. Pfetsch and Christin R. Müller

As children, adolescents and young adults' access to mobile phones and computers has increased, so has their time on social networking sites (SNS) such as Facebook, MySpace, Twitter and Instagram. In the US, 97 per cent of youth access the Internet at least intermittently (Tokunaga, 2010), and 80 per cent own mobile phones or other connectivity devices (David-Ferdon & Hertz, 2007), thus potentially allowing adolescents to be 'plugged in' constantly (Thomas et al., 2012; Turkel, 2011). Currently, mobile phone text messaging is the preferred mode of communication between teens, with one in three adolescents, and especially 14- to 17-year-old girls, sending more than 100 texts per day (Lenhart et al., 2010). SNS, email, texts, and more broadly, the Internet, allow children, adolescents and adults to create possible selves, develop friendships with peers in other geographical locations, plan activities and share information with their friends, and stay plugged into peer networks in their schools, neighbourhoods and communities (Salimkhan et al., 2010; Thomas, et al., 2012). High levels of connectivity have positive and negative implications for communication between peers and friends of all ages. However, it is especially relevant to discuss these implications for adolescent boys and girls because the meaning of friendship and peer relationships is of special significance during this age period (Azmitia et al., 2005).

Electronic communications can compensate for difficulties in in-person communication. For example, individuals who find in-person interactions difficult or students who have difficulty participating in the fast-paced discussions in the classroom can benefit from SNSs, classroom discussion boards or chat rooms (Holfeld & Grabe, 2012; Kraut et al., 2002; Valkenburg & Peter, 2011). Although the *social compensation hypothesis* has received some empirical support, the majority of research has supported the *'rich get richer' hypothesis,* wherein the Internet becomes an additional interaction context for socially competent children, adolescents and young adults (Peter et al., 2005). Valkenburg et al. (2011) found, for example, that children and adolescent boys and girls use online self-disclosures to rehearse offline self-disclosure and maintain their closeness to friends (Valkenburg & Peter, 2007).

Electronic communication can also provide emotional support during transitions to new schools or new countries. In a recent study with adolescent *third culture* adolescents (i.e. adolescents who frequently move from country to country with their parents), more than two thirds of the sixty-four participants reported that the Internet was the most effective way of staying in touch and feeling connected with their families, who are often spread out around the globe (Ittel & Sisler, 2012). They also shared that the Internet helped them feel less lonely and isolated once they moved (yet again) to a new country where they lacked the immediate support of the friends they have left behind.

The Internet can also be a source of political mobilization, linking adolescents and young adults across geographical locations in the US and around the world, as evident by the Occupy Movement in the US, the recent revolution in Egypt and, more locally, adolescents and young adults at schools and universities joining together to work towards social justice causes. Facebook, the most popular SNS, has 845 million monthly active users, 57 per cent female (Infographic Labs, 2012), and most politicians and key figures around the world have a personal page on Facebook and other SNSs (e.g. Twitter, Tumbler) in which they post their views and solicit contributions.

While the Internet can provide useful and positive developmental opportunities for youth around the globe in terms of interpersonal alliance, social engagement and general exchange of information, there is also a dark side to this high level of constant connectivity. In the US the average 8- to 18-year-old spends about seven and a half hours per day on the Internet (Lewin, 2010). While the average rate is much lower in in Europe, with currently two hours per day spent on the Internet, (JIM, 2012), connectivity has been globally blamed for lack of attention to schoolwork and exercise, thus contributing to academic problems and obesity worldwide (Ittel & Drury, 2011). Research has not only revealed negative associations between time spent online and academic and physical development, some studies also confirm the negative associations between psychosocial adjustment and the amount of time children and adolescents spend online. For example, in a study of early adolescents conducted in Berlin, Germany, Ittel and Drury (2011) showed that time spent online was associated with poorer body image and lower overall confidence. Interestingly, this association was stronger for boys than for girls, a result which is contrary to the extensive literature on the association between media, body image and internalization disorders in adolescent girls and young women (Grabe et al., 2008).

As noted by Holfeld and Grabe (2012), while many parents give their children mobile phones to keep them safe, paradoxically, the high level of (expected) connectivity, the lack of training on Internet safety and the ease with which messages spread on SNSs and the Internet make it difficult for them to escape the dark side of cyber-communication. Conflicts and rumours can spread easily on the Internet, and because texts are often decontextualized, they are easily misinterpreted, thus increasing their recipients' distress (Allen, 2012; Tokunaga, 2010; Underwood & Rosen, 2011).

Research has also shown that boys and girls and men and women express more anger and aggression on the Internet than offline (Erdur-Baker, 2010; Subrahmanyam et al., 2001; Ybarra & Mitchell, 2004; Valkenburg & Peter, 2011). Especially in the case of adolescents and young adults, aggressive and often degrading messages are often sent anonymously or – alternatively – another person's screen name is used to bully others (Kowalski & Limber, 2007) lowering the fear of negative ramifications. As a consequence, cyberbullying, a term which refers to a multitude of online behaviours that aim to have a negative impact on another person, has increasingly been at the centre of attention by media, educators, parents, policymakers and scholars due to its potential role in negative psychosocial development. In a telephone, nationally representative survey of children 12–17 years old living in the US, Mitchell et al. (2011) found that sexual harassment and bullying were the two most frequently reported negative forms of cyber-communication. Because cyberbullies can more easily remain anonymous, their messages can be more hostile and difficult to track than in-person bullies (LeBlanc, 2012). Since 2003, cyberbullying has been implicated in the suicides of at least forty-one adolescents in the United States, Canada and the UK and very likely even more incidents worldwide. However, because most of these adolescents and young adults were also harassed at school, their neighbourhood or their community, it is difficult to identify a single trigger – 'real' or 'virtual' – that led them to end their lives (LeBlanc, 2012).

In what follows, we briefly review similarities and differences between in-person and cyberbullying. We then discuss gender variations in cyberbullying as it relates to children's and adolescents' friendships and peer relationships and present data from a study that examined gender variations in online communication habits and the individual factors that were associated with cyberbullying. We conclude with suggestions for future research and guidelines for in- or out-of schools programmes that may help increase awareness and prevent, or at least mitigate, the negative psychological and developmental effects of cyberbullying.

In-person and cyber bullying: an overview

Bullying has many different forms, such as insults, spreading rumours, threats of physical harm or sexual harassment. Cyberbullying also refers to many different destructive behaviours on the Internet such as *flaming* (mutual denigration), *harassment* (recurrent insults), *denigration* (spreading rumors), *outing and trickery* (blaming), *exclusion*, *impersonation* (taking on a different identity), *happy slapping* (publishing embarrassing pictures/movies of someone) and *cyberstalking* and *cyberthreatening* (Kowalski et al., 2008). In a recent qualitative study with thirty adolescents (49 per cent boys) aged 14–17, focus group discussions concerning participants' cyberbullying experiences revealed that most adolescents had heard of these different cyberbullying behaviours or knew someone who had been a victim to one or more of these behaviours. In addition, almost all of the participants had personally experienced a wide range of in-person and cyberbullying behaviours (Pfetsch, 2012).

In-person and cyberbullying are similar in that the bully asserts his or her power over the victim and the victim often feels helpless because of the lack of strategies to stop the bullying, isolated because often victims do not want to talk to their peers, friends, parents or teachers about what is happening to them, and powerless because of their perceived lack of status among their peers or in their friendship cliques; most incidents of bullying and cyberbullying reoccur over time, increasing victims' isolation and distress (Gordon, 2012; Ittel & Rosendahl, 2007; Valkenburg & Peter, 2011). However, unlike in-person bullying, cyber-victims can retaliate against their aggressor through text messaging or SNSs, and many do (Holfeld & Grabe, 2012). Victims' anguish can be increased or decreased by bystanders' direct or perceived support for the bully or victim (Williams & Guerra, 2007), a finding that is consistent with the predictions of in-group solidarity derived from Tajfel and Turner's (1979) social identity theory (e.g. Jones et al., 2011).

In-person and cyberbullying peak in middle school (Goldbaum et al., 2007) but also occur in high rates in high school (Allen, 2012) as peer groups are reconfigured, friendships shift, romantic relationships begin, and puberty increases adolescents' insecurities and social comparisons (Eccles, 1999). Although girls report higher incidences of in-person bullying and friendship conflicts than do boys (Azmitia et al., 2005; Underwood et al., 2011), boys' reticence to self-disclose victimization or conflicts with friends makes getting accurate reports of from them difficult (Azmitia et al., 1998).

In a European survey designed to be representative for German adolescents, more than 20 per cent of the participating adolescent boys and girls reported that they either had experienced or witnessed cyberbullying (JIM, 2012). Consistent with this finding, in their review of empirical studies of bullying published between 1990 and 2009 in a broad range of countries, Rigby and Smith (2011) found that although in-person bullying between school-age children and adolescents has decreased, cyberbullying has increased as mobile phones and the Internet have become more accessible. In support of this proposal, after surveying 12- to 17-year-old adolescents, Juvonen and Gross (2008) reported that 72 per cent of their respondents had been cyberbullied at least once, with name calling and insults being the most common forms of cyber-aggression. Rates of cyberbullying were lower (12 to 35 per cent) in studies that included nationally representative samples (e.g. Lenhart et al., 2010; Ybarra et al., 2007). Consistent with these US rates, in Germany between 4 and 36 per cent of adolescents report that they have experienced cyberbullying or negative interactions on the Internet (Livingstone et al., 2010; Techniker Krankenkasse, 2011). Rates vary with the sample characteristics and the criteria and method (research design) used to identify cyberbullying behaviours or negative Internet communication (Pfetsch et al., 2013).

Between-study variations in the incidence of cyberbullying may also reflect variations in the specificity of the questions or definitions used to assess cyberbullying and victimization (Holfeld & Grabe, 2012). Nevertheless, there is wide agreement about the need to increase cybersecurity[1] (Suzuki et al., 2012) and growing evidence of the links between cyber-victimization and lasting damage to adolescents' mental health (Holfeld & Grabe, 2012; Perren et al., 2010; Suzuki et al., 2012; Wang et al., 2011).

In spite of the growing concern about the developmental and mental health correlates of cyberbullying, well-known experts on bullying, and most notably

Olweus (2012), have suggested that cyberbullying is not as serious as in-person bullying because cyber-victims have the option of turning off their connectivity devices, a strategy that is not available to victims of in-person bullies. For this reason, Olweus has proposed that the focus of theory, research and intervention should continue to be on in-person bullying. Olweus has spent decades developing effective anti-bullying curricula for schools, and his programme is perhaps the most widely used intervention in elementary and middle schools in the US and Europe. Programmes that draw on his curricula, such as those developed by www.nobully.com and www.thebullyingproject.com, focus specifically on middle schools and provide training and curricula for administrators and teachers who want to implement anti-bullying programmes in their schools. In 2011, the documentary *Bully* received considerable attention in the US, where it was shown in theatres, teacher in-service training and during parent–teacher meetings. Films about bullying in childhood and adolescence are not new, but seldom has one of these films generated the amount of attention generated by *Bully*. In schools, teachers and administrators encouraged children and adolescents to make a pledge against bullying and demonstrations and marches by concerned citizens and families often followed showings of the documentary. Moreover, in the US 8 February has been designated by the federal government as anti-bullying day, further highlighting the centrality of bullying to policy debates and children's, adolescents' and young adults' lives.

In our view, Olweus' proposal to devote more attention to in-person than cyberbullying seems premature because research on cyberbullying – especially concerning effective intervention and prevention strategies – is still in its infancy. Moreover, while cyberbullying often occurs in conjunction with in-person bullying, it may have different predictors and correlates. For example, in a recent study, Müller (2013) found that the degree to which adolescents engaged in cyberbullying depended on the degree to which they used media in general. That is, the more media usage the adolescents reported, the more likely it was that they engaged in cyberbullying behaviours. These results suggest that different factors play a role in whether (or not) adolescents engage in cyberbullying or in-person aggression. These results are also relevant to the development of prevention and intervention programmes because they suggest that parents, teachers and other concerned adults need to find better ways to limit or supervise children and adolescents' connectivity. Therefore, and contrary to Olweus, we propose that more research is needed to understand the similarities and differences in factors that foster or hinder high levels of in-person and cyberbullying behaviour (see also Hinduja & Patchin, 2012). Further, there is very little research that systematically addresses gender variations in the factors that predict cyberbullying and their associations with mental health, academic performance and other developmental issues. In one of the few longitudinal studies on cyberbullying and victimization, Schultze-Krumbholz et al. (2012) investigated gender differences in the association between cyberbullying and victimization and internalizing and externalizing disorders in German middle school students. For girls, over time cyber-victimization was associated with increases in depressive symptoms and reactive (i.e. hostile) aggression, but loneliness remained unchanged. In contrast, for boys the rate of cyber-victimization did not predict internalizing or externalizing disorders, but cyberbullying predicted increases in depressive symptoms and loneliness. Importantly, boys who had been both perpetrators and victims of cyberbullying increased in loneliness from Time 1 to Time 2, perhaps because their peer status declined as a result of their aggressive behaviours. These results show that there seem to be gender-typical patterns in the association of cyberbullying and adjustment. However, more research needs to be conducted in the area to draw any sort of causal conclusions.

One difficulty in assessing the prevalence of cyberbullying is that children and adolescents are especially wary to talk to other people about their negative online experiences; unlike in-person bullying, which can sometimes be observed by others, peers and adults are often not privy to many forms of cyberbullying. In Juvonen and Gross's (2008) study, 90 per cent of the victimized youth had not reported the incident to their parents or teachers or taken steps to increase their cybersecurity (see also Perren et al., 2010). Holfeld and Grabe (2012) also found that their early adolescent participants seldom reported cyberbullying to teachers, school administrators or their parents, with most only disclosing the incident to their friends. Holfeld and Grabe's (2012) participants did not report the incidents to adults primarily because they felt they could handle the incident on their own, perhaps because contrary to the view that the Internet encourages anonymous victimization, most were victimized by classmates, friends or former friends and romantic partners. Another reason why victims or bystanders of cyberbullying do not report their experiences to adults is that they are worried about the consequences that will befall them when they admit to their parents or teachers that they have been victimized or witnessed others being victimized (Pfetsch, 2012). For example, in an effort to protect them, parents may take away their children's mobile phones, thus limiting their communication with friends, or teachers and parents may contact the bully's parents, which children and adolescents fear will impact their peer status or lead to bullies finding new ways to victimize them. It is vital that adults talk with their children/students about their activities on the Internet and encourage them to report their negative experiences. Teachers and other adults also need to understand the nature, processes and consequences of cyberbullying and dispel the myths that teasing, insulting and gossiping are typical behaviours of childhood and adolescence, i.e. 'boys will be boys' or 'girls are mean' and that 'sticks and stones may break my bones but words will never hurt them'. During her extensive experience in conducting teacher educational seminars on cyberbullying, Ittel has often found that many teachers do not take their students' negative experience seriously and react to their reports of victimization with the oversimplistic advice to turn off their device in order to stop the cyberbullying process. Adults (teachers, parents, mentors and other community agents) need to be sensitive to the reality of children's and adolescents' worlds, in which the Internet has become an extension of adolescents' peer networks and identities and a context of socialization in its own right. Bystanders also need to know that it is vital that they support the victim by reporting what they have witnessed. In any case, much like bullies, cyberbullies fly 'under the radar' of parents, teachers and school administrators and even 'under the radar' of their peers. Victims' attempts to retaliate against cyberbullies and the consequences in the non-virtual world of friendships and peer relationships have not received much attention by researchers or educational practitioners, and this is an important gap in the literature and an area for future research.

Another area that has not received enough attention is the role of bystanders in the cyberbullying process (Pfetsch, 2012). Bystanders can be part of the problem or part of the solution (Willard, 2006). That is, bystanders can reinforce and support the behaviour of the bully (e.g. they can forward a link to a degrading video or chat or add negative comments to an ongoing exchange or they can support the victims by helping them find solutions to the ongoing problem). Unfortunately, only a handful of studies have investigated the role of bystanders in cyberbullying (Pfetsch, 2012). For example, provided with online digital animations of cyberbullying, adolescents differ in their understanding of who is a bystander in these cases (Spears et al., 2012). Further, in reaction to hypothetical written scenarios, adolescents report that they would tell the bully to stop, support the victim or do nothing (Fawzi & Goodwin, 2011). Also a classification of real behaviours of bystanders – as reported in focus groups – includes the categories of reinforcers/assistants, defenders and outsiders (Pfetsch & Ittel, 2012). It seems that a considerable part of cyberbullying takes place in (semi-)public areas of the Internet and therefore the behaviour of bystanders can deflect or channel the attack of a cyberbully.

Gender and in-person bullying and cyberbullying

The results of the handful of studies that have explored gender variations in cyberbullying are mixed, with some reporting that girls and women are more likely than boys and men to be victims and perpetrators of cyberbullying (Keith & Martin, 2005; Snell & Englander, 2010), other studies reporting higher prevalence in males than females (Erdur-Baker, 2009; Li, 2006), and others finding no gender differences (Müller, 2013; Tokunaga, 2010). For males, but not females, in-person and cyberbullying are correlated (Erdur-Baker, 2009). Possibly, these gender differences are age-related, with studies focusing on early adolescents (e.g. Snell & Englander, 2010) finding higher prevalence of cyberbullying in females, but studies focusing on young adults reporting higher prevalence in males.

To explore more deeply gender variation in (cyber)bullying and individual factors that are associated with its occurrence, in the following section we report data from a longitudinal study, CyberEmp, recently conducted by Pfetsch (2012) in Berlin, Germany. CyberEmp focused on the associations between the development of empathy and cyberbullying. The ongoing longitudinal study, which began in the winter of 2011, consists of four measurement points (each 6 months apart) and includes a questionnaire that addresses adolescents' media usage, empathy, moral disengagement and participation in cyberbullying behaviour in primary and secondary schools in Berlin, Germany.

Empathy as the ability to understand and share others' emotional state was analysed as a potential protection factor against cyberbullying behaviour, because research has linked empathy to lower aggressive behaviour, in-person bullying and offending (Espelage et al., 2004; Jolliffe & Farrington, 2004; Miller & Eisenberg, 1988), but in some studies only for boys (Gini et al., 2007). Moral disengagement, on the other hand, is the cognitive restructuring of aggressive into benign behaviour by processes like moral justification, euphemistic labelling, and diffusion or displacement of personal responsibility (Bandura et al., 1996). Studies with adolescents have shown that the level of moral disengagement was related to more in-person bullying (Hymel et al., 2005; Menesini et al., 2003). Therefore, this construct was analysed as a potential facilitation factor for cyberbullying behaviour.

Method

The analyses draw on the data focusing on the association between empathy and participation in cyberbullying behaviour collected in eleven schools and sixty-seven classrooms during the first measurement point. The parents of the participating students were informed about the purpose, content, and all relevant organizational details concerning the study; 75 per cent of the parents gave their consent for their children to participate in the research. Trained graduate students and trained master's student assistants informed the adolescents about the purpose, content and all relevant organizational details concerning the study. Participants were also informed that their privacy would be protected and their responses would not be linked to their names, thus protecting their anonymity. Most adolescents completed the questionnaire in about thirty to forty-five minutes. The graduate students, who were present during the session, answered the adolescents' questions and provided clarifications as needed.

Sample description

There were a total of 979 adolescents (54.9 per cent female) who completed the questionnaire. 326 (33.3 per cent) early adolescent fourth and fifth graders enrolled in primary schools, 237 (24.2 per cent) seventh and eighth graders enrolled in integrated high schools (vocational and university track), and 416 (42.5 per cent) seventh and eighth graders who attended a Gymnasium (university track). The average age of the students was 12.01 (SD = 1.68, range 8–16 years), and 49.2 per cent of the participants indicated that either one or both of their parents or they themselves were born in a country other than Germany. Preliminary analyses revealed no gender variations in age, school type or ethnic heritage, so the data were aggregated over these categories, for the subsequent analyses.

Measures

The questionnaire used at the first measurement point of the study, CyberEmp, contained five sections. Section 1 gathered demographic data, such as school type, grade, age, gender, dominant language and immigration status; Section 2 contained questions concerning the usage of mobile phone and Internet; Section 3 assessed moral disengagement; Section 4 indexed adolescents' participation in traditional bullying and cyberbullying; and Section 5 gathered self- and peer estimates of affective and cognitive empathy.

Cyberbullying and cyber-victimization was assessed through the Berlin Cyberbullying-Cyber-victimization Questionnaire (BCyQ; Schultze-Krumbholz & Scheithauer, 2009a). The BCyQ assesses how often certain behaviours in the context of cyberbullying occurred during the last 6 months on a 5-point Likert scale ranging from (1) 'it never happened' through (5) 'it has happened several times a week'. We classified students as cyberbully or cyber-victim when they reported that certain behaviours had occurred two to three times in one week or more often.

The cyberbullying subscale was reduced from eighteen to twelve items due to low discriminatory power and low reliability of the scales in its original version. With Cronbach's $\alpha = .83$ the modified version of the scale had moderate reliability. Based on the recommendations of Schultze-Krumbholz and Scheithauer (2009b) three subscales were established: 1) relational cyberbullying (six items, $\alpha = .76$) measured behaviours such as outing, social exclusion, defamation and impersonation ($M = 1.11$, $SD = 0.28$); 2) picture-based cyberbullying (three items, $\alpha = .78$) measured behaviours that intend to change and distribute pictures and videos depicting other people or happy slapping ($M = 1.04$, $SD = 0.25$); 3) direct cyberbullying ($\alpha = .69$) entailed threats, abusive language and insults ($M = 1.08$, $SD = 0.31$).

Cyber-victimization was measured with seventeen items, which included topics such as how often a person has received a message that entails threats, abusive language and insults. After conducting a factor analysis, we excluded four items of the original scale due to low discriminatory power ($< .30$) or low reliability. The modified scale had moderate reliability, $\alpha = .76$. Three subscales were again established: direct cyber-victimization ($\alpha = .75$) was concerned with the experience of threats, blackmailing, insults in chats or text messages ($M = 1.12$, $SD = 0.35$). Relational cyber-victimization ($\alpha = .69$) contained six items that measured the experience of having personal rumours spread around the Internet, social exclusion in chats and online games, and outing ($M = 1.10$, $SD = 0.27$). Illegal cyber-victimization (three items, $\alpha = .58$) described illegal online activities such as abuse of passwords, impersonation and happy slapping ($M = 1.04$, $SD = 0.19$).

Traditional bullying and traditional victimization was measured by one item each after a definition was given which explained the meaning of bullying, namely 'repeated negative behaviour intended to harm psychologically or physically a student who cannot easily defend himself or herself including behaviours like hitting, insulting, excluding, or spreading rumors'. The participants indicated on a 6-point scale ranging from (1) 'not at all' through (6) 'almost daily' how often they bullied and were bullied within the past 6 months.

Empathy was measured with a modified version of the two dimensional Basic Empathy Scale (BES) developed by Jolliffe and Farrington (2006), which measures the degree of cognitive (nine items) and affective empathy (eleven items) on a 4-point scale. A sample item for cognitive empathy is: 'I can understand my friend's happiness when she/he does well at something.' A sample item for affective empathy includes: 'I tend to feel scared when I am with friends who are afraid.' After conducting factor analyses (SPSS 19), it was evident that in this sample a solution that included six items for cognitive empathy ($\alpha = .69$, $M = 3.18$, $SD = 0.51$) and six items for affective empathy ($\alpha = .63$, $M = 2.46$, $SD = 0.63$) was the best solution. We also calculated a general empathy score with all twelve items ($M = 2.82$, $SD = 0.48$), which was moderately reliable with $\alpha = .77$.

Media use was measured with four items on a 7-point scale (1 = rarely or never through 7 = more than 50 times a day; $M = 3.00$, $SD = 1.34$, $\alpha = .77$).

Moral disengagement ($\alpha = .89$) was measured with a scale from Bandura and colleagues (1996), translated and adapted by Pfetsch (2012). On fifteen items participants answered with 1 (not true at all) through 4 (is exactly true) whether – for example – they think that 'It is alright to fight when your group's honour is threatened' ($M = 1.62$, $SD = 0.53$).

Results

Descriptive results: media usage

MOBILE PHONE USAGE

As other studies have shown, we found that the mobile phone is a popular device for communication; only 8.0 per cent of the participating students did not have their own mobile phones. On average, adolescents used their mobile phones to make phone calls and send text messages several times a week, typically 1–2 times a day. Looking more specifically at the gender variations in the patterns of mobile phone usage, we conducted Mann-Whitney-U analysis and found that while boys and girls do not differ in the extent to which they used their mobile phone to make phone calls (81.6 per cent girls and 77.4 per cent boys), on average girls ($M = 2.66$) called others more often than boys ($M = 2.45$) (Mann-Whitney-U = 97107.500, $z = -2.67$, $p = .008$). In agreement with previous research, we also found that significantly more girls (66.1 per cent) than boys (50.5 per cent) used their phones to communicate via text messages ($\chi^2 (1) = 24.57$, $p = .000$) and that on average, girls ($M = 2.82$) sent text messages more frequently than boys ($M = 2.21$ (Mann-Whitney-U = 85912.000, $z = -5.44$, $p = .000$). In addition, we found that of all participants more girls (53.4 per cent) than boys (37.8 per cent) used their phone to surf the Internet ($\chi^2 (1) = 23.91$, $p = .000$), but there was no difference in the average frequency of Internet surfing via mobile phone between those boys and girls who used their phones to surf the Internet. No differences were found in the percentage of boys and girls who used their phone to record and forward videos, music and pictures (23.3 per cent) or in the frequency with which the phone was used for these activities.

Only 5.9 per cent of the participating students had no Internet access. Boys (7.3 per cent) and early adolescents (fourth and fifth grade students; 14.4 per cent) more frequently reported they had no internet access than girls (4.8 per cent) and secondary school students (seventh and eighth grade, 1.7 per cent). On average, boys and girls who had access (94.1 per cent) used the Internet about one hour per day. Overall descriptive results revealed that 65.6 per cent viewed pictures and videos, 63.8 per cent used it to seek for information, and 62.9 per cent look up information that helped them with their homework, 52.5 per cent listened to music, 49.7 per cent used the Internet to communicate via email, and 43.6 per cent were actively involved in social media sites (SNS) such as Facebook several times a week. SNS included Facebook, Skype, MSN, schülerVZ, Jappy, YouTube, Hotmail, Twitter, Google+ and GMX. Finally, 36.4 per cent used the Internet to chat, 27.9 per cent play games and 27.4 per cent make phone calls through Internet providers.

There were some interesting gender variations in these patterns of Internet usage. As in other studies (e.g. Ittel & Rosendahl, 2007) more girls (41.3 per cent) used the Internet to chat than boys (30.3 per cent), (χ^2 (1) = 12.73, p = .000), to participate in social networks (girls = 48.2 per cent versus boys = 38.0 per cent, χ^2 (1) = 10.31, p = .001), to read and send emails (girls = 54.0 per cent versus boys = 44.6 per cent, χ^2 (1) = 8.63, p = .003), to look up information (girls = 68.0 per cent versus boys = 58.8 per cent, χ^2 (1) = 8.78, p = .000), and to prepare for homework or school-related presentations (girls = 68.0 per cent versus boys = 56.8 per cent, χ^2 (1) = 13.00, p = .000). Taken together, these results suggest that girls are more active users of the Internet, although boys may be more actively engaged in browser games and Massively Multiplayer Online Role Playing Games (MMORPGs) such as World of Warcraft (see Yee, 2006).

Descriptive results: cyberbullying and cyber-victimization

In all, 57.5 per cent of the students reported no incidence of cyberbullying within the last six months; 32.7 per cent were actively involved once or twice, 4.0 per cent up to three times, 1.5 per cent once a week and 4.3 per cent several times a week. Some 90.2 per cent of the students were classified as non-cyberbullies and 9.8 per cent (n = 96) as cyberbullies. The frequencies for boys and girls are listed separately in Table 3.1. There were an equal number of boys and girls in the group of cyberbullies. No gender variations were revealed in the response patterns in any of the cyberbully subscales (see Table 3.2); that is, girls and boys did not differ in their activities revolving around cyberbullying.

Altogether, 55.9 per cent of the participating boys and girls (*n* = 547) did not experience any kind of cyber-victimization within the last six months; 36.6 per cent (*n* = 358) reported 1 or 2 incidences of cyber-victimization; 3.3 per cent of the participating boys and girls reported being victimized 2 or 3 times within the past six months;

Table 3.1 Frequency of cyberbullying

		Girls (n = 537) (%)	Boys (n = 442) (%)
Frequency of cyberbullying	Not at all	57.9	57.0
	1 or 2 times	34.8	30.1
	2 or 3 times	4.3	3.6
	Once a week	0.7	2.5
	Several times a week	2.2	6.8

Table 3.2 Mean and standard deviation for cyberbullying activities separated by gender and results of nonparametric group comparisons using the Mann-Whitney statistic

		M	SD	U	r
CB (all items)	Girls	1.08	0.23	116299.5 n.s.	−.01
	Boys	1.10	0.28		
Relational CB	Girls	1.11	0.24	110801.5 [#]	−.06
	Boys	1.11	0.33		
Picture CB	Girls	1.03	0.23	114986.5 n.s.	−.04
	Boys	1.04	0.27		
Direct CB	Girls	1.05	0.14	111862.5 n.s.	−.05
	Boys	1.12	0.43		

Note. M = mean; SD = standard deviation; U = Mann-Whitney statistic; r = effect size; CB = cyber bullying; [#]$p < .06$ (2-tailed), n.s. = not significant; $436 < N < 535$.

1.6 per cent once a week and 2.7 per cent several times a week within the last 6 months. In all, 92.4 per cent of the participating boys and girls were classified as not being a victim of cyberbullying, and 7.6 per cent (n = 74) were classified as cyber-victims. Compared to former research, this prevalence rate is slightly lower than, for example, in the study by Schultze-Krumbholz and Scheithauer (2009b), who found 15.5 per cent cyber-victims and 16.9 per cent cyberbullies. Although these authors also classified students with regular experiences as cyber-victims and cyberbullies, they surveyed a sample of older adolescents with a mean age of 14 years compared to the current sample who had a mean age of 12 years. On the other hand, a European study found 4 per cent of victims of internet bullying among German adolescents (Livingstone et al., 2010), which is slightly less than the prevalence rate in the current sample. But this study included fewer forms of cyberbullying and did not comprise bullying via mobile phones, for example.

Table 3.3 shows that cyber-victims were more often harassed through relational and direct bullying than through illegal cyber-activities (χ^2 (2) = 101.035, $p = .000$). Also, girls were more often victimized through relational cyberbullying than boys ($M_{girls} = 1.11$, $M_{boys} = 1.09$, Mann-Whitney-U = 107339.0, $z = -2.65$, $p_{2\text{-sided}} = .008$, $r = -.09$) (see Table 3.4.)

Table 3.3 Cyber-victimization means and standard deviations

		M	SD
Cyber-victimization	Scale	1.09	0.19
	Relational	1.10	0.27
	Illegal	1.04	0.19
	Direct	1.12	0.35

Note. M = mean; SD = standard deviation; $967 < N < 976$.

Table 3.4 Cyber-victimization means and standard deviation for boys and girls and results of nonparametric group comparisons

		M	SD	U	r
CV (all items)	Girls	1.09	0.18	115241.5 n.s.	−.02
	Boys	1.09	0.21		
Relational CV	Girls	1.11	0.22	107339.0*	−.09
	Boys	1.09	0.32		
Illegal CV	Girls	1.04	0.14	114078.0 n.s.	−.01
	Boys	1.05	0.24		
Direct CV	Girls	1.10	0.30	115629.5 n.s.	−.03
	Boys	1.13	0.39		

Note. M = mean; SD = standard deviation; U = Mann-Whitney statistic; r = effect size; CV = cyber-victimization; $*p < .01$ (2-tailed), n.s. = non-significant; $437 < N < 535$.

Potential risk and protective factors as correlates of cyberbullying: gender-specific commonalities and variances

This section focuses on our correlational analyses of factors that are related to the occurrence of cyberbullying such as age of participants, media use, moral disengagement, empathy, and their associations with cyberbullying and traditional bullying, cyber-victimization and traditional victimization (see Table 3.5).

Table 3.5 Correlations between potential risk and protective factors of cyberbullying: gender-specific commonalities and variances

		Overall	Girls	Boys
Risk factors	Traditional bullying	.402***	.427***	.392***
	Traditional victimization	.114***	.141**	.080*
	Cyber-victimization	.487***	.563***	.393***
	Moral disengagement	.352***	.379***	.332***
	Age	.364***	.342***	.390***
	Media use	.448***	.437***	.467***
Protective factors	Empathy	.014 n.s.	.042 n.s.	−.036 n.s.
	Empathy (affective)	.014 n.s.	.025 n.s.	−.009 n.s.
	Empathie (cognitive)	.002 n.s.	.038 n.s.	−.045 n.s.
	Media-based empathy	−.055*	−.090*	−.015 n.s.
	(Empathy with real life figures)	(−.138***)	(−.187***)	(−.088*)

Note. $*p < .05$, $**p < .01$, $***p < .001$, n.s. = non-significant; $407 < N < 975$.

The results of the correlational analyses generally replicated the existing literature. However, the finding that general empathy was not significantly associated with the frequency of cyberbullying was unexpected and did not replicate previous work. In addition, the frequency of using mobile devices was associated with cyberbullying. Also traditional bullying was positively associated with the occurrence of cyberbullying. In regard to cyber-victimization, a Fischer z-Test revealed a significant gender difference in the frequency of cyberbullying ($z = 3.44$, $p_{(1\text{-sided})} = .000$). In particular, the association between cyber-victimization and cyberbullying was stronger for girls than for boys.

Summary and discussion

Our results show that there are more similarities than differences in adolescent girls' and boys' media usage and cyberbullying behaviour. However, because the measure we used differentiated between different types of media usage, we were able to depict small but interesting gender variations in terms of usage of mobile phones and the Internet. In summary, while there was no gender gap in frequency of usage, girls use the media more frequently for social reasons, such as keeping in touch with their friends and chatting and for school-related work, while boys report being more involved in entertainment-related activities such as online gaming and in downloading of music.

The higher rates of relational cyberbullying and relational cyber-victimization for girls than boys may be due to text messaging being a form of indirect (relational) aggression, which is more common in girls than boys, socialization practices wherein girls are often discouraged from expressing anger in face-to-face interactions (but may feel comfortable expressing it in online), and because on average, girls (and women) send more texts and make more posts on SNSs than boys (Infographic Labs, 2012; Lenhart et al., 2010). However, these gender differences may not generalize to other cultures. For example, Tomada and Schneider (1979) found that Italian 14-year-old boys reported higher rates of physical and indirect (relational) aggression than girls.

While reports of gender differences in indirect aggression are not new, many studies have failed to replicate the differences and found that, contrary to most research, boys engage in more relational aggression than girls, or when more than one age group is studied, found either an increase or a decrease in gender variations in in-person and cyberbullying. Early adolescent girls, for example, use gossip in face-to-face conversations to evaluate others or clarify group norms (Eder & Sanford, 1986; Underwood, 2003), and in a recent longitudinal study, Reynolds and Juvonen (2011) found that early puberty and popularity with boys and teachers increased early adolescent girls' risk of being targeted by peer gossip and rumours, which in turn heightened their propensity for depressive symptoms.

There is some evidence in the literature that adolescent boys and girls varied in their preferred form of cyberbullying: girls are more likely than boys to engage in indirect aggression, exhorting peers to exclude others, forming coalitions, gossiping or planting rumours (Allen, 2012; Underwood & Rosen, 2011); and boys are more likely than girls to engage in name calling and threats of physical aggression (Allen, 2012; Valkenburg & Peter, 2011). These findings are consistent with research on in-person bullying, which has shown that boys are more likely than girls to engage in physical aggression and name calling and girls are more likely than boys to engage in indirect aggression (Björkqvist, 1994; Pepler, 2006; Underwood, 2003). Although the empirical evidence is sparse, some forms of cyberbullying that require a higher competency in computer/media skills (e.g. happy slapping) may occur more frequently in late adolescence and young adulthood. Cyberbullying may also be associated with boys' and girls' pro-social skills.

In our study, cognitive empathy was only marginally inversely related to boys' but not girls' cyberbullying behaviour. That is, low levels of cognitive empathy increased the likelihood for boys to engage in cyberbullying (risk factor) while high levels of cognitive empathy were related to lower levels of cyberbullying behaviours in girls (protective factor). These results point to the importance of gender-sensitive analyses as well as gender-sensitive prevention and intervention programmes.

Prevention and intervention

Taken together, our research and the available studies support the proposal that effective prevention and intervention strategies need to include gender-sensitive strategies to increase their effectiveness. Although females less often physically attack their victims, their gossip and rumour spreading on the Internet has been implicated in their victims' mental health and suicide. In June 2011, for example, Jason Medley, an attorney in Texas, filed a lawsuit against three middle-school girls who had posted a video on Facebook that falsely accused his daughter of sexual improprieties and promised to physically harm her; and cyberbullying was implicated in Jenna Bowers-Bryanton's suicide in Canada, 13-year-old Erin Gallagher and 15-year-old Ciara Pugsley's suicides in Ireland, 13-year-old Ryan Patrick Halligan's suicide in the US and forty other suicides. Moreover, cyberbullying is not confined to teens. In 2008, Lori Drew, a mother in Missouri, was tried (but acquitted) in the federal court for felony computer hacking and conspiracy for collaborating with her daughter Sarah (13) and their employee Ashley (18) to create a false profile of a 16-year-old boy (Josh Evans) on MySpace because they wanted to find out what Megan Meier (13, Sarah's peer) would say online about Sarah; 'Josh' developed an online romantic relationship with Megan and then taunted her, contributing, federal prosecutors argued, to Megan's suicide. Although the jury convicted Ms. Drew of three misdemeanors for violating MySpace policies, her acquittal underscores the slippery slope underlying taking legal action against cyberbullies.

There currently are very few prevention and intervention programmes that have been systematically evaluated, and the empirical evidence of the effectiveness of these programmes is rare (for an overview see Perren et al., 2012; Pfetsch et al., 2013). Programmes that help victims and bystanders report incidences of in-person and cyberbullying are crucial, and research evaluating the effectiveness and consequences of reporting these kinds of aggression is an essential goal for the future. However, beyond the reaction to cyberbullying (intervention), the need for preventive strategies will increase as the rate with which children and adolescents use online media increase worldwide. The factors that need to be addressed in effective cyberbullying prevention programmes are complex: the ecological and social context of the individual, the relevant risk and protective factors, and systematic consideration of age, gender, ethnicity/race, social class, sexual orientation and media usage as they relate to the frequency, process and consequences of in-person and cyberbullying. This research needs to be coupled with frank discussions among the stakeholders – parents, teachers, administrators, policymakers, children, adolescents and adults that use research findings to develop effective prevention and intervention programmes.

Note

1   In a yearly German survey adolescent participants indicated that, in 2012, only 10 per cent of the participating adolescents felt safe when using the Internet, but more than 40 per cent reported that they did not feel safe when connected (JIM, 2012).

References

Allen, K. P. (2012). Off the radar and ubiquitous: text messaging and its relationships to drama' in an affluent, academically rigorous, U.S. high school. *Journal of Youth Studies, 15*, 99–17.

Azmitia, M., Kamprath, N. A., & Linnet, J. (1998). Intimacy and conflict: the dynamics of friendships during middle childhood and early adolescence. In Meyer, L., Grenot-Scheyer, B., Harry, B., Park, H., & Schwartz, I. (Eds), *Understanding the social lives of children and youth* (pp. 171–187), New York: Brookes Publishing Company.

Azmitia, M., Ittel, A., & Radmacher, K. A. (2005). Narratives of friendship and self in adolescence. *New Directions for Child and Adolescent Development, 2005* (107), 23–39.

Bandura, A., Barbaranelli, C, Caprara, G. V., & Pastorelli, C. (1996). Mechanisms of moral disengagement in the exercise of moral agency. *Journal of Personality and Social Psychology, 71*, 364–374.

Björkqvist, K. (1994). Sex differences in physical, verbal, and indirect aggression: a review of recent research. *Sex Roles, 30*, 177–188.

David-Ferdon, C., & Hertz, M. H. (2007). Electronic media, violence, and adolescents: an emerging public health problem. *Journal of Adolescent Health, 41*, S1–S5.

Eccles, J. (1999). The development of children ages 6-14. *The Future of Children, 9*, 30–44.

Eder, D., & Sanford, S. (1986). The development and maintenance of interactional norms among early adolescents. *Sociological Studies of Child Development, 1*, 283–300.

Erdur-Baker, O. (2009). Peer victimization, rumination, and problem solving as risk contributors to adolescents' depressive symptoms. *Journal of Psychology, 143*(1), 78–90.

Erdur-Baker, O. (2010). Cyberbullying and its correlation to traditional bullying, gender, and frequent and risky usage of internet-mediated communication tools. *New Media and Society, 12*, 109–125.

Espelage, D. L., Mebane, S. E., & Adams, R. S. (2004). Empathy, caring, and bullying: toward an understanding of complex associations. In Espelage, D. L. & Swearer, S. M. (Eds), *Bullying in American schools: a social-ecological perspective on prevention and intervention* (pp. 37–61). Mahwah, NJ: Erlbaum.

Fawzi, N., & Goodwin, B. (2011). *Witnesses of the offense. What influences the behaviour of bystanders of cyberbullying?* Unpublished manuscript. München: Ludwig-Maximilians-Universität.

Gini, G., Albiero, P., Benelli, B., & Altoè, G. (2007). Does empathy predict adolescents' bullying and defending behaviour? *Aggressive Behaviour, 33*, 467–476.

Goldbaum, S., Craig, W. M., Pepler, D., & Connolly, J. (2007). Developmental trajectories of victimization: identifying risk and protective factors. In Goldbaum, S., Craig, W. M., Pepler, D., & Connolly, J. (Eds), *Bullying, victimization, and peer harassment: a handbook of intervention* (pp. 143–160). New York: Hawthorne Press.

Gordon, D. (2012, October). Keeping kids cybersafe. UCLA Online Magazine, Los Angeles, CA: University of California.

Grabe, S., Ward, L. M., & Hyde, J. S. (2008). The role of media in body image concerns among women: a meta-analysis of experimental and correlational studies. *Psychological Bulletin, 134*, 460–476.

Hinduja, S., & Patchin, J. W. (2012). *School climate 2.0: preventing cyberbullying and sexting one classroom at a time.* Thousand Oaks, CA: Sage Publications.

Holfeld, B. B., & Grabe, M. (2012). An examination of the history, prevalence, and characteristics of reporting cyberbullying in the United States. In Li, Q., Cross, D., & Smith, P. K (Eds), *Cyberbullying in the global playground: research from international perspectives* (pp. 117–142). New York: Wiley.

Hymel, S., Rocke-Henderson, N., & Bonnano, R. A. (2005). Moral disengagement: a framework for understanding bullying among adolescents. *Journal of Social Sciences, 8*, 1–11.

Infographic Labs (2012). Facebook 2012: the latest on everybody's favorite social network. Available at http://infographiclabs.com/news/facebook-2012.

Ittel, A. & Rosendahl, Y. (2007). Internetnutzung und soziale Integration im frühen Jugendalter. In Mikos, L., Hoffmann, D., &Winter, R. (Eds), *Mediennutzung, Identität und Identifikationen. Die Sozialisationsrelevanz der Medien im Selbstfindungsprozess von Jugendlichen* (pp. 183–206). Weinham, Germany: Weinham Press.

Ittel, A., & Drury, K. (2011). The meaning of media and body issues of girls and boys. *MERZ - Zeitschrift für Medienpädagogik, 55*, 35–52.

Ittel, A., & Sisler, A. (2012). Third culture kids: adjusting to a changing world. *Diskurs Kindheits- und Jugendforschung Heft, 4*, S. 487–492.

JIM (2012). *JIM-Studie 2012: Jugend, Information, (Multi-) Media.* Stuttgart, Germany: Medienpädagogischer Forschungsverbund Südwest.

Jolliffe, D., & Farrington, D. P. (2004). Empathy and offending: a systematic review and meta-analysis. *Aggressive and Violent Behaviour, 9*, 441–476.

Jolliffe, D., & Farrington, D. P. (2006). Development and validation of the Basic Empathy Scale. *Journal of Adolescence, 29*, 589–611.

Jones, S. E., Manstead, A. S. R., & Livingstone, A. G. (2011). Ganging up or sticking together: group processes and children's responses to text-message bullying. *British Journal of Psychology, 102*, 71–96.

Juvonen, J., & Gross, E. F. (2008). Extending the school grounds? Bullying experiences in cyberspace. *Journal of School Health, 78*, 496–505.

Keith, S., & Martin, S. E. (2005). Creating a culture of respect in a cyber world. *Crisis Prevention Briefs, 13*, 1–6.

Kowalski, R. M., & Limber, S. P. (2007). Electronic bullying among middle school students. *Journal of Adolescent Health, 41*, S22–S30.

Kowalski, R. M., Limber, S. P., Agatson, S. P., & Malden, P. W. (2008). *Cyberbullying: bullying in the digital age.* New York: Blackwell.

Kraut, R., Kiesler, S., Boneva, B., Cummings, J. N., Hegelson, V., & Crawford, A. M. (2002). Internet paradox revisited. *Journal of Social Issues, 58*(1), 49–74.

Lenhart, A., Purcell, K., Smith, A., & Zickur, K. (2010). Social media and mobile internet use in teens and young adults. Pew Internet & American Life Project, Pew Research Center, www.pewinternet.org.

LeBlanc, J. C. (2012). *Cyberbullying and suicide: a retrospective analysis of 22 cases.* Paper presented at the October meeting of the American Association of Pediatrics, New Orleans, LA.

Lewin, T. (2010). If your kids are awake, they are probably online. *The New York Times,* 20 January.

Li, Q. (2006). Cyberbullying in schools: a research of gender differences. *School Psychology International, 27*, 157–170.

Livingstone, S., Haddon, L., Görzig, A., & Ólafsson, K. (2010). Risks and safety on the internet. The perspective of European children. Initial findings from the EU Kids Online survey of 9-16 year olds and their parents. EU Kids Online II report, The London School of Economics and Political Science.

Menesini, E., Sanchez, V., Fonzi, A., Ortega, R., Costabile, A., & Lo Feudo, G. (2003). Moral emotions and bullying: a cross-national comparison of differences between bullies, victims and outsiders. *Aggressive Behaviour, 29,* 515–530.

Miller, P. A., & Eisenberg, N. (1988). The relationship of empathy to aggressive and externalizing/antisocial behaviour. *Psychological Bulletin, 103*, 324–344.

Mitchell, K. J., Finkelhor, D., Wolak, J., Ybarra, M. L., & Turner, H. (2011). Youth internet victimization in a broader victimization context. *Journal of Adolescent Health, 48(2),* 128–134.

Müller, C. R. (2013). *Empathie und Cyberbullying. Zum Zusammenhang von selbst- und fremdeingeschätzter Empathie, Medienempathie, Cyberbullying und.* Unpublished master's thesis, TU Berlin, Germany.

Olweus, D. (2012). Cyberbullying: an overrated phenomenon? *European Journal of Developmental Psychology, 9,* 520–538.

Pepler, D. (2006). Bullying interventions: a binocular perspective. *Journal of the Canadian Academy of Child and Adolescent Psychiatry, 15*(1), 16–20.

Perren, S., Dooley, J., Shaw, T., & Cross, D. (2010). Bullying in school and cyberspace: associations with depressive symptoms in Swiss and Australian adolescents. *Child and Adolescent Psychiatry and Mental Health, 4*(28), 1–10.

Perren, S., Vorcoran, L., Cowie, H., Dehue, F., Garcia, D., McGuckin, C., Sevcikova, A., Tsatsou, P., & Völlink, T. (2012). Tackling cyberbullying: review of empirical evidence regarding successful responses by students, parents and school. *International Journal of Conflict and Violence, 6*(2), 283–293.

Peter, J., Valkenburg, P. M., & Schouten, A. P. (2005). Developing a model of adolescent friendship formation on the Internet. *CyberPsychology and Behaviour, 8*, 423–430.

Pfetsch, J. (2012). *CyberEmp.* Unpublished research report, TU Berlin, Germany.

Pfetsch, J., & Ittel, A. (2012). *Adolescents' view on cyberbullying: behaviour and motives of bystanders.* Presentation at the XVIIth Workshop Aggression. Walferdange: University of Luxembourg, 1–17 July 2012.

Pfetsch, J., Mohr, S., & Ittel, A. (2013). Prävention und Intervention bei Cyberbullying. In Pieschl, S. & Porsch, T. (Eds), *Neue Medien und deren Schatten. Mit neuen Medien kompetent umgehen.* Göttingen: Hogrefe.

Reynolds, B. M., & Juvonen, J. (2011). The role of early maturation, perceived popularity, and rumors in the emergence of internalizing symptoms among adolescent girls. *Journal of Youth and Adolescence, 40,* 1407–1422.

Rigby, K., & Smith, P. K. (2011). Is school bullying really on the rise? *Social Psychology of Education, 14,* 441–445.

Salimkhan, G., Manago, A. M., & Greenfield, P. M. (2010). The construction of the virtual self on MySpace. *Journal of Psychosocial Research on Cyberspace, 4*(1), 446–458.

Schultze-Krumbholz, A., & Scheithauer, H. (2009a). *Measuring cyberbullying and cyber-victimization using behavioral categories: The Berlin Cyberbullying and cybervictimization questionnaire (BCyQ).* Poster presented at the Post Conference Workshop 'COST ACTION IS0801': Coping with negative and enhancing positive uses of new technologies in educational settings', August, Vilnius.

Schultze-Krumbholz, A., & Scheithauer, H. (2009b). Social behavioral correlates of bullying in a German sample. *Zeitschrift fur Psychology [Journal of Psychology], 217*(4), doi:10.1027/0044-3409.

Schultze-Krumbholz, A., Jakel, A., Schultze, M., & Scheithauer, H. (2012). Emotional and behavioural problems in the context of cyberbullying: a longitudinal study of German adolescents. *Emotional and Behavioural Difficulties, 17*(3–4), 329–345.

Snell, P. A., & Englander, E. K. (2010). Cyberbullying victimization and behaviours among girls: applying research findings in the field. *Journal of Social Sciences, 6,* 510–514.

Spears, B. A., Johnson, B., Johnson, A., Scrimgeour, M., Price, D., Geer, R., & Green, D. (2012). *Cyberbullying and bystanders: using digital animations to access attitudes and beliefs about cyberbullying and bystander behaviour.* Presentation at the XXth ISRA World Meeting. Walferdange: University of Luxembourg, 17–21 July 2012.

Subrahmanyam, K., Greenfield, P., Kraut, R., & Gross, E. (2001). The impact of computer use on children and adolescents' development. *Journal of Applied Developmental Psychology, 22*(1), 7–30.

Suzuki, K, Asaga, R., Sourander, A., Houven, C. W., & Mandell, D. (2012). Cyberbullying and adolescent mental health. *International Journal of Adolescent Medicine and Mental Health, 24,* 27–35.

Tajfel, H., & Turner, J. C. (1979). An integrated model of intergroup conflict. The social psychology of intergroup relations. In Austin, W. G. & Worchel, S. (Eds), *The social psychology of intergroup relations* (pp. 33–47). Monterrey, CA: Brooks/Cole.

Techniker Krankenkasse (2011). Gesundheitsreport 2011. Veröffentlichungen zum Betrieblichen Gesundheitsmanagement der TK, Band 26, Techniker Krankenkasse, Hamburg.

Thomas, V., Whittaker, S., & Azmitia, M. (2012). *Unplugged: exploring the costs and benefits of constant connection.* Unpublished manuscript, University of California at Santa Cruz.

Tokunaga, R. S. (2010). Following you home from school: a critical review and synthesis of research on cyberbullying victimization. *Computers in Human Behaviour, 26,* 277–287.

Tomada, G., & Schneider, B. H. (1979). Relational aggression, gender, and peer acceptance: invariance across culture, stability over time, and concordance among informants. *Developmental Psychology, 33*(4), 601–609.

Turkel, S. (2011). *Alone together.* New York: Basic Books.

Underwood, M. K. (2003). *Social aggression in girls.* New York: Guilford.

Underwood, M. K., & Rosen, L. (2011). Gender and bullying: moving beyond mean differences to consider conceptions of bullying processes by which bullying unfolds, and cyberbullying. In Espelage, D., & Sweaer, S. (Eds), *Bullying in North American schools* (2nd ed.) (pp. 13–22). New York: Routledge.

Underwood, M. K., Beron, K. J., & Rosen, L. H. (2011). Joint trajectories for social and physical aggression as predictors of adolescent maladjustment: internalizing symptoms, rule-breaking behaviours, and borderline and narcissistic personality features. *Development and Psychopathology, 23,* 659–678.

Valkenburg, P. M., & Peter, J. (2007). Preadolescents' and adolescents' online communication and their closeness to friends. *Developmental Psychology, 43,* 267–277.

Valkenburg, P. M., & Peter, J. (2011). Online communication among adolescents: an integrated model of its attraction, opportunities, and risks, *Journal of Adolescent Health, 48*(2), 121–127.

Valkenburg, P. M., Sumter, S. R., & Peter, J. (2011). Gender differences in online and offline self-disclosure in preadolescence and adolescence. *British Journal of Developmental Psychology, 29,* 253–269.

Wang, J, Nansel, T. R., & Iannotti, R. J. (2011). Cyber and traditional bullying: differential association with depression. *Journal of Adolescent Health, 48,* 415–417.

Willard, N. (2006). *Cyberbullying and cyberthreats: responding to the challenge of online social cruelty, threats, and distress.* Champaign, IL: Center for Safe and Responsible Internet Use.

Williams, K. R., & Guerra, N. G. (2007). Prevalence and predictors of internet bullying. *Journal of Adolescent Health, 41,* s14–s21.

Ybarra, M. L., & Mitchell, K. Y. (2004). Online aggressor/targets, aggressors, and targets: a comparison of associated youth characteristics. *Journal of Child Psychology and Psychiatry, 45,* 1308–1316.

Ybarra, M. L., Diener-West, M., & Leaf, P. J. (2007). Examining the overlap between Internet harassment and school bullying: implications for intervention, *41*(6), S42–S50.

Yee, N. (2006). The demographics, motivations, and derived experiences of users of massively multi-user online graphical environments. *Presence: Teleoperators and virtual environments, 15*(3), 309–329.

4   Is having an older sister or older brother related to younger siblings' gender typing?

A meta-analysis

Timea Farkas and Campbell Leaper

In one of our classes on the psychology of gender, a regular question raised by students is whether having an older brother or older sister has an impact on individuals' gender development. Studies that have tested for sibling gender effects have considered various aspects of children's gender typing including social behaviours, activity preferences, self-concepts and attitudes (see Wagner et al., 1993, 1996). To consider the overall significance of older siblings' gender on younger siblings' gender typing, we carried out a quantitative meta-analysis.

When evaluating the older sibling's gender as a predictor of gender typing, we included studies investigating multiple aspects of gender development. According to the multidimensional view of gender (Liben & Bigler, 2002; Spence, 1993), gender typing occurs in several domains. These include self-perceived traits (agency and communion), social behaviours (e.g. nurturance, aggression), and activity preferences (e.g. dolls, trucks). Furthermore, because gender development does not end in childhood (see Ruble et al., 2006 Leaper, 2013) and older siblings may have an ongoing influence, we included studies investigating participants from early childhood to preadolescence and late adolescence.

The potential importance of older siblings

For most people, sibling relationships will be the longest relationships of their lives. These relationships are often characterized by high emotional intensity and high intimacy, a combination that creates much opportunity for mutual influence (Dunn, 2002). Although some work has looked at the potential influence of younger sibling gender (e.g. Rosenberg & Sutton-Smith, 1971), from a socialization perspective the influence of older siblings is more relevant. Social cognitive theory emphasizes the importance of observational learning during gender development (Bussey & Bandura, 1999). Older siblings can be role models and also facilitate opportunities for younger siblings to practise particular behaviours (e.g. through shared play). Research guided by this approach indicates that higher-power and higher-status models may be especially salient and effective as role models (e.g. Bussey & Bandura, 1984; Revels & Gutkin, 1983). Accordingly, past research has found that younger siblings more often observe older siblings than the other way around (Stoneman et al., 1985). Social cognitive theory also emphasizes the importance of direct tuition in gender socialization. Indeed, older siblings have been shown to play the role of teacher and younger siblings the role of learner more often than the reverse (Stoneman et al., 1986).

The impact of older siblings may partly depend on their gender. Brothers may have a stronger effect than do sisters on younger siblings' gender typing. Much research suggests that gender functions as a status marker with higher status typically accorded to males than females (see Ridgeway & Bourg, 2004). Although enacting masculine-stereotyped behaviours can sometimes enhance girls' status, adopting feminine-stereotyped behaviours typically diminishes boys' status (Leaper, 1994). For example, one study found that children rated boys higher than girls in competence in a classroom task despite there being no objective evidence of differences in performance (Lockheed et al., 1983). Thus, children are likely aware that they could gain status by acting in masculine-stereotyped ways and lose status by acting in feminine-stereotyped ways; therefore, both girls and boys may choose to adopt more masculine gender-typed characteristics when a male sibling is available as a role model. By contrast, they may choose not to adopt more feminine gender-typed characteristics even if a female sibling is available as a model.

We also hypothesized that there would be differences in the extent to which sibling gender was related to gender typing among girls and boys. There is ample evidence that girls and women are often more gender-flexible than are boys and men (e.g. Katz & Ksansnak, 1994; Signorella et al., 1993; Twenge, 1997). It is not uncommon for girls to identify as tomboys (see Gottschalk, 2003). Also, adults are more likely to condone cross-gender activities for girls than boys (Cahill & Adams, 1997; Martin, 1990). Boys tend to experience much stricter gender boundaries and feel significantly more pressure to conform to gender stereotypes than do girls (Egan & Perry, 2001; Leaper, 2013). Given the strong pressure from society, parents and peers to conform to traditional gender roles, it is plausible that boys may be less prone to influence from any one source of socialization (e.g. older sibling). Thus, we may find a stronger effect of sibling gender on gender typing for girls compared to boys.

Two alternative hypotheses were considered regarding the possible relation of the older sibling's gender to the younger sibling's gender typing. One possibility is that younger siblings are more likely to differentiate themselves from their older siblings' gender (e.g. a boy with an older sister becomes more gender-typed). Several decades ago, Schachter et al. (1976) proposed that younger siblings often differ from older siblings because they want to carve out their own identities. In a similar manner, Sulloway (1996) advanced an evolutionary argument that younger siblings are motivated to find their own unique niche in a family and therefore tend to differ in personality from older siblings. Thus, to highlight her differences with her older brother, a girl would be more likely to adopt feminine gender-typed characteristics and less likely to adopt masculine gender-typed qualities.

An alternative hypothesis is that younger siblings tend to move toward the gender-typed pattern associated with the older sibling's gender (e.g. a girl with an older sister becomes more feminine gender-typed). According to social cognitive theory (Bussey & Bandura, 1999) one of the main processes of gender socialization is observational learning. Thus, children observe their older siblings and imitate their gender-typed behaviours, self-perceptions and preferences. Although past research shows that children are more likely to imitate same-gender models, they also can and do imitate cross-gender models, especially if the models are perceived as powerful (Bussey & Bandura, 1984). Thus, a girl with an older brother may be more likely to adopt masculine-stereotyped characteristics compared to a girl with an older sister; in contrast, a girl with an older sister may be more likely to adopt feminine-stereotyped characteristics.

Further support for this hypothesis can be inferred from findings of a 'social dosage effect' in same-gender peer groups (Martin & Fabes, 2001). Martin and Fabes (2001) observed that preschool children who spent more time playing with same-gender peers in autumn were more likely to increase their gender-typed behaviours later in the spring. For example, boys who spent more time playing with other boys in autumn were more likely to play in masculine-typed ways in spring; they were also more likely to be aggressive and to engage in rough-and-tumble play. Thus, interactions with peers enhanced the propensity to be gender-typed in various domains (e.g. play, social behaviour). Although this research investigated relationships with same-age, non-sibling peers, it is plausible that analogous effects would be found with siblings. That is, spending time with older siblings may lead to adopting some of their behaviours. Indeed, researchers find that children generally spend considerable time interacting with their siblings (see Dunn, 2002; McHale & Crouter, 1996). For example, children with a same-gender older sibling may be more likely than children with other-gender older siblings to spend time in gender-typed activities; conversely, children with an other-gender older sibling may spend more time than children with same-gender older siblings in cross-gender-typed activities. Indeed, some research has found that the time boys spent with brothers was positively associated with their own instrumentality (a masculine-stereotyped trait) and the time girls spent with sisters was negatively associated with their own instrumentality (McHale et al., 2004).

Moderators

Whether or not there is an overall effect across studies, there might be effects within different gender domains; for example, older siblings' gender may predict younger siblings' gender-typed activity preferences but not self-perceived traits. Further, effects may vary by the age of participants. Thus, we consider gender-typing domain and participant age as potential moderators.

Gender domain

A multidimensional view of gender suggests that individuals may develop and exhibit gender-typed characteristics in some domains (e.g. self-perceived traits) less so, or not at all, compared to others (e.g. activities). Accordingly, studies investigating sibling gender influences have included various gender-related outcome variables such as self-perceived traits (e.g. expressivity, instrumentality; McHale et al., 2001), leisure activity preferences and behaviours (e.g. Leventhal, 1970; McHale et al., 2001), social behaviours (friendship intimacy, friendship control; Updegraff et al., 2000), adjustment (externalizing/internalizing behaviours and symptoms; e.g. Buist, 2010), and occupational interests (e.g. engineering; Leventhal, 1970). For the present review, we coded the outcome measures of studies for each of these dimensions. In addition, there are some studies that utilized a global measure of gender typing (e.g. Bigner, 1972; Leventhal, 1970; Rust et al., 2000).

Unfortunately, the small number of studies in each category did not allow for testing the categories separately as moderators. Therefore, we compared two types of studies. In one set, we considered studies using global measures of gender typing. In the other set, we included studies examining specific domains of gender typing (e.g. leisure activities). Children are often inconsistent across domains in their gender typing (Liben & Bigler, 2002); that is, they may prefer traditional play activities but endorse non-traditional attitudes about occupations. Given these common inconsistencies in gender typing across domains within individuals, we reasoned that global measures would be more reliable indices of gender typing. Accordingly, we hypothesized that sibling-gender effects would be stronger among studies using global measures than those using domain-specific measures of gender typing.

Age group

We include studies in the meta-analysis with participants ranging in age from early childhood to emerging adulthood. Sibling gender may be more strongly related to gender typing earlier in life compared to later. Children's social interactions with peers increase steadily through childhood and adolescence (Ellis et al., 1981). The importance of siblings may thus be weakened with the addition of so many other potential sources of socialization. However, it is also possible that siblings constitute such important and pervasive relationships (see Dunn, 2002), that their influences last equally through development.

Summary

Based on theory and past empirical evidence, we hypothesize the following: 1) older sibling gender will predict younger siblings' gender typing among both girls and boys, with a possibly stronger effect among the younger girls; 2) younger siblings will be more likely to be gender-typed toward (rather than away from) the pattern associated with their older sibling's gender; 3) younger siblings will be more likely to adopt their brothers' masculine-stereotyped traits rather than their sisters' feminine-stereotyped traits; and 4) effects of older sibling gender may be moderated by domain of gender typing and age of participants. All of the hypothesized patterns are correlational in nature. It is not possible to test for causality in the meta-analysis.

Method

Literature search

Seven relevant studies were identified to use in the meta-analysis (see Appendix Table 4a for the characteristics of each study). They included six independent samples of younger female siblings and ten independent samples of younger male siblings. The studies were found through the PsycINFO database using the search terms 'gender' and 'sibling'. All journal article abstracts in the search results were then skimmed for relevant measures and analyses: sibling gender as a predictor and gender typing as outcome. Additional studies were found in literature reviews and reference lists of relevant journal articles. Dissertation abstracts found using the same search terms were also inspected, but none was found to be useable based on our selection criteria (described later). Three other studies were found that measured older sibling gender as predictor and gender typing as outcome, but they were excluded because of insufficient statistical information regarding the findings (Rosenberg & Sutton-Smith, 1968, 1971; Vroegh, 1971).

Coding moderators

Outcome measures were coded into several categories based on domain of gender typing. These included self-perceived traits (e.g. expressivity, instrumentality), leisure activities/interests (e.g. sports, handicrafts), occupational interests (e.g. engineering), social behaviours (e.g. intimacy behaviours, controlling behaviours) and global measures of gender typing (i.e. measures comprising multiple gender domains; It Scale for Children; Preschool Activities Inventory; Minnesota Multiphasic Personality Inventory (MMPI) Femininity-Masculinity Scale). In addition, we classified the domain (or global) as either feminine- or masculine-stereotyped. The first author and an undergraduate research assistant independently coded studies' outcome measures according to these categories; inter-coder reliability was excellent (Cohen's kappa = .81).

Many domain categories were represented by only one study due to the limited number of available studies. Therefore, we could not consider specific domains of gender typing as a moderator. Instead, we made a comparison between samples that were based on a measure of a specific gender-typing domain with those that were based on global measures of gender typing.

We tested younger sibling's age as a possible moderator using age as both a continuous and categorical variable. Three categories of age groups were used: early childhood (ages 3–6), preadolescence (ages 9–13), and late adolescence (ages 18–20). There were no samples of girls in the late adolescence age group.

Statistical analyses

Unit of analysis

Analyses were carried out using the Comprehensive Meta-Analysis statistical software package. For all analyses, except those testing gender domain as moderator, independent samples were used as the unit of analysis. Thus, if a study reported more than one outcome measure for the same sample, effect sizes were averaged across outcomes. When testing domain as a moderator, we used the statistical test as the unit of analysis. This means that studies that measured more than one domain for the same independent sample were included more than once in the analysis of domain as a moderator.

Effect sizes

Most effect sizes were computed from means, standard deviations and sample sizes for each comparison group (i.e. girls with older brothers, girls with older sisters, boys with older brothers, boys with older sisters). In some cases, standard deviations were not available; if so, then means, sample sizes and F or t values were used. Finally, in a few cases, only means, sample sizes and p-values were available to impute the effect size. In these cases, if the finding was reported as non-significant, we entered $p = .99$; if the finding was reported as significant at the $p < .05$ level, we entered $p = .049$. These estimates are conservative and may underestimate the effect size. However, only three statistical tests from a single study (Leventhal, 1970) had imprecise statistics.

As a measure of effect size, we calculated and report Cohen's d (i.e. the standard difference in means). Guidelines for interpreting Cohen's d are the following: a value of less than .20 is considered a negligible difference between groups, a value between .20 and .49 is considered a small difference, a value between .50 and .79 is considered a medium difference, and a value of .80 or higher is considered a large difference.

Random-effects model

Overall analyses of effect sizes were conducted separately for girls and boys using a random-effects model. A random-effects model assumes that effect sizes vary among sample studies not just because of differences among participant samples (as assumed by a fixed-effects model), but also because of measurement differences among studies. A mixed-effects model was used when analysing the effects of moderators. In a mixed-effects model, the effect sizes of studies within a subgroup are combined using a random-effects model, whereas the effect sizes of the subgroups are analysed using a fixed-effects model.

Results

Overall analyses

All analyses were conducted separately for girls and boys. There were six independent samples of girls comprising a total sample size of 1698. There were ten independent samples of boys comprising a total sample size of 2773. Results are reported in Table 4.1. There was an overall positive effect of older sibling gender

Table 4.1 Effect of older sibling's gender on younger sibling's gender typing: overall effects and effects by gender typing dimension

Analysis	k	N	d	95% CI	Z	Q_W
Overall						
Females	6	1708	.22*	.00/.43	1.97*	15.58**
Males	10	2773	.17	−.06/.41	1.45	68.18***
Masculine-stereotyped						
Females	6	1708	.31*	.07/.55	2.57*	19.51**
Males	8	2384	.21+	−.01/.44	1.87+	38.69***
Feminine-stereotyped						
Females	3	1255	−.02	−.42/.39	−.09	9.64**
Males	6	1764	.16	−.21/.57	−.79	57.16***

Note. Independent sample was the unit of analysis, and *k* refers to the number of relevant independent samples for each condition. Positive effect sizes indicate a higher mean score for participants with older brothers for masculine-stereotyped outcomes and participants with older sisters for feminine-stereotyped outcomes. Q_W is a test for homogeneity of variance in effect sizes within a condition for a particular moderator.

+p = .06; *p < .05; **p < .01; ***p < .001.

on gender typing that was significant for girls (d = .21, 95% CI = [−.01/.43], p = .049). Thus, there was a small combined effect for girls' gender typing in the direction of their older sibling's gender. There was no significant effect for boys (d = .17, 95% CI = [−.06/.41], p = .145).

To gain a better understanding of this overall effect we conducted separate analyses for masculine-stereotyped and feminine-stereotyped outcomes. For masculine-stereotyped outcomes, results showed a significant positive effect for girls (d = .31, 95% CI = [.07/.55], p = .010), and a marginal positive effect for boys (d = .21, 95% CI = [−.01/.44], p = .062). Thus, girls and boys with an older brother tended to be somewhat more masculine-stereotyped than their counterparts with an older sister. There were no significant effects of older sibling gender on feminine-stereotyped outcomes.

Test of publication bias

To test for publication bias, we used funnel plots (see Figures 5.1 and 5.2). In a funnel plot, effect sizes are plotted against standard error. If studies scatter relatively symmetrically around the overall effect size, the chance of publication bias is low. The funnel plots of effect sizes for girls and boys in the studies included in this meta-analysis indicate that publication bias is not a likely problem. However, they should be interpreted with some caution because of the small number of studies.

Moderator analyses

Domain

Because the test of heterogeneity of variance was significant among samples of girls and boys (see Table 4.1), we tested the effects of potential moderators.

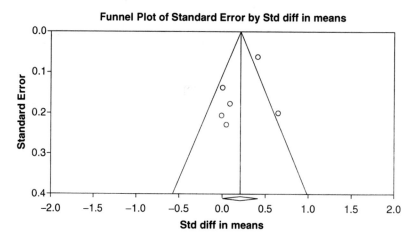

Figure 4.1 Funnel plot of effect size as a function of standard error for samples of girls

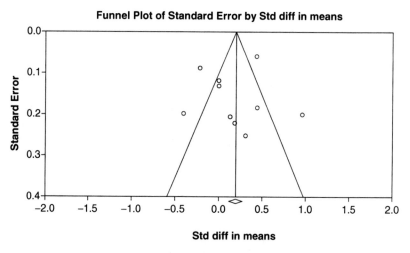

Figure 4.2 Funnel plot of effect size as a function of standard error for samples of boys

Results from the moderator analyses are summarized in Table 4.2. Gender-typing domain was a significant moderator of the relationship between gender typing and older sibling gender for girls. For boys, there was a marginal effect for the same moderator. Specifically, girls tended to be more gender-typed in the direction of their sibling's gender in studies using global measures ($d = .45$) compared to domain-specific measures ($d = .03$). For boys, the combined effect size for global measures was larger ($d = .44$) than that for domain-specific measures ($d = .04$).

Table 4.2 Effect of older sibling's gender on younger sibling's gender typing: effects by domain and younger sibling's age

Analysis	k	N	d	95% CI	Z	Q_W	Q_B
Domain							
Females							11.43**
Global	2	1186	.45***	[.28, .62]	5.22***	1.23	
Specific domain	4	522	.03	[−.14, .21]	.36	.16	
Males							
Global	3	1539	.44*	[.02, .85]	2.07*	19.52***	2.82+
Specific domain	7	1222	.04	[−.18, .25]	.32	17.85**	
Age							
Females							11.47**
Young child	2	1186	.45***	[.28, .62]	5.22***	1.23	
Preadolescence	4	522	.03	[−.14, .21]	.36	.16	
Males							8.54*
Young child	2	1255	.66*	[.15, 1.18]	2.53*	6.37*	
Preadolescence	4	530	.16	[−.04, .36]	1.61	3.85	
Late adolescence	4	976	.11	[−.33, .11]	−1.00	7.01	

Note. For tests of domain as moderator, statistical test was the unit of analysis, and k refers to the number of relevant statistical tests for each condition. For tests of age as moderator, independent sample was the unit of analysis, and k refers to the number of relevant independent samples for each condition. Positive effect sizes indicate a higher mean score for participants with older brothers for masculine-stereotyped outcomes and participants with older sisters for feminine-stereotyped outcomes. Q_B is an overall test of significance for a particular moderator. Q_W is a test for homogeneity of variance in effect sizes within a condition for a particular moderator.

+$p = .10$; *$p < .05$; **$p < .01$; ***$p < .001$.

Age

Age group was significantly and negatively correlated with effect size for both girls ($r = -.87$) and boys ($r = -.70$). Because ages tended to cluster in three distinct groups, we also tested age as a categorical moderator using three age groups: early childhood, preadolescence and late adolescence (see Table 4.2). For girls, studies with samples of children in early childhood ($d = .45$) found an overall stronger effect compared to studies of preadolescents ($d = .03$). (There were no samples of girls at the late adolescence age level.) For boys, studies with samples of children in early childhood ($d = .66$) indicated an overall stronger effect compared to studies of preadolescents ($d = .16$) and late adolescents ($d = -.11$).

Caveat

The domain and the age moderators were confounded. Among the studies using global measures, all of the samples of girls and most of the samples (two out of three) of boys were based on young children. Thus, it is not possible to determine which of the two moderators may have accounted for the differences in findings.

Discussion

Our findings indicate that across multiple studies there was a small yet statistically significant effect of older sibling's gender on gender typing among girls; the effect was not significant among boys. These results are in line with our hypothesis that girls would be more prone than boys to sibling influence regarding gender typing. Girls, compared to boys, tend to enjoy more allowances for gender-role flexibility both from themselves (Katz & Ksansnak, 1994) and from others in their lives (Cahill & Adams, 1997; Martin, 1990). Compared to boys, girls also tend to feel less pressure in general to conform to traditional gender-roles (Egan & Perry, 2001; Leaper, 2013).

In addition, the overall effect for girls was in the direction of, rather than in contrast to, the older sibling's gender. This finding supports the hypothesis that younger siblings would emulate older siblings' self-perceptions, behaviours, interests and attitudes. Past theoretical and empirical work also corroborates this finding. Social cognitive theory predicts that children learn from others by observation and imitation, and that this is especially true of children observing higher-status models such as older siblings (Bussey & Bandura, 1999). In addition, research on the social dosage effect suggests that when children spend more time with same-gender peers, they tend to exhibit proportionally more gender-typed behaviour later. Because siblings are peers with whom children spend a considerable amount of time, it makes sense for this effect to apply to them. Finally, research investigating the time spent with siblings indicates that children who spend more time with brothers or sisters score higher and lower on masculine-typed traits, respectively (McHale et al., 2004).

We next analysed the overall effect of older sibling gender on masculine- and feminine-stereotyped outcomes separately. As expected, there was a stronger (though small) overall effect for masculine-stereotyped outcomes compared to feminine-stereotyped outcomes for both girls and boys. Thus, girls and boys were more likely to be masculine-stereotyped if they had an older brother than if they had an older sister. However, girls and boys were not likely to have more feminine-stereotyped outcomes if they had an older sister than if they had an older brother. These findings make sense when we consider that gender functions as a status characteristic in our society. Boys and men often enjoy higher perceived and actual status compared to girls and women (see Leaper, 1994; Ridgeway & Bourg, 2004). Thus, members of both genders may feel that they gain status by acting in more masculine-stereotyped ways and lose status by acting in more feminine-stereotyped ways. In a related manner, higher status and higher power models tend to be more effective teachers than their lower status and lower power counterparts (Bussey & Bandura, 1984; Revels & Gutkin, 1983); older brothers may represent models who occupy an even higher status than older sisters, and thus their behaviours, traits and preferences may be more likely to be emulated by younger siblings.

In addition, we found that the type of outcome measure (domain-specific or global) and age (younger children versus early adolescence and older) moderated the effects of the older sibling's gender on the younger siblings' gender typing.

Unfortunately, these two factors were confounded. Nearly all of the studies using global measures were based on younger children and most studies using domain-specific measures were based on older children or adolescents. We discuss below the potential influences of domain and age as moderators, but our interpretations should be viewed cautiously.

When domain was tested as a moderator, the association between sibling gender and gender typing was significantly stronger when the study used a global measure compared to a domain-specific measure. This finding indicates that for both girls and boys older siblings may influence younger siblings somewhat in multiple domains. Furthermore, measuring any individual domain alone may not yield large effects; however, when these effects are pooled using a global measure, they may become more prominent. Perhaps pooling across multiple domains may allow for greater reliability in assessment.

With regard to age, it was significantly and negatively correlated with effect size for both girls and boys. In addition, when we tested age as a categorical moderator, there was a stronger overall effect among samples of young children compared to older ages for both genders. These findings support our prediction that sibling-gender effects would be more likely for younger than older children. As children grow, they are exposed to more and more peers and outside influences (Ellis et al., 1981); thus, the impact of a sibling may partly be overshadowed by the many other sources of influence in a child's life.

Because age and type of measure were confounded in the sample of available studies included in the meta-analysis, it is unclear whether just one or both of these variables moderated the sibling gender effects. As we have suggested, there are reasons to suspect that both may be true. With more studies, this relationship may become clearer.

Limitations and future directions

The present meta-analysis is the first to statistically synthesize the findings of research on older sibling's gender and younger sibling's gender typing. Our findings suggest that older siblings' gender may be related to younger siblings' gender typing and this relationship seems to vary based on several variables (e.g. participant gender, masculine- or feminine-stereotyped outcome). Despite this potentially helpful information, the meta-analysis needs to be viewed cautiously.

The most important limitation of the present meta-analysis is the small number of available studies that we could use. There have been surprisingly few studies testing for the association between older sibling's gender and younger siblings' gender typing. Among those studies that have been conducted on this topic, many of them (especially older studies) did not provide adequate statistical information about the effects. Interest in the topic of siblings and gender, however, appears to have increased. Most of the studies included in the meta-analysis were published after 2000. Thus, despite this limitation, the present study offers researchers who are increasingly interested in this area of study a first systematic look at the statistical effects of older sibling's gender on younger sibling gender typing.

A second limitation was that we could not consider whether the older sibling's gender was related to specific domains of gender typing more than others. Many domains of gender typing were only considered in one or two samples that we found. We did compare studies using comprehensive measures of gender typing with all studies testing specific domains of gender typing, and we found a stronger effect size with the former than the latter. However, if it was possible to compare effect sizes associated with different gender-typing domains, perhaps there would be some in which sibling-gender effects are stronger than others. For example, because siblings often play together, perhaps one would find stronger effects associated with gender-typed activities than other domains such as personality traits or academic/occupational interests.

A third limitation is that we could not address causal influences in our review. Although there are theoretical reasons to presume a causal link between sibling gender and participants' gender typing, the findings from the meta-analysis are exclusively correlational. The use of longitudinal studies can help to highlight possible causal relationships in this regard (e.g. McHale et al., 2001).

Another important and related point is that we only investigated the effect of older siblings' gender on younger siblings' gender typing. The relationship between older sibling gender and younger siblings' gender typing is likely complex. If there is a causal link between these factors, it may happen through modelling and direct tuition by the older sibling. If this is the case, past research suggests that other important factors to consider are amount of time spent with the older sibling (McHale et al., 2004), the level of gender typing of older sibling (McHale et al., 2001) and the age spacing between siblings (Bigner, 1972; Koch, 1956; Pepler et al., 1981). Further, in accordance with the social dosage hypothesis, a few studies have investigated the effects of having fewer or more siblings of a certain gender (e.g. Grotevant, 1978; Hines et al., 2002) or interacting less or more with siblings of a certain gender (e.g. Colley et al., 1996). As more research is conducted on these topics, future reviews should summarize the effects of these variables in addition to sibling gender.

Authors' note

The research was supported by a grant to Campbell Leaper from the Academic Senate of the University of California, Santa Cruz. We thank Harriet R. Tenenbaum for her suggestion to conduct this meta-analysis. We also appreciate Rachael Robnett for assistance with the statistical software and Chaconne Tatum-Diehl for help with searching for studies and coding.

Address for correspondence: Timea Farkas (timeafar@gmail.com) or Campbell Leaper (cam@ucsc.edu), Department of Psychology, University of California, Santa Cruz, Room 277 Social Sciences 2, 1156 High Street, Santa Cruz, CA 95064.

Appendix Table 4a Meta-analysis study characteristics by younger sibling's gender

Study	N	Mean age	Outcome measure	Direction for high scores	Statistical value	d
Female samples						
Bigner (1972)	104	5.25	Global	Masculine-stereotyped	M & SD	.96
Buist (2010)	128	12	Externalizing	Masculine-stereotyped	M & SD	.09
McHale et al. (2001)	97	10.25	Self-perceptions	Masculine-stereotyped	M & SD	.07
McHale et al. (2001)	97	10.25	Self-perceptions	Feminine-stereotyped	M & SD	-.11
McHale et al. (2001)	96	10.25	Leisure	Masculine-stereotyped	M & SD	.31
McHale et al. (2001)	96	10.25	Leisure	Feminine-stereotyped	M & SD	-.19
Rust et al. (2000)	1082	3	Global	Masculine-stereotyped	M & SD	.55
Rust et al. (2000)	1082	3	Global	Feminine-stereotyped	M & SD	.28
Updegraff et al. (2000)	77	12.42	Social behaviour	Masculine-stereotyped	M & SD	.41
Updegraff et al. (2000)	77	12.42	Social behaviour	Feminine-stereotyped	M & SD	-.31
Williams et al. (2007)	210	12.11	Externalizing	Masculine-stereotyped	M & SD	0
Male samples						
Bigner (1972)	112	5.25	Global	Masculine-stereotyped	M & SD	.65
Buist (2010)	128	12	Externalizing	Masculine-stereotyped	M & SD	.44
Leventhal (1970) – Study 1	105	19	Self-perceptions	Feminine-stereotyped	F = 4.20	-.40
Leventhal (1970) – Study 2	522	18.5	Leisure	Masculine-stereotyped	F = 8.70	-.26
Leventhal (1970) – Study 2	509	18.5	Occupational Interests	Masculine-stereotyped	p = .049	-.18
Leventhal (1970) – Study 3	56	20.2	Internalizing	Feminine-stereotyped	F = 5.29	.62
Leventhal (1970) – Study 3	78	20.2	Self-perceptions	Masculine-stereotyped	p = .99	0
Leventhal (1970) – Study 4	284	18.3	Global	Feminine-stereotyped	p = .99	0
McHale et al. (2001)	96	10.25	Self-perceptions	Masculine-stereotyped	M & SD	-.04
McHale et al. (2001)	96	10.25	Self-perceptions	Feminine-stereotyped	M & SD	-.03
McHale et al. (2001)	94	10.25	Leisure	Masculine-stereotyped	M & SD	.39
McHale et al. (2001)	94	10.25	Leisure	Feminine-stereotyped	M & SD	.21
Rust et al. (2000)	1143	3	Global	Masculine-stereotyped	M & SD	.17
Rust et al. (2000)	1143	3	Global	Feminine-stereotyped	M & SD	.70
Updegraff et al. (2000)	77	12.42	Social behaviour	Masculine-stereotyped	M & SD	.40
Updegraff et al. (2000)	77	12.42	Social behaviour	Feminine-stereotyped	M & SD	-.04
Williams et al. (2007)	231	12.11	Externalizing	Masculine-stereotyped	M & SD	0

Note. N = Number of participants; M & SD = effect size computed from reported means and standard deviations; d = aggregate effect size.

References

Bigner, J. J. (1972). Sibling influence on sex-role preference of young children. *Journal of Genetic Psychology, 121*, 271–282.

Buist, K. L. (2010). Sibling relationship quality and adolescent delinquency: a latent growth curve approach. *Journal of Family Psychology, 24*, 400–410.

Bussey, K., & Bandura, A. (1984). Influence of gender constancy and social power on sex-linked modeling. *Journal of Personality and Social Psychology, 47*, 1292–1302.

Bussey, K., & Bandura, A. (1999). Social cognitive theory of gender development and differentiation. *Psychological Review, 106*, 676–713.

Cahill, B., & Adams, E. (1997). An exploratory study of early childhood teachers' attitudes toward gender roles. *Sex Roles, 36*, 517–529.

Colley, A., Griffiths, D., Hugh, M., Landers, K., & Jaggli, N. (1996). Childhood play and adolescent leisure preferences: associations with gender typing and the presence of siblings. *Sex Roles, 35*, 233–245.

Dunn, J. (2002). Sibling relationships. In Smith, P. K., & Hart, C. H. (Eds), *Blackwell handbook of childhood social development* (pp. 223–237). Oxford: Blackwell.

Egan, S. K., & Perry, D. G. (2001). Gender identity: a multidimensional analysis with implications for psychosocial adjustment. *Developmental Psychology, 37*, 451–463.

Ellis, S., Rogoff, B., & Cromer, C. (1981). Age segregation in children's social interactions. *Developmental Psychology, 17*, 801–821.

Gottschalk, L. (2003). Same-sex sexuality and childhood gender non-conformity: a spurious connection. *Journal of Gender Studies, 12*, 35–50.

Grotevant, H. D. (1978). Sibling constellation and sex typing of interests in adolescence. *Child Development, 49*, 540–542.

Hines, M., Johnston, K. J., Golombok, S., Rust, J., Stevens, M., Golding, J., & ALSPAC Study Team. (2002). Prenatal stress and gender role behavior in girls and boys: a longitudinal, population study. *Hormones and Behavior, 42*, 126–134.

Katz, P. A., & Ksansnak, K. R. (1994). Developmental aspects of gender role flexibility and traditionality in middle childhood and adolescence. *Developmental Psychology, 30*, 272–282.

Koch, H. L. (1956). Sissiness and tomboyishness in relation to sibling characteristics. *Journal of Genetic Psychology, 88*, 231–244.

Leaper, C. (1994). Exploring the consequences of gender segregation on social relationships. In Leaper, C. (Ed.), *Childhood gender segregation: causes and consequences* (New Directions for Child Development, No. 65). San Francisco, CA: Jossey-Bass.

Leaper, C. (2013). Gender development during childhood. In Zelazo, P. D. (Ed.), *Oxford handbook of developmental psychology* (Vol. 2) (pp. 327–377). New York: Oxford University Press.

Leventhal, G. S. (1970). Influence of brothers and sisters on sex-role behaviour. *Journal of Personality and Social Psychology, 16*, 452–465.

Liben, S. L., & Bigler, R. S. (2002). The developmental course of gender differentiation: conceptualizing, measuring, and evaluating constructs and pathways. *Monographs of the Society for Research in Child Development, 67*(2), vii–147.

Lockheed, M. E., Harris, A. M., & Nemceff, W. P. (1983). Sex and social influence: does sex function as a status characteristic in mixed-sex groups of children? *Journal of Educational Psychology, 76*, 877–888.

Martin, C. L. (1990). Attitudes and expectations about children with nontraditional and traditional gender roles. *Sex Roles, 22*, 151–165.

Martin, C. L., & Fabes, R. A. (2001). The stability and consequences of young children's same-sex interactions. *Developmental Psychology, 37*, 431–446.

McHale, S. M., & Crouter, A. C. (1996). The family contexts of children's sibling relationships. In Brody, G. (Ed.), *Sibling relationships: their causes and consequences* (pp. 173–195). Norwood, NJ: Ablex.

McHale, S. M., Updegraff, K. A., Helm-Erikson, A., & Crouter, A. C. (2001). Sibling influences on gender development in middle childhood and early adolescence: a longitudinal study. *Developmental Psychology, 37,* 115–125.

McHale, S. M., Kim, J., Whiteman, S. & Crouter, A. C. (2004). Links between sex-typed time use in middle childhood and gender development in early adolescence. *Developmental Psychology, 40,* 868–881.

Pepler, D. J., Abramovitch, R., & Corter, C. (1981). Sibling interaction in the home: a longitudinal study. *Child Development, 52,* 1344–1347.

Revels, O. H., & Gutkin, T. B. (1983). Effects of symbolic modeling procedures and model status on brainstorming behaviour. *Journal of School Psychology, 21,* 311–318.

Ridgeway, C. L., & Bourg, C. (2004). Gender as status: an expectation states theory approach. In Eagly, A. H., Beall, A. E., & Sternberg, R. J. (Eds), *The psychology of gender* (pp. 217–241). New York: Guilford Press.

Rosenberg, B. G., & Sutton-Smith, B. (1968). Family interaction effects of masculinity-femininity. *Journal of Personality and Social Psychology, 8,* 117–120.

Rosenberg, B. G., & Sutton-Smith, B. (1971). Sex-role identity and sibling composition. *The Journal of Genetic Psychology: Research and Theory on Human Development, 118,* 29–32.

Rust, J., Golombok, S., Hines, M., Johnston, K., Golding, J., & The ALSPAC Study Team. (2000). The role of brothers and sisters in the gender development of preschool children. *Journal of Experimental Child Psychology, 77,* 292–303.

Schachter, F. F., Shore, E., Feldman-Rotman, S., Marquis, R. E., & Campbell, S. (1976). Sibling deidentification. *Developmental Psychology, 12,* 418–427.

Signorella, M. L., Bigler, R. S., & Liben, L. S. (1993). Developmental differences in children's gender schemata about others: a meta-analytic review. *Developmental Review, 13,* 147–183.

Spence, J. T. (1993). Gender-related traits and gender ideology: evidence for a multifactorial theory. *Journal of Personality and Social Psychology, 64,* 624–635.

Stoneman, Z., Brody, G. H., MacKinnon, C. E., & MacKinnon, R. (1985). Role relationships and behaviour between preschool-aged and school-aged sibling pairs. *Developmental Psychology, 21,* 124–129.

Sulloway, F. J. (1996). *Born to rebel: birth order, family dynamics, and creative lives.* New York: Pantheon.

Twenge, J. (1997). Changes in masculine and feminine traits over time: a meta-analysis. *Sex Roles, 36,* 305–325.

Updegraff, K. A., McHale, S. M., & Crouter, A. C. (2000). Adolescents' sex-typed friendship experiences: does having a sister versus a brother matter? *Child Development, 71,* 1597–1610.

Vroegh, K. (1971). The relationship of birth order and sex of siblings to gender role identity. *Developmental Psychology, 4,* 407–411.

Wagner, M. E., & Schubert, H. J. P., & Schubert, D. S. P. (1993). Sex-of-sibling effects: part I. Gender role, intelligence, achievement, and creativity. In Reese, H. W. (Ed.), *Advances in child development and behaviour* (pp. 181–214). San Diego, CA: Academic Press.

Wagner, M. E., Schubert, H. J. P., & Schubert, D. S. P. (1996). Sex-of-sibling effects: a review, part II. Personality and mental and physical health. In Reese, H. W. (Ed.), *Advances in child development and behaviour* (pp. 139–179). San Diego, CA: Academic Press.

Williams, S. T., Conger, K. J., & Blozis, S. A. (2007). The development of interpersonal aggression during adolescence: the importance of parents, siblings, and family economics. *Child Development, 78,* 1526–1542.

5 The developing relationship between gender and pro-social behaviour

Benjamin Hine and Patrick J. Leman

Introduction

Empirical studies typically indicate that girls both perform more pro-social behaviour and are judged as more pro-social than boys from as young as 2 years (Fabes & Eisenberg, 1996). However, although many studies find similar gender differences in judgement and behaviour, recent research has suggested that the link between gender and pro-sociality may not be quite as clear-cut as first thought. For example, gender differences in pro-social behaviour may vary as a function of type of behaviour, the recipient of behaviour, the age of participant and study methodology (Eisenberg et al., 2007). Furthermore, studies using self- and other-reports yield much larger effect sizes for gender differences in pro-social behaviour than those using observational methods (Fabes & Eisenberg, 1996). These variations suggest, among other things, that the stereotype that girls are 'nicer' (or more pro-social) than boys might influence reports of pro-social behaviour. This influence may, in turn, act as a socializing force that creates and sustains these gender differences in behaviour and the stereotype itself.

Surprisingly, little research has sought to investigate children's and adolescents' *understanding* of the links between gender and pro-social acts. Yet there are important questions for the field, both for gender theory and for work into moral judgement, about how children may appropriate gender knowledge to think about pro-sociality. In this chapter we give a brief description of key studies that have investigated gender differences in pro-social behaviour and judgements, and outline some of the difficulties in reliably interpreting these results. We then describe findings from a research programme of three studies that explore gender and pro-social behaviour. In the first study, we investigated how children and adolescents associate pro-social behaviour with gender across development (i.e. are there age differences in gender norms regarding pro-social behaviour?). We then assessed what some of the consequences of these norms might be (i.e. how children and adolescents judge others who perform or fail to perform pro-social behaviours). And in the third and final study, we explored in more detail the reasoning and justification processes that help create and maintain gender typing of pro-social behaviour. Additionally, findings from the first study suggest that early adolescence may be a sensitive period with regards to the internalization and application of gender norms that have a specific influence on judgements about pro-social acts. The final study explored this idea further.

Gender differences in pro-social behaviour

Studies conducted across a number of cultures have tended to show that girls are more pro-social than boys (Carlo et al., 2001; Russell et al., 2003; Whiting & Whiting, 1973). However, researchers have increasingly questioned whether such a broad, universal pattern is accurate (Dovidio et al., 2006; Eisenberg et al., 2007). Many authors have noted a pro-social gender stereotype, and an assumption that girls are inherently more pro-social than boys (Eisenberg & Mussen, 1989; Eisenberg et al., 2007; Serbin et al., 1993), that may influence both the way research is designed and conducted and also how participants report pro-social behaviour. Indeed the early nineteenth-century nursery rhyme 'What are little boys made of?' popularized the notion of girls as made of 'sugar and spice and all things nice' (Opie & Opie, 1997). Certainly aggregated studies of gender differences in pro-social behaviour suggest some empirical grounds for the existence of gender differences. Fabes and Eisenberg (1996) conducted a meta-analysis using 450 effect sizes (from 259 studies) which indicated gender differences (albeit with a modest effect size, .18) with girls both judged by participants and observed to be more pro-social. However, when the studies were separated into different categories – behaviour type, age of participant and study design – the effect size for gender differences changed dramatically. For instance, when separated by type of pro-social behaviour, behaviours such as being kind or considerate yielded much larger effect sizes (.42) than others, such as sharing or donating (which produced only small effect sizes, .13). This finding suggests that different pro-social behaviours are performed (or, at least, are perceived to be performed) in different frequencies by boys and girls.

Moreover, this suggestion is supported by empirical research. When adolescents are asked to report about their pro-social behaviours, girls tend to report relational pro-social behaviours (such as providing emotional support or playing peacemaker), whereas boys are more likely to report pro-social tendencies in public scenarios, and ones that involve risk and chivalry (Carlo et al., 2003). These results reflect a similar pattern seen in adulthood, with women gravitating towards more communal and empathic pro-social behaviours, and men towards more agentic and performance based pro-social behaviours (Eagly, 2009). Thus, different types of pro-social behaviour may be associated with boys and girls. Zarbatany et al. (1985) found that different items elicited different ratings for boys and girls, based on whether the activity used within the item was regarded as traditionally masculine or feminine. Masculine (male-typed) items (such as climbing to save a cat that is stuck in a tree) were judged to be more likely of boys than girls by children's classmates. In contrast, feminine items such as caring for or comforting another child, and neutral items such as sharing, were judged to be more likely to be performed by girls, again by classmates. Zarbatany et al. argued that measures used to evaluate children's pro-social behaviour include a disproportionate number of female-typed items. This stereotyping may contribute to the fact that an overwhelming amount of studies find that girls are more pro-social than boys.

The possibility that boys and girls (and men and women) express pro-sociality in different ways is an intriguing one. Moreover, it is one that appears to sit well with the research evidence in gender differences in moral reasoning. For instance, although there has been a good deal of research attention given to establishing the extent of gender differences in moral reasoning (e.g. Gilligan & Attanucci, 1988), several studies suggest that any differences that might exist are either negligible (Jaffee & Hyde, 2000) or can be accounted for by gender differences in reporting or other experiences (e.g. Haviv & Leman, 2002; Wark & Krebs, 1996). Some researchers have suggested that gender differences in pro-social behaviour are a consequence of underlying differences in causally related processes, specifically empathy (Lennon & Eisenberg, 1987). However, if gender roles funnel pro-social behaviours into differing forms of expression by boys and girls, the gender differences that have been assumed in pro-social reasoning may be little more than an artefact of the methods and measures used in studies investigating pro-sociality.

The extent of gender differences in reported and observed pro-social behaviour also varies as a function of age. In their meta-analysis, Fabes and Eisenberg (1996) separated studies into four age categories: early childhood (0–6 years), childhood (7–12 years), early adolescence (13–15 years) and late adolescence (16–18 years). The effect sizes for gender differences in pro-social behaviour in those four categories were .19, .17, .28 and .35 respectively, suggesting an exaggeration of gender differences with age. Specifically, while girls appear to perform more pro-social behaviour across all age ranges, the effect sizes substantially increase in early and late adolescence compared to those in early, middle and late childhood, and were found to be significantly different (Fabes & Eisenberg, 1996; Fabes et al., 1999). There is good evidence that boys and girls increasingly diverge at the onset of adolescence with regards to behaviours and social choices (Balk, 1995; Galambos et al., 1990). At a time of personal and social uncertainty, as young adolescents' bodies begin to change and mature and their interest in dating increases, there may be an increased pressure to act in ways that are consistent with gender-role expectations (Fabes et al., 1999). Thus if pro-social behaviour has been recognized as female-typed behaviour throughout childhood, the strength of any association between gender and pro-sociality may increase in adolescence as boys and girls seek to emphasize the differences between them.

Another source of support for the suggestion that gender differences in pro-sociality stem, at least in part, from self-presentational and intergroup concerns comes from methodological comparisons. In this respect, differences in effect sizes all but disappear when study design or reporting measures are controlled. Perhaps because of practical research concerns, there is a large proportion of self-report studies with adolescent populations.

Why might study design have such a large impact? When studies were split (self-report versus other-report versus observational methods) the effect sizes for gender differences varied greatly (Fabes & Eisenberg, 1996). Studies that relied on self- and other-reports showed significantly greater effect sizes (.33 and .28

respectively) than those that used observational methods (.13). These findings are underscored by further empirical studies that continue to find gender differences in reports of children's pro-social behaviours (Bosacki, 2003; Caprara et al., 2001), with fewer differences found in observational studies (Fabes et al., 2002). Therefore, when participants are allowed to report on behaviour, they may be influenced by an extraneous factor (such as gender norms) that is not as pervasive in more objective methodology (for example, when an impartial observer codes behaviour). Specifically, when participants report on their own and others' behaviour, they may be reporting what they feel they *should* be reporting, and how children are supposed to behave. For example, peers, parents and teachers have been shown to perceive girls as more pro-social than boys, in contrast to behavioural data, that show smaller differences or none at all, for the same interactions (Bond & Phillips, 1971; Shigetomi et al., 1981). Thus there is a danger that these reports may be based on stereotypes, or gender norms about pro-social behaviour and that any changes in early adolescence are a methodological artefact.

It is therefore important to investigate the gender typing of pro-social behaviour, especially from a developmental perspective, as self- and other-reports, as well as blind observational studies, may be influenced by gender norms. In other words, children's changing gender knowledge may influence these reports. In childhood, gender stereotypes are often characterized as rather basic or rigid and inflexible (Martin & Ruble, 2009). However, by adolescence, gender norm knowledge has become increasingly complex, influencing activities and behaviours to a much greater extent. This extended knowledge allows for judgements to be made about personality and character (Maccoby, 2002; Martin & Ruble, 2009). Therefore, as children grow older their increasing knowledge of the stereotype that girls are more pro-social than boys may be reflected more strongly in reports about pro-social behaviour. Furthermore, group dynamics and peer pressures also change across development. In childhood, whilst boys are judged harshly if they choose to engage in cross-gender activities or play with opposite-gender toys (Fagot, 1985), intolerance remains restricted to certain domains (such as toy choice or what to wear). However, in adolescence, pressure to conform to gender norms is arguably at its strongest (McHale et al., 2004; Rae Clasen & Brown, 1985), and influences a much wider variety of behaviours and activities. The reinforcement of pro-social behaviour as feminine, and conversely as not masculine, may therefore be reflected in adolescents' reports and judgements of pro-social behaviour.

The gender typing of pro-social behaviour may also affect how adolescents judge pro-social behaviour in a moral context. If pro-social behaviour is judged as feminine, when boys perform this behaviour, will they be judged differently? In childhood, stereotypes regarding personality characteristics and behaviours may not be strong enough for children to change their judgements about a moral behaviour. However, in early adolescence, strong peer pressures regarding gender norms (Rae Clasen & Brown, 1985), and greater knowledge of gender norms regarding appropriate behaviours (Serbin et al., 1993), may lead peers to judge pro-social behaviour differently when performed by boys. For example, studies on inclusion and exclusion have shown that children in early adolescence judge exclusion less negatively than at other ages when presented with additional (social) information (e.g. Killen & Stangor, 2001).

The studies in this chapter investigated the association between gender and pro-sociality in a developmental context. In study 1a we investigated how far children and adolescents judge that boys or girls will be more likely to perform different pro-social behaviours. The goal of this first study was to clarify at what ages children may distinguish between boys and girls in terms of the frequency (typicality) of their pro-social behaviour and to establish a cross-sectional picture of gender typing of pro-social behaviour. Study 1b examined some of the consequences of the gender typing of pro-social behaviour at different ages. If pro-social behaviour is associated with girls more than boys (and we predict it will be because of the stereotype of girls as more pro-social), then does this affect peers' moral judgements about boys and girls when they perform pro-social acts? Study 2 uses focus groups to explore the relation between gender norms and judgements about pro-social behaviour further – using discussions with early adolescents. This qualitative approach was taken because it allowed us to gain important insight into the complex nature of the judgements and reasoning that help mould pro-social behaviour by boys and girls at this age.

Study 1a: children and adolescents think girls are more likely to be pro-social

Many studies have been conducted on how children allocate personality characteristics to boys and girls (Powlishta, 1995, 2000). Children have been shown to allocate characteristics such as *gentle* and *affectionate* to girls, and *strong* and *dominant* to boys at 5 years (Best et al., 1977; Williams et al., 1975). These allocations become increasingly sophisticated as children age, with children aged 8 years allocating characteristics such as *emotional* and *soft-hearted* to girls, and *cruel, independent* and *coarse* to boys (see again, Best et al., 1977; Williams et al., 1975). A clear distinction can be seen between the types of characteristics allocated, with girls more closely associated with interpersonal characteristics and personality aspects that are 'softer' and 'nicer', whereas boys are associated with less interpersonal, more autonomous and 'harder' and 'harsher' characteristics.

It is tempting to draw a comparison between the gendered characteristics associated with personality and those associated with pro-social behaviour because many pro-social acts encourage qualities such as awareness of others' needs, feelings and attention to emotional states. These qualities may also contribute to the stereotypes that girls are more empathic than are boys (Lennon & Eisenberg, 1987) and are generally better behaved (Hastings et al., 2007). However, it is important to investigate whether the allocation of specific pro-social behaviours follows this pattern, to see if children gender-type pro-sociality as they do for many other behaviours and attributes. If children and adolescents female-type pro-social behaviour, this gender typing could account for the increased gender differences we see with age in self- and other-report studies as children respond to pressures to conform in adolescence. It may also change how children and adolescents judge peers who perform these behaviours, specifically boys, who would be performing a gender-incongruent behaviour.

Studies that use sociometric methods (such as nomination studies) indicate that children and adolescents aged 9–14 years nominate more girls as pro-social classmates than boys (Veenstra et al., 2008; Warden & MacKinnon, 2003; Warden et al., 2003; Wentzel, 2002; Wentzel et al., 2007). These studies typically ask children who is the most pro-social child or children. One danger with such an approach is that nominations could be a representation of the gender norm that pro-social behaviour is a feminine thing to do, and so girls are simply viewed as 'nicer' than boys (Serbin et al., 1993). Thus, it is necessary to investigate in a more general sense whether pro-social behaviour is gender-typed when asking about all children (rather than specific classmates), because gender norm knowledge helps children predict future behaviours and informs the judgements they make towards peers.

Our initial study investigated whether children and adolescents associate pro-social behaviours with either girls or boys (or with both). It is different from previous studies in two important ways. First, we asked whether boys or girls are more likely to perform pro-social behaviour; a measure of gender likelihood. Most previous studies have tended to infer gender typing of pro-social behaviour by examining the attributions that participants make to real peers. Here, we sought to determine the association to a gender group (i.e. boys or girls). Gender likelihood questions, arguably, are a clearer assessment of children's and adolescents' explicit gender associations with pro-sociality. Additionally, gender likelihood questions were used to explore what *expectations* children have about others performing behaviours based on their membership to a gender group. This in contrast with several other studies where participants are asked about specific behaviours (by specific classmates) that have already occurred (e.g. Warden et al., 2003; Wentzel, 2002; Wentzel et al., 2007). Second, we asked children to rate the likelihood that either boys or girls would perform *pro-social* behaviours specifically (rather than asking them to ascribe traits or personality characteristics to each gender). This measure provided an indication of whether children believe gender is an important factor in the performance of pro-social behaviour.

Knowledge of stereotypes regarding personality traits and characteristics are acquired during childhood (Martin & Ruble, 2009) and reach adult levels by age 9 (Serbin et al., 1993). Therefore, we expected that all participants would judge pro-social behaviours as more likely of girls. We also explored whether boys and girls rated boys' and girls' pro-social behaviour as more or less likely. Previous research has shown that girls nominate more girls as pro-social classmates than boys do (Warden & MacKinnon, 2003; Warden et al., 2003), girls place greater emphasis on pro-social goal pursuit and pro-social values (Beutel & Johnson, 2004), girls have greater knowledge of gender stereotypes than boys (Serbin et al., 1993), and finally that girls are likely to emphasise the pro-social stereotype about girls (Powlishta, 2004). We therefore expected that, whereas boys and girls would both rate girls as more likely to be pro-social (because of knowledge of stereotypes by both), girls would rate girls as more likely to be pro-social to a greater extent than boys would across all age groups.

Method

Participants

We interviewed 121 boys and 114 girls ranging from 5 to 15 years, in three age groups: early childhood ($n = 55$, $M = 6.91$, min = 5.86, max = 7.80, $SD = .53$, 27 boys, 28 girls), middle childhood ($n = 96$, $M = 9.86$, min = 7.94, max = 11.68, $SD = 1.02$, 51 boys, 45 girls), and early adolescence ($n = 84$, $M = 13.76$, min = 11.85, max = 15.78, $SD = 1.17$, 43 boys, 41 girls). Participants were from two schools in the South-East of England located in a predominantly middle-class area. Most participants were white British (88 per cent), with the remaining percentage from ethnic minorities (mostly Black African or Caribbean, South Asian, or another Asian background). These figures are similar to population ethnic group proportions across the United Kingdom.

Materials

Each participant was presented with four brief vignettes depicting pro-social acts. These vignettes were adapted to written stories for the older age group (because cartoons may have been thought of as childish by adolescents). The four scenarios were based on examples of sharing, giving, comforting and aiding/helping. For instance, for sharing: 'There are two children sitting in a classroom together drawing. One of the children needs a red pencil that the other child is using. The child using the pencil gives it to the other child to borrow.' The scenarios represented equivalent pro-social acts across age groups, but some details were altered to make the scenarios more realistic for participants. For example, for the oldest age group the scenarios concerned the sharing of a magazine, whereas for the youngest age group the scenarios involved sharing a pencil.

Procedure

Each participant read all four scenarios. After reading each scenario, participants were asked the question, 'Who is more likely to [behaviour]?' for each act. They could choose from boys, girls or either. Boys were coded as −1, either as 0, and girls as 1 thus creating a gender likelihood scale ranging from −1 to 1.

Results

A mixed design analysis of variance (ANOVA) was computed to explore the impact of age, gender and behaviour type on likelihood ratings of pro-social behaviours. There was a significant main effect for behaviour type, $F (3, 227) = 16.26$, $p < 0.001$. The means and standard deviations for gender likelihood judgements are presented in Table 5.1. Whilst the means for giving, sharing and helping are relatively similar, participants judged comforting as much more likely of girls than the other behaviours. Post hoc same sample t tests (using Bonferroni correction) showed that gender likelihood ratings for all behaviours were significantly different from 0 (the gender neutral option). Therefore, all behaviours were judged as more likely of girls than boys and, in addition to this, comforting was particularly strongly associated with girls.

There was a main effect for gender, $F(1, 229) = 38.06, p < 0.001, \eta p^2 = 0.143$, showing that girls ($M = 0.46, SD = 0.33$) gave significantly higher ratings (i.e. that girls would perform the actions) than boys ($M = 0.19, SD = 0.42$). Two one-sample t-tests, again applying a Bonferroni correction, were computed to assess whether boys' and girls' gender likelihood ratings were significantly different from 0 (the gender neutral option). Both boys', $t(120) = 4.96, p < 0.001$, and girls', $t(113) = 15.09, p < 0.001$, ratings were positive and significantly different from 0, indicating that while both boys and girls consider pro-social behaviour more likely of girls, girls judge this to a greater extent than boys.

There was also a main effect for age group, $F(2, 229) = 12.40, p < 0.001, \eta p^2 = 0.098$. Post hoc analysis using a Tukey HSD test ($p < .05$) revealed a significant difference comparing responses from children (i.e. early childhood and middle childhood) with the older, early adolescent group. Furthermore, three Bonferroni corrected, one-sample t tests were computed to assess whether participants' gender likelihood ratings were significantly different from 0 (the gender neutral option). At all ages, participants judged girls to be more likely to be pro-social than boys. Taken together these results indicate that while participants judged pro-social behaviour as more likely of girls at all ages, adolescent participants judged pro-social behaviour as more likely of girls than at other ages.

Finally, there was an interaction between gender and age group, $F(2, 234) = 3.05, p < 0.05, \eta p^2 = 0.026$. Three post hoc t-tests were computed to assess the differences between boys and girls ratings in each age group. In early childhood, $t(53) = -3.42, p < 0.001$, in middle childhood, $t(94) = -2.04, p < 0.05$, and in early adolescence, $t(82) = -5.12, p < 0.001$, girls rated pro-social behaviour as more likely of girls than boys did. Furthermore, six corrected one-sample t-tests were computed to assess whether boys and girls ratings were significantly away from 0 in each age group. With the exception of boys in early childhood, boys and girls in each age group judged pro-social behaviour to be significantly more likely of girls (shown in Table 5.2). These results reveal that across development, while all children judge that girls will be more likely to act pro-socially than boys, girls regard it as more likely that girls will perform pro-social acts than boys do.

Table 5.1 Descriptive statistics for likelihood judgements for each behaviour type

Behaviour type	N	Mean	Standard deviation
Giving	235	.30	.75
Sharing	235	.22	.70
Helping	235	.21	.68
Comforting	235	.55	.63

Table 5.2 The means (standard deviations) for boys and girls gender likelihood judgements at each of the four age groups

	Early childhood	Middle childhood	Early adolescence	All ages
Boys	.00 (.41)	.22* (.40)	.27* (.41)	.17* (.41)
Girls	.34* (.32)	.36* (.28)	.66* (.29)	.46* (.33)
Total	.17* (.40)	.28* (.35)	.46* (.41)	.32* (.40)

Note. *$p < 0.001$. -1 = more likely of boys through to $+1$ = more likely of girls.

Discussion

In this study we investigated how and to what degree children associate specific pro-social behaviours with boys or girls. We predicted that all children, at all ages, would judge all pro-social behaviour as more likely of girls, and this was supported. In addition, children increasingly judged pro-social behaviour as more likely of girls as they grew older. As predicted, at all ages girls judged pro-sociality as more likely of girls to a greater extent than boys. This study provides important insight into how children view pro-social behaviour as related to gender, and who boys and girls expect to perform pro-social behaviour. These results suggest that children and adolescents make a clear association between pro-social behaviour and femininity and view pro-social behaviour as female-typed.

It is clear that children and adolescents give consistent judgements that girls are more likely than boys to act pro-socially. In this sense we can view pro-social behaviour, or at least these broad behaviours, as female-typed. This could mean that pro-social behaviour is incorporated into children's and adolescents' gender schemas as a behaviour set that is identified as a 'girl thing to do' (Martin & Halverson, 1981). Gender typing of pro-social behaviour increased in early adolescence. This could be as a result of children's increasing social knowledge about gender norms (Martin & Ruble, 2009). Alternatively, a specific period of stereotype intensification in early adolescence could account for this difference (Galambos et al., 1990). Whatever the explanation, female typing of pro-social behaviour is stronger in adolescence than in childhood.

Girls also judged their own gender as more pro-social to a greater extent than boys at all ages. This may be a consequence of girls being particularly aware of the pro-social gender stereotype (Serbin et al., 1993), or perhaps having more of their identity invested in conforming to this stereotype (Beutel & Johnson, 2004). Alternatively, girls may merely display greater own-sex favouritism than boys (Serbin et al., 1993). Considering these results, it seems likely that children and adolescents use knowledge about gender to make predictions about children's current and future behaviour; when they evaluate how likely boys and girls are to perform pro-social behaviour, they will expect it more from girls than from boys.

An important practical consideration is how children and adolescents may react to pro-social behaviour when performed by boys. Children and adolescents use their gender schemas to assess the appropriateness of actions both for themselves and others (Martin, 2000). As pro-social behaviour appears to be female-typed, when boys perform this behaviour it may be deemed by peers as incongruent with their gender role. Classic research shows that boys are often judged harshly by peers for playing with gender-incongruent toys and engaging in cross-gender activities (Fagot, 1985). So if a boy chooses to display pro-social behaviour he may face social difficulties in interactions with his peers and therefore be discouraged from doing so in the future. Interestingly, greater sex role flexibility has been correlated with greater displays of pro-social behaviour from boys (Doescher & Sugawara, 1990) suggesting that when boys view gender roles less rigidly they may feel more able to perform pro-social actions.

The female typing of many pro-social acts could provide strong motivation for boys to perform fewer pro-social behaviours, particularly under certain circumstances (for instance, public interactions) where they may suffer social consequences for engaging in 'feminine' acts. This motivation may be felt more keenly at times in development when the pressure to conform to gender norms is often thought to become greater, for example in early adolescence (Fabes et al., 1999; McHale et al., 2004; Rae Clasen & Brown, 1985). Peers at this age often encourage others to act in a highly gender-congruent fashion. This could be a result of pubertal hormones helping to emphasize sex and gender as an integral and salient part of the self in the context of peer relationships (Fabes et al., 1999). These influences lead to a period in development during which gender roles become a great deal stricter and more rigid (McHale et al., 2004). Of course, the results from this initial study indicate that female typing of pro-social behaviour is present throughout childhood. Thus, whilst peers may be active reinforcers of gender norms across development, their impact in early adolescence may be particularly powerful.

Peers across childhood discourage gender atypical behaviour (that is, behaviour that does not conform to expectations regarding gender norms) (Carter & McCloskey, 1984). Therefore, it is important to explore whether boys will be judged negatively when they act pro-socially, as this is a female-typed behaviour. Our next study (study 1b) sought to determine whether social knowledge (such as gender role norms) about pro-social behaviour might influence how these actions are morally evaluated. Study 1b takes inspiration from work on inclusion and exclusion that showed that children aged 13 years judge exclusion as less bad than at other ages when presented with social information (gender and experience with the activity) about the person wishing to join the group (Killen & Stangor, 2001).

Study 1b: children in early adolescence judge boys being pro-social as less good than at other ages

Domain theory (Smetana, 2006) proposes that an important and developmentally relevant task for children is to acquire different domains of social knowledge, specifically, those concerning moral, social–conventional and personal issues. In the moral domain are rules (e.g. that it is wrong to steal or to harm others) that are universal and have a necessity to them. In the social–conventional domain are rules that are context dependent, such as it may be appropriate to wear one set of clothes at home, but more formal dress is required at another occasion. Matters in the personal domain are at the discretion and choice of individuals. These strands coexist and follow different developmental trajectories. Rules in different domains may be used together but may also be subordinated to each other in different contexts. This subordination arises when there are conflicts between rules or when events cannot be cleanly separated into moral or social–conventional components. In these 'mixed domain scenarios', events that have typically been construed in moral terms may be evaluated in social–conventional or personal terms (Killen, 1990; Smetana et al., 1991). If moral judgements about pro-social behaviours change depending on the gender of the protagonist performing the action, it could be suggested that social–conventional reasoning concerning gender typing of pro-social behaviour may affect moral judgements and become a source of reasoning alongside, or in competition with, the moral domain.

To date, no studies have explicitly examined age differences in how gender affects moral judgements about pro-social acts. However, work on children's judgements about including and excluding other children from groups has shown that social information can affect moral judgements (Theimer et al., 2001). Ordinarily, exclusion is consistently judged as wrong, and inclusion as right from childhood onwards. Furthermore, moral justifications (appealing to moral rules and norms such as fairness and turn taking) are given in support of these decisions (Theimer et al., 2001). These moral justifications are given based on the beliefs held by children about fairness and rights, equal treatment and equal access (Damon, 1983; Turiel, 1998). These scenarios are classified as *straightforward*, because children make a simple evaluation that employs only the moral domain. However, when additional information is provided this creates multifaceted scenarios. Killen and Stangor (2001) suggest that when decisions about potential exclusion from a group are made, these decisions involve coordination of moral judgements about the wrongfulness of exclusion with a range of social–conventional judgements and social group functioning, group identity and group stereotypes. Put simply, adolescents must weigh these two competing sources of information against each other when making decisions about exclusion.

Killen and Stangor (2001) find age-related variations in judgements made about multifaceted scenarios. For instance, when choosing between a same-sex child with more experience with the group activity, and an opposite-sex child with less experience exclusion of an opposite sex peer was judged as less wrong at 13 years than at 11 years (see again, Killen & Stangor, 2001). At 13 years, social–conventional reasoning was often used. This form of reasoning is based on beliefs held by children about group identity (Brown, 1989), group stereotypes (Carter & Patterson, 1982; Liben & Signorella, 1993; Stangor & Ruble, 1989; Stoddart & Turiel, 1985), and, particularly salient in Killen and Stangor (2001), beliefs about group functioning (Turiel, 1978, 1983, 1998). The researchers argued that this change represented a shift in the dominant domain being used in this age group.

In some respects a certain 'confusion' between moral and conventional reasoning at 13 years is somewhat surprising, given that children from a very young age can make clear distinctions between which actions are right and wrong (Vaish et al., 2011). This suggests a specific influence or salience of social–conventional reasoning at this age. Research on children's reasoning about social conventions has shown that social–conventional concepts change with age, particularly so in reference to social group roles and expectations and taking these into account (Helwig, 1995, 1997; Killen, 1991; Turiel, 1978, 1983, 1998). Whereas young children reason about social conventions in terms of social conformity (e.g. 'It's wrong to call a teacher by her first name because there is a rule about it'), older children reason about social group customs in terms of societal standards and social coordination (e.g. 'It's wrong to call a teacher by her first name because maybe the other students would think of her as a peer instead of someone with authority and higher status'; see Turiel, 1983, p. 103). With age, children become increasingly concerned about the nature of social groups and the norms and expectations that go along with the structure and functioning of the group. Killen and Stangor (2001) argued that the changes in adolescents' judgements about exclusion at 13 years represented a shift in the dominant domain being used in this age group, and may represent increased importance of social–conventional knowledge to adolescents at this age.

This shift in judgements at 13 years might also reflect children's underlying awareness of intra- (as well as inter-) group characteristics in making judgements (Killen et al., 2012) or, not necessarily unrelated, more specific changes in children's gender relations and gender knowledge (Martin & Ruble, 2009; Serbin et al., 1993). In support of this, whilst some researchers argue that gender stereotype flexibility increases throughout late childhood and adolescence (Carter & Patterson, 1982; Katz & Ksansnak, 1994), others argue that gender stereotype knowledge intensifies at this age (Hill & Lynch, 1983) and that gender flexibility decreases (Bartini, 2006; Galambos et al., 1990; Stoddart & Turiel, 1985). Increased gender stereotype saliency at this age could be responsible for the increased use of social–conventional reasoning in justifying intergroup exclusion based on gender.

In the present study we extended the work of Killen and colleagues to establish whether gender affects children's evaluations of pro-social actions at different ages. In line with previous research, we expected that children will judge that pro-social actions are 'good' or morally right. However, including gender information produced scenarios that were *multifaceted*, because there is a competing opportunity to frame judgements in social–conventional as well as moral terms. Thus our second study investigated if varying the gender of the protagonist performing pro-social behaviour affected the moral judgements made by participants about that behaviour. Again, we explored these judgements at different age groups. We predicted that at 12–13 years children would judge boys who acted pro-socially in a less positive manner than girls who acted pro-socially because, in a mixed scenario, individuals at this age may be more likely to invoke gender role (social–conventional) knowledge when making judgements about pro-social behaviour than at other ages.

Methods

Participants

The study included 265 boys and 234 girls between 6 and 16 years. Participants were in five age groups: 6–7 years ($n = 134$, $M = 6.7$, min = 6.27, max = 7.26, $SD = .29$, 70 boys, 64 girls), 8–9 years ($n = 125$, $M = 8.7$, min = 8.29, max = 9.33, $SD = .29$, 62 boys, 63 girls), 10–11 years ($n = 110$, $M = 10.8$, min = 10.29, max = 11.58, $SD = .29$, 62 boys, 48 girls), 12–13 years ($n = 70$, $M = 13.0$, min = 12.41, max = 13.34, $SD = .29$, 36 boys, 34 girls), and 14–15 years ($n = 60$, $M = 14.8$, $SD = .30$, 35 boys, 25 girls). Participants were from two schools (the same schools used in Study 1a).

Material

Each participant was shown two vignettes (6–7, 8–9 and 10–11 years), or read two text-based scenarios (12–13 and 14–15 years), of either boys or girls performing pro-social behaviour or failing to act pro-socially (creating four scenarios: boys acting pro-socially, boys failing to act pro-socially, girls acting pro-socially and girls failing to act pro-socially). In these vignettes (or written scenarios) a male or female protagonist was acting pro-socially (shown sharing and then helping) or failing to act pro-socially (shown not sharing and then not helping) towards two other children (a girl and a boy). For example, for the boys acting pro-socially scenario, children were shown a vignette of a boy called Simon sharing his book with another boy and girl. They were then shown a vignette of Simon helping another girl and boy (Sarah and Shaun) to pick up some balls they had dropped.

Procedure

Each participant only saw one of the four different types of scenario. Following the vignettes participants judged the vignettes in terms of how good or bad the behaviour was. Specifically they were asked, 'How good or bad is this?' and were reminded to answer regarding what they had seen happen in the vignettes. They made judgements using a standard 5-point Likert scale (1 = Very Bad, 5 = Very Good).

Results

A 2 (gender) × 5 (age group) × 4 (scenario) ANOVA was completed to assess the differences in participants' judgements of how good or bad an action was if performed by a boy or a girl. As expected, there was a significant main effect for scenario, $F(3, 498) = 837.29$, $p < 0.001$, $\eta p^2 = .845$, indicating that participants rated pro-social acts more positively ($M = 4.73$, $SD = 0.67$) than instances where an individual failed to act pro-socially ($M = 1.53$, $SD = 0.64$). Neither participant gender nor age group showed significant effects on judgements. However, the interaction between age group and scenario was significant, $F(12, 498) = 3.17$, $p < 0.001$, $\eta p^2 = .077$.

Four one-way ANOVAs were computed to assess age group differences in judgements for each scenario. The means and standard deviations at each age for each behaviour type are shown in Table 5.3. When participants made judgements about a boy acting pro-socially, there was a significant age difference, F (4, 125) = 2.85, p < 0.05, ηp^2 = .086. Post hoc analyses using a Tukey HSD (p < .05) test indicated that at 6–7 years children judged boys' pro-social behaviour to be morally better than at 12–13 years for these pro-social acts. When participants made judgements about a boy failing to act pro-socially, there was also a significant difference in judgements, F (4, 119) = 4.15, p < 0.01, ηp^2 = .126. Post hoc analyses showed that 8–9 year olds judged a boy's failure to act pro-socially as morally worse than 12–3 year olds did. There was no significant difference in judgements relating to girls' being pro-social or failing to be pro-social.

Discussion

Our second study investigated whether the gender of a protagonist performing pro-social behaviour affected moral judgements about these behaviours by children and adolescents. As we expected, the results indicated that participants at all ages judged pro-social behaviour as morally good and failing to act pro-socially as morally bad. However, also as expected, at 12–13 years of age adolescents judged boys acting pro-socially as 'less good' than at other ages (and boys failing to act pro-socially as 'less bad' than at other ages).

Our first study demonstrated the gender typing of pro-social behaviour as feminine. In this study we see evidence that, in early adolescence, participants may

Table 5.3 The means (standard deviations) for children's and adolescents' judgements about the morality of pro-social behaviour (and failing to be pro-social) at each age group

	7 year olds	9 year olds	11 year olds	13 year olds	15 year olds	All ages
Boys being pro-social	4.85 (0.36)$_a$	4.72 (0.84)$_{a,b}$	4.72 (0.63)$_{a,b}$	4.21 (0.92)$_b$	4.67(0.65)$_{a,b}$	4.67 (0.70)
Boys failing to be pro-social	1.56 (0.80)$_{c,d}$	1.39 (0.56)$_c$	1.35 (0.63)$_{c,d}$	2.13 (0.96)$_d$	1.85 (0.55)$_{c,d}$	1.58 (0.74)
Girls being pro-social	4.88 (0.33)	4.74 (0.89)	4.79 (0.69)	4.80 (0.41)	4.63 (0.62)	4.78 (0.63)
Girls failing to be pro-social	1.44 (0.50)	1.25 (0.44)	1.67 (0.48)	1.60 (0.59)	1.63 (0.49)	1.49 (0.52)

Note. Subscript with different letters are significant at the p < 0.05 level or below. 1 = Very bad through to 5 = Very good.

not have made judgements about pro-social actions in purely moral terms because gender may influence moral evaluations of the situation. A possible explanation for this age effect relates to the well-established observation that in early adolescence stereotypes regarding gender roles are consolidating and possibly intensifying (Hill & Lynch, 1983), gender typing becomes rigorous and inflexible (McHale et al., 2004), and gender flexibility may decrease (Bartini, 2006; Galambos et al., 1990). Thus while children at all ages seem to regard pro-social behaviour as feminine, at 12–13 years this intensification of gender roles exerts a more powerful pressure on judgements and, for boys, pro-social acts are affected not only by moral concerns, but also influenced by group (gender) norms and considerations. Furthermore, all children (i.e. boys and girls at this age) appear to recognize the tensions or difficulties that may be experienced by boys engaging in pro-social acts at this age.

These results fit with previous work suggesting that, in early adolescence, children may invoke social–conventional knowledge to justify excluding a child of the opposite gender (see Killen & Stangor, 2001). In the present study, only judgements about boy's pro-social behaviour change at this age, not those made about girls. Moreover, the judgements of both boys and girls reflect recognition of the tension between acting pro-socially and being male at this age. This suggests that the specific knowledge regarding gender norms, and the female typing of pro-social behaviour, is influencing judgements about boys in these scenarios. Both genders appear to be aware of the costs of transgressing gender boundaries and therefore judge boys negatively when they are shown performing a feminine behaviour.

It is also noteworthy that the changes in moral judgements about boy's pro-social acts are specific to early adolescence. Our first study indicated that, broadly, pro-social behaviour is female-typed from age 6–15 years (study 1a). Yet there is no simple relation between gender typing and moral evaluations because children judge boys and girls similarly (in moral terms) when they perform pro-social acts at all other ages. However, it is certainly true that at 12–13 years, when stereotypes are most intense (Hill & Lynch, 1983) and pressure to conform to gender role expectations is likely at a peak (Rae Clasen & Brown, 1985), moral judgements become affected. Whatever the source of the age-specific association, our results indicate that after this age (from 14 years) participants no longer interpret pro-social acts as a 'mixed scenario' when judging boys behaviour.

Our first two studies clarified a number of important developmental considerations about the relations among gender, age and pro-sociality. Firstly, we found that four key types of pro-social behaviour (i.e. sharing, helping, giving and comforting), are female-typed by both children and adolescents (as opposed to more general personality characteristics – see Powlishta, 1995, 2000). In other words, up to 15 years of age participants felt it was more likely that girls rather than boys would perform pro-social acts. However, while this association extends across development, it strengthens and entails specific consequences in early adolescence when, compared with children at other ages, boys are judged less positively when they are performing these female-typed behaviours. Our finding of a specific difference in terms of boys' judgements at 12–13 years suggests that something specific about children's gender knowledge or gender roles affects judgements in early adolescence. Specifically, because pro-social behaviour is regarded as feminine and early adolescents are more accepting of peers who conform to more traditional gender norms (Horn, 2007), the pressure to conform peaks at around age 13 (Fabes et al., 1999; McHale et al., 2004; Rae Clasen & Brown, 1985). Thus peer acceptance may mediate the relation between self-perceived gender typicality and self-worth (Smith & Leaper, 2006). Consequently boys at 12–13 years may feel social pressure not to perform pro-social behaviours for fear of being judged as too 'girly' or 'sissy' or may shy away from pro-social behaviour altogether. Furthermore, if they are discouraged from pro-social behaviour, they may also be discouraged from other behaviours that are traditionally thought of as feminine, such as showing empathy towards others (Lennon & Eisenberg, 1987).

The feminization of pro-social behaviour has important implications for moral reasoning, development and moral identity, or in other words, the sense of self as a good or bad person (Blasi, 2004; Reed & Aquino, 2003). Children and adolescents are likely to be acutely aware of the positive moral status of pro-social behaviour, and from an early age (Vaish et al., 2011). However, at 12–13 years children recognize that gender introduces a relevant element into judgements about pro-sociality and, specifically, that boys are to some extent absolved from adhering to or acting in accordance with these moral rules. Boys may also want to distance themselves from particular pro-social behaviours, possibly as a result of the negative (or less positive) judgements they receive from peers when performing these behaviours. How, then, do boys reconcile this with broader moral reasoning and, in turn, moral behaviour?

Study 2: there are 'masculine' and 'feminine' pro-social behaviours in early adolescence

Children and adolescents recognize a strong motivation to perform pro-social behaviours. However, around 13 years of age there is tension between the female typing of many pro-social acts and these moral motivations for boys. In other words, at 13 years boys may experience ambiguity between their moral role (to be a good individual) and their gender role (to be a good example of a boy). However, this conflict of roles appears to diminish at 14–15 years, and moral judgements return to patterns seen at younger ages where pro-social behaviour is judged as good, regardless of gender. This implies two things. Firstly, that the ambiguity between roles seen at 12–13 years is somehow resolved for boys by age 14–15 years. Secondly, that 12–13 years old is a particularly sensitive period in terms of the relationship between gender and pro-social behaviour. We must therefore ask what processes are involved at this age that might allow this ambiguity (or incongruence in beliefs) to be overcome.

The answer may lie in research using adults. Eagly (2009) suggests that gender roles can be used as a tool for understanding gender differences in pro-social behaviour. In concepts originally proposed by Bakan (1966) men are traditionally thought of as more agentic – that is, assertive, competitive and dominant, whilst women are thought of as more communal – that is friendly, unselfish and emotionally expressive. Men are also thought of as chivalrous and heroic, and women more empathic. Eagly (2009) suggests that these qualities may influence the ways in which men and women choose to be act pro-socially. For example, pro-social behaviours such as comforting someone when upset and providing community service are congruent with the relational emphasis within the female gender role. In contrast, behaviours such as providing physical assistance and defending others are congruent with the concepts of dominance and chivalry traditionally associated with men.

By examining the qualities that define traditional gender roles, Eagly provides a persuasive argument that men and women can be equally pro-social, but may express pro-sociality in different ways. However, to date, little research has addressed the developmental origins of these gender differences in the expression of pro-social behaviours. As we have seen, gender stereotypes consolidate and intensify in early adolescence (Hill & Lynch, 1983), and gender norms become more rigid and inflexible at this age (McHale et al., 2004). Our findings of a sensitive period in terms of gender consolidation at 13 years suggest that this age could represent a pivotal point in development where girls and boys are learning gendered ways of expressing pro-social behaviour.

For our final study we wanted to look more closely at the reasoning processes that underlie judgements *of* and reasoning *about* pro-social behaviour at 13 years of age. We therefore used a qualitative approach to explore whether early adolescents (specifically aged 13 years old) believed that girls and boys behave in different ways when it comes to pro-social behaviour. We chose to use focus groups because they allow participants, in interaction with each other, to speak for themselves, based on their own experiences, and in their own language (Patton, 1990). Moreover, there is greater opportunity within such a setting for peers to question, confront and explore reasoning and attitudes in greater depth than might be possible using questionnaire or even adult–child interview techniques. In essence, our reasons for using focus groups were similar to those discussed by Bergin et al. (2003). Specifically, focus groups were desirable because individual pro-social behaviours have a low frequency of occurrence; the presence of adults undoubtedly changes adolescents' behaviours, often rendering observations invalid; pro-social acts are often subtle, hard to detect and involve a number of variables that change performance likelihood; and pro-social behaviour is situation specific and is open to interpretation by the performer. This is particularly important for this study, which seeks to extensively explore how judgements and gender norm beliefs influence levels and types of pro-social behaviour in boys and girls. Using this more detailed and open format, the final study investigated whether adolescents felt that specific behaviours were performed more by boys or girls, behaviours could only be performed by either boys or girls, whether peers were judged for performing behaviours that were not expected of them, and whether any factors altered the acceptability of boys and girls performing certain pro-social behaviours.

Method

Participants

Twenty-seven 12 year olds were randomly selected and invited to take part in discussions. The school was located in a predominantly middle-class area of South-East England. The participants were predominantly white, with four of the participants coming from other ethnic backgrounds. Participants were allocated at random into two same-sex groups (one with seven boys, one with seven girls), one mixed-sex groups of seven (three boys, four girls), and one mixed-sex group of six (three boys, three girls). The composition of the groups was varied in order to cater for differences in conversational dynamics (Leman et al., 2005).

Materials and procedure

The sessions began with the selected participants coming to a small, quiet room away from distractions. The adult moderator (the first author) then outlined the plans and rules for the fifty minute session. These plans included a number of tasks for discussions to follow. The sessions roughly corresponded to the length of a class session at the school. Participants were reminded that there were no 'right' or 'wrong' answers to the tasks and that they should try and discuss each choice to reach a consensus (but if they did disagree then this could be discussed also).

The moderator then outlined the first task. This involved placing a masculinity–femininity decision task on the table in front of the participants. The task involved the groups using a scale which was divided into three sections, the far left labelled masculine, the middle labelled as neutral and the far right labelled as feminine. They were then presented with sixteen objects, eight traditionally viewed as feminine (e.g. dollhouse, make-up) and eight traditionally viewed as masculine (e.g. football, cowboy guns) and asked to place these along the scale, and to discuss their choices. This discussion was kept brief, as the first task was designed to get them thinking about gender stereotypes and was not for analysis. Following completion of the task, the moderator led a discussion on why participants had placed objects where they had.

When discussion had reached a natural conclusion, the moderator then outlined the second task. This involved placing twenty-four pro-social behaviours along the same masculinity–femininity scale. Pro-social behaviours were defined by the moderator as 'voluntary behaviour intended to benefit another', and as 'positive interactions with others'. The moderator asked the participants to name a few pro-social behaviours and, when confident they knew what defined a pro-social behaviour, gave them the twenty-four behaviours to place on the scale. The behaviours used were taken from a focus group study that explored the complexity of pro-social behaviour in adolescence (Bergin et al., 2003). These behaviours are presented in Table 5.4. Once they had placed these on the scale, the moderator then encouraged discussion about their placements.

Participants also completed two further tasks to encourage discussion about social judgement following the performance of pro-social behaviours by boys and girls. In each task the participants had to place the twenty-four pro-social behaviours along a good–bad scale, one time responding as if a boy was performing these actions, another time responding as if a girl was. After they had placed the behaviours, they were again encouraged to discuss their placements and whether judgements might change based on different factors. Examples of factors included audience (i.e. whether the behaviour was performed in public or in a one-to-one setting), urgency (i.e. how serious the problem was) and relationship (i.e. was the recipient a stranger or a friend). The moderator ensured that discussions were open, free flowing and honest, by providing prompts but not dictating the nature or direction of conversation. The groups were audiotaped, and the audio tapes were transcribed by the first author.

Results

Thematic analysis, which is the most common form of analysis for qualitative data (Guest et al., 2012), was conducted (by the first author) on the data set in order to identify and establish patterns in adolescents' discussions. This was achieved following the steps outlined for researchers using this approach (Braun & Clarke, 2006; Guest et al., 2012), involving a number of stages. In the first stage, each focus group recording was transcribed to form a data item. In the second stage, each data

Table 5.4 Male- and female-typed pro-social behaviours as identified in focus group discussions

Male-typed pro-social behaviours	Neutral	Female-typed pro-social behaviours
Provides physical assistance	Helps others develop skills	Provides emotional support
Willing to play	Humorous	Avoids fights
Stands up for others	Shares	Peacemaker
Confronts others when wrong	Keeps confidences	Provides community service
Inclusive	Expresses happiness	Avoids hurting feelings
	Coaches others in social skills	
	Honest	
	Admits mistakes	
	Apologizes	
	Does not make fun of others	
	Does not brag	
	Good sport	
	Calm – does not yell	
	Compliments and encourages others	

item was read through at least two times, and initial codes were generated based on recurring concepts (this included coding any extracts that had nothing to do with gender and pro-social behaviour, and excluding these from further analysis). In the third stage, the codes generated were collated and compared to generate potential themes. In stage four, data items were re-read to check whether potential themes corresponded with the data extracts indentified in stage two, and with the data set as a whole. In stage five, themes were defined and named. Six themes emerged from this analysis: 1) that anybody can act pro-socially; 2) there are specific gendered pro-social behaviours; 3) the features of masculine pro-sociality; 4) the features of feminine pro-sociality; 5) judgements about pro-social behaviour; and 6) context of pro-social behaviour. The next section provides extracts from the data set that demonstrate the existence of these themes.

Anybody can act pro-socially

Adolescents were quick to point out that anybody was capable of being pro-social, regardless of their sex:

> I think there are also things that are expected of all genders . . . they're [pro-social behaviours] seen as good things for all genders whether you're a man or a woman you should, you're seen as good if you do those things, and if you don't do those things you are generally seen as a bad person.

There are specific gendered behaviours

A number of behaviours were classified as explicitly more appropriate for boys or girls to perform, or in other words were gender-typed. Those identified as masculine were willing to play (i.e. willing to play a game or in a group), confronting others when wrong, inclusive, standing up for others and providing physical support. Behaviours identified as feminine were avoiding fights, avoiding hurting feelings, providing community service, peacemaker and providing emotional support (see Table 5.4).

The features of masculine pro-sociality

Discussions revealed that there were certain characteristics that helped to group behaviours identified as masculine above. Discussions revealed that masculine behaviours are direct/physical:

> [in reference to pro-social behaviour] whereas with boys it's like physical.

Involve possible confrontation:

> I think because it's like provides physical assistance, that's more like, like if your mates being bullied and he's like upset, boys are more likely to walk up to whoever's bullying them and punch them in the face.

And are largely performed in public/in front of larger audiences:

> I think boys are like . . . the bigger the crowd the better. The bigger the crowd they can show off more.

The features of feminine pro-sociality

Discussions revealed that characteristics that group feminine pro-social behaviours are that they involve emotion:

> Because, like girls, you kind of expect them . . . to . . . erm . . . provide emotional support because it's kind of a girly thing to do, because they do it with their mates.

Are focused on relationships:

> Because like I think, boys are more likely to just be like, oh I'll just leave it, it'll calm down in a bit, but girls are more like kind of worried, so they don't want their friends to be upset and argue and stuff, they just want everything to be happy.

Avoid confrontation:

> I think the avoids fights one is feminine, because most girls like to talk things over than rather getting physical to each other.

And are more interpersonal and private:

> [Who works behind the scenes] Like the girls, they like don't actually say it, face to face, but they try and make it alright.

These results show that adolescents may label pro-social behaviours based on characteristics that fit with broader gender stereotypes, the most obvious distinction being between agency and physicality (masculine) versus communality and emotionality (feminine).

Peer judgements of pro-social behaviour

As well as key themes regarding likelihood and acceptability of pro-social behaviours by boys and girls, specific themes regarding appropriateness and judgement emerged. Participants discussed in great depth what their reactions would be if they saw a peer performing behaviours typically associated with the other gender. For example, if they saw a boy providing community service:

> Like if a boy did something for the community, they would get . . . A lot of stick.

Or why a girl wouldn't provide physical assistance:

> But the thing is, I do notice that, say, say someone's done something to hurt someone and I've seen it happen and then a lot of the girls will just stand there, their close friends will just stand there and be like, they're too worried to do anything, because of the way they'll be perceived by the others.

Furthermore, adolescents at this age may make predictions about peers' expected and future behaviour in pro-social scenarios based on their gender. For example, focus groups agreed that a boy would be unlikely to comfort a friend when they are crying, because that transgresses gender boundaries and is seen as too 'sissy' or 'girly':

> [Why would coaching others in social skills be bad] . . . It would make them more girly . . . It would make them different.

Discussions also revealed that peers may have a significant role in shaping adolescents' gender-typed pro-social behaviours, by providing negative judgements when peers perform gender atypical behaviours. This also appears to be more severe for boys:

> [When doing community service] . . . He'd get a lot of banter and stick for it. Say a guy went out and like, worked in a nursing home or something, he'd a get a load of stick for it when he come back to school.

Adolescents may therefore be driven away from certain types of pro-social behaviour because they are deemed inappropriate for their gender role and the characteristics of that gender role. For example, boys may be driven away from providing emotional support because this is deemed as too feminine, or not sufficiently masculine. Conversely, there appear to be behaviours that are deemed as highly appropriate for each gender role, and it can be assumed that these will be positively reinforced by peers.

Context of pro-social behaviour

Discussions also revealed key contextual factors that influenced how acceptable certain behaviours were for boys or girls. The most important distinction was between a public and a personal setting (for example, in a group of friends or in a one-to-one scenario). Although it wasn't specifically discussed, it can be assumed that children could perform behaviours that were typical for their gender in any situation, as they are viewed as gender congruent. However, for atypical behaviours, children were more likely to perform these in one-to-one settings (assumingly to avoid judgement from peers). In other words typically feminine behaviours, such as providing emotional support, were more/only acceptable for boys to perform if they were in one-to-one scenarios, but not in groups:

> Boys like would be comforting to people if their friends weren't around.

Typically masculine behaviours, such as providing physical assistance, were also more acceptable for girls to perform if they were in one-to-one scenarios rather than in front of a large group:

> I wouldn't like that, like I know it sounds really horrible but it's really hard to help someone when there is loads of people around, cos you've gotta act, like you've got to conform to what the others are doing, you know if everyone else like doesn't do anything, it's like well I'm not gonna do anything.

Discussion

Our third and final study used focus groups to investigate whether adolescents aged 12 felt that specific behaviours were performed more by boys or girls, behaviours could only be performed by either boys or girls, whether peers were judged for performing behaviours not expected of them, and whether any factors altered the acceptability of boys and girls performing certain pro-social behaviours. Focus groups were chosen as they allowed adolescents to speak openly and freely about the topics presented, and in their own words.

There were a number of pro-social behaviours (from the twenty-four used) that were identified as specifically masculine or feminine (or something that boys or girls 'do', or do more). Study 1b showed that at 12–13 years boys experience a moral ambiguity caused by competition between their moral pressures (to be a good boy) and their social pressures (to be a good example of a boy) with regards to pro-social behaviour. One possible way in which boys may resolve this conflict is for boys to identify and perform pro-social behaviours that are more consonant with a masculine gender role, in order to satisfy both the moral obligation to be 'good' and their social obligation to conform to gender norms and roles.

In further support of this argument is that the behaviours identified as masculine or feminine are characterized by qualities that are congruent with the male and female gender role respectively. For example, participants categorized feminine behaviours as relational, involving emotion, avoidant of confrontation and more interpersonal/private. Masculine behaviours were categorized as involving confrontation, being direct/physical and being more likely to be performed in public. The characteristics of these behaviours are parsimonious with the characteristics that define the differences between the male and female gender roles, namely as agentic versus communal respectively (Bakan, 1966). The increasing division between masculine and feminine pro-social behaviours in adolescence could be the precursor to the divisions highlighted in research using adults (Eagly, 2009).

Peers also appear to be important in the gender typing of pro-social behaviour, as adolescents at this age readily chastised peers who performed pro-social behaviours associated with the other sex, and did so much more harshly with male peers than female peers. Boys are discouraged by peers across childhood not to engage in cross-gender activities and to not play with other gender toys to a much greater extent than are girls (Fagot, 1985). Boys have also been shown to feel much greater pressure to not be like the other sex than girls (Egan & Perry, 2001), and that the pressure to conform to gender roles is greatest in early adolescence (around age 12/13 years, Rae Clasen & Brown. 1985). This study shows that discouragement and reinforcement by peers also applies to pro-social behaviour (a moral behaviour). The importance of peer judgement is further reflected in adolescents' discussions of the context in which pro-social behaviours are performed. Adolescents highlighted that gender atypical behaviours could be performed in private, presumably as it avoids social judgement incurred when performing these behaviours in public (or in front of an audience of some kind).

A key message from this study is one which is reflected in adult research. It may not be that women and girls are more pro-social than boys and men; it is that women and girls are different in their pro-social behaviour compared to boys and men. In other words, children think it is all right for both boys and girls to be pro-social; however, they are also aware of the constraints on boys (and to a certain extent girls) performing certain pro-social behaviours. This study provided valuable insight into how pro-social behaviours are gender-typed, how this gender typing occurs in relation to broader gender role characteristics, and how peer judgements help to create and maintain this gender typing.

General discussion

The aim of this chapter was to explore the relation between gender and pro-social behaviour across development. Results from meta-analyses on gender differences in pro-social behaviour have indicated that studies using self- and other-reports have larger effect sizes than studies that use observational methods (Fabes & Eisenberg, 1996). This suggests that a confounding factor influences participants in report studies (and to a lesser extent observation studies) – possibly the stereotype that girls are more pro-social than boys (Serbin et al., 1993). We have investigated not only how children and adolescents gender-type pro-social behaviour, but also what the consequences of this gender typing might be in early adolescence. Our qualitative analysis indicates that, even at 12 years, adolescents have a firm knowledge of gendered forms of pro-social behaviour and may be beginning to apply them.

The studies detailed in this chapter have provided some important new insights into the relation between gender and pro-social behaviour. Our initial study demonstrated that children and adolescents judge that girls are more likely than boys to perform broad categories of pro-social behaviour commonly used in previous studies (such as sharing and comforting). These judgements add weight to the suggestion made by other researchers that there is a gender stereotype regarding pro-social behaviour that girls are 'nicer' than boys (Eisenberg & Mussen, 1989; Eisenberg et al., 2007; Serbin et al., 1993). A further study followed this up by exploring how children and adolescents evaluated the moral dimension to pro-social behaviour in mixed scenarios involving gender. At 12–13 years, judgements about the moral status of actions may be influenced by social knowledge about the gender norms regarding pro-social behaviour, but only for boys. Specifically, at 12–13 years all participants felt it less morally wrong for a boy to fail to act pro-socially and less morally right to act pro-socially.

On the basis of findings from the initial studies, our final study probed underlying elements of reasoning about gender and pro-social behaviour at 12–13 years. This age was chosen due to the increased gender typing of pro-social behaviour at this age in study 1a, the changes in moral judgements seen in study 1b, and because this represents a time when gender stereotypes are particularly salient (Hill & Lynch, 1983), and pressure to conform to gender norms peaks (Fabes et al., 1999; McHale et al., 2004; Rae Clasen & Brown, 1985). A close analysis of the themes emerging from our focus groups indicates that when more specific or detailed pro-social behaviours are considered adolescents make more fine-grained judgements about the appropriateness of boys or girls performing specific types of social act. Specifically, in our focus group study, while participants labelled some pro-social behaviours as feminine there were also pro-social behaviours that were deemed to be masculine.

These studies demonstrate how the relation between gender and beliefs about pro-social behaviour changes across development. Generally, pro-social behaviour is consistently gender-typed from 5 years. However, at 12–13 years (early adolescence) the association appears to strengthen and extend to influence evaluations of boys' moral behaviour. Therefore, a key message from this chapter is the existence of a 'sensitive' period in early adolescence, where gender roles and norms appear to create an ambiguity between acting morally and acting in a gender congruent way for boys. This period of conflict was highlighted by using mixed scenarios that evoked the use of social knowledge about gender that competed with the moral domain. Girls can act pro-socially free of this role conflict, whereas boys may wish to be morally good and perform pro-social behaviours, but fear being labelled as feminine for doing so. Key elements in this conflict may be resolved after 14 years when adolescents begin to think less rigidly about gender roles (Katz & Ksansnak, 1994). However, it may also be resolved as a consequence of adolescents adapting to the pressures presented by gender roles, and appreciating that pro-social behaviour may become less about *who* is doing more, but more about *how* they are doing it. For example while adolescents in study 2 identified a number of pro-social behaviours that are deemed as appropriate for both boys and girls to perform (and that may not present a moral–social conflict for adolescents to perform), discussions showed that some pro-social behaviours become more finely discriminated in line with traditional gender roles.

These 'masculine' and 'feminine' pro-social behaviours fit with broader concepts about gender roles and gender stereotypes and how boys and girls (and men and women) are supposed to act, similar to patterns seen in studies using adults (Eagly, 2009). For example a meta-analysis into studies of adult helping found that men helped more than women (Eagly & Crowley, 1986), and this effect size was much larger when the person requiring help was in the presence of onlookers (or in a public scenario). In contrast, studies that have investigated pro-social behaviours that take place in close relationships, and involve more empathic and communal behaviours, have shown that women perform these behaviours much more than men (see again, Eagly, 2009).

In empirical studies, if specific behaviours are not defined (or if the categories are too broad) participants may automatically be cued towards girls and women, in judging who performs these behaviours more (seen in study 1a). However, if more specific pro-social behaviours are used (seen in study 2) there may be more precise associations and relationships between gender and pro-social behaviour, particularly in adolescence. Very few studies use such a diverse range of pro-social behaviour as used in study 2 of this chapter. This is more understandable in studies using younger children, as research has shown that pro-social behaviour becomes more complex as children grow older (Bergin et al., 2003). However, it is clear that the use of a wide range of specific behaviours is important. Some behaviours have specific associations with gender, and some none at all. Studies that investigate helping (providing physical assistance) may garner different effect sizes for gender differences in behaviour, and even different relationships, than studies investigating providing emotional support.

These studies support the suggestion that there is a consistent stereotype that girls are more pro-social than boys. Building on the stereotypes that girls are 'nicer' than boys (Serbin et al., 1993), and that girls are better behaved than boys (Hastings et al., 2007), these studies have shown that children allocate specific pro-social behaviours to girls when asked about likelihood of behaviour; they expect girls to be more pro-social. Secondly, we considered the possible consequences when children (specifically boys) break this stereotype and engage in behaviours that are seen as incongruent with children's and adolescents' gender stereotypes. In early adolescence, boys displaying certain pro-social behaviours may lead to problems in terms of peer perceptions of gender norms, as they may be performing behaviours that are broadly judged as feminine (whereas girls are free to perform pro-social behaviours, as these behaviours are congruent with their gender role).

Finally, early adolescence is a time when boys are conflicted between doing what is right morally and what is right for them as a boy. As the focus group study (study 2) only utilized adolescents aged 12 years, we can only draw conclusions from this study with reference to this age group, and the small sample it used. However, broader gender role expectations may help mould adolescents' pro-social behaviours, with peers acting as willing enforcers of these stereotypes. This diversification of pro-social behaviours may provide boys with a way to resolve the conflict they face, by embracing pro-social behaviours that are more masculine.

Participant responses from study 2 suggest that adolescents (especially boys) may not attempt behaviours in public that are deemed inappropriate for them by peers. This may limit some moral behaviours that should be considered good to perform, such as providing emotional support (for boys) and providing physical assistance (for girls). Therefore, the first key task is to employ a comprehensive quantitative research design to concretely identify patterns of gender typing for the twenty-four pro-social behaviours used in study 2. A further research question is whether it is possible to change adolescents' pro-social behaviour by labelling behaviours differently. For instance, would it be possible to present a feminine behaviour with a masculine label, in order to cue different associations to gender roles? Would this make these behaviours more appealing to each gender? And would it be possible to manipulate the associations made between pro-social behaviours and gender to encourage gender atypical pro-sociality? It is an ambitious task, especially with behaviours such as 'providing emotional support' that seem to evoke such strong reactions from peers (for boys), but it is worth exploring.

In addition to specific research questions, there are broader issues to tackle. Research using adults has shown that men and women may not necessarily be that different in their levels of pro-social behaviour, but may be pro-social in different ways (Dovidio et al., 2006; Eagly, 2009). The research in this chapter suggests that this separation of pro-social behaviour may occur much earlier than adulthood, and that there is a compelling argument that early adolescence represents the beginning point of this process. To this end, future research needs to account for the differences within pro-social behaviour, and the number of behaviours involved when using this broad term.

Pro-social behaviour is often more closely associated with girls than boys. In their review, Radke-Yarrow and Zahn-Waxler (1986) stated that until researchers 'give up reliance on the very innocuous and almost conventionalized pro-social behaviours that reappear in studies . . . this field of research will be relatively limited in predicting or controlling pro-social behaviour in ways that make a difference in the lives of individuals and groups' (p. 230). Part of the challenge that continues to lie ahead is to move towards considering a more diverse range of behaviours and contexts for understanding pro-social behaviour. For example, if early adolescents can appreciate that boys and girls are both pro-social, but just in different ways, then they will also understand that there is plenty of 'sugar and spice' to go around.

References

Bakan, D. (1966). *The duality of human existence: isolation and communion in Western man.* Boston, MA: Beacon Press.

Balk, D. E. (1995). *Adolescent development: early through late adolescence.* Pacific Grove, CA: Brooks/Cole.

Bartini, M. (2006). Gender role flexibility in early adolescence: developmental change in attitudes, self-perceptions, and behaviours. *Sex Roles, 55,* 233–245.

Bergin, C., Talley, S., & Hamer, L. (2003). Prosocial behaviours of young adolescents: a focus group study. *Journal of Adolescence, 26,* 13–32.

Best, D. L., Williams, J. E., Cloud, J. M., Davis, S. M., Robertson, L. S., Edwards, J. R., & Fowles, J. (1977). Development of sex-trait stereotypes among young childen in the United States, England and Ireland. *Child Development, 48,* 1375–1384.

Beutel, A. M., & Johnson, M. K. (2004). Gender and prosocial values during adolescence: a research note. *The Sociological Quarterly, 45*(2), 379–393.

Blasi, A. (2004). Moral functioning: moral understanding and personality. In Lapsley, D. K., & Narvaez, D. (Eds), *Moral development, self and identity: essays in honor of Augusto Blasi.* Mahwah, NJ: Lawrence Erlbaum & Associates.

Bond, N. D., & Phillips, B. N. (1971). Personality traits associated with altruistic behaviour of children. *Journal of School Psychology, 9*, 24–34.

Bosacki, S. L. (2003). Psychological pragmatics in preadolescents: sociomoral understanding, self-worth, and school behaviour. *Journal of Youth and Adolescence, 32*, 141–155.

Braun, V., & Clarke, V. (2006). Using thematic analysis in psychology. *Qualitative Research in Psychology, 3*, 77–101.

Brown, B. B. (1989). The role of peer groups in adolescent's adjustment to secondary school. In Berndt, T., & Ladd, G. (Eds), *Peer relationships in child development* (pp. 188–215). New York: Wiley.

Caprara, G. V., Barbaranerlli, C., & Pastorelli, C. (2001). Prosocial behaviour and aggression in childhood and pre-adolescence. In Bohart, A. C., & Stipek, D. J. (Eds), *Constructive and destructive behaviour: implications for family, school, and society* (pp. 187–203). Washington, DC: American Psychological Association.

Carlo, G., Roesch, S. C., Knight, G. P., & Koller, S. H. (2001). Between- or within-culture variation? Culture groups as a moderator of the relations between individual differences and resource allocation preferences. *Applied Developmental Psychology, 22*, 559–579.

Carlo, G., Hausmann, A., Christiansen, S., & Randall, B. A. (2003). Sociocognitive and behavioural correlates of a measure of prosocial tendencies for adolescents. *Journal of Early Adolescence, 23*, 107–134.

Carter, D. B., & McCloskey, L. A. (1984). Peers and the maintenance of sex-typed behaviour: the development of children's conception of cross-gender behaviour in their peers. *Social Cognition, 2*, 294–314.

Carter, D. B., & Patterson, C. J. (1982). Sex roles as social conventions: the development of children's conceptions of sex-role stereotypes. *Developmental Psychology, 18*(6), 812–824.

Damon, W. (1983). *Social and personality development*. New York: Norton.

Doescher, S. M., & Sugawara, A. I. (1990). Sex role flexibility and prosocial behaviour among preschool children. *Sex Roles, 22*, 111–123.

Dovidio, J. F., Piliavin, J. A., Schroeder, D. A., & Penner, L. A. (2006). *The social psychology of prosocial behaviour*. Mahwah, NJ: Lawrence Erlbaum.

Eagly, A. H. (2009). The his and hers of prosocial behaviour: an examination of the social psychology of gender. *American Psychologist, 64*(8), 644–658.

Eagly, A. H., & Crowley, M. (1986). Gender and helping behaviour: a meta-analytic review of the social psychological literature. *Psychological Bulletin, 100*(3), 283–308.

Egan, S. K., & Perry, D. G. (2001). Gender identity: a multidimensional analysis with implications for psychosocial adjustment. *Developmental Psychology, 37*, 451–463.

Eisenberg, N., & Mussen, P. H. (1989). *The roots of prosocial behaviour in children*. New York: Cambridge University Press.

Eisenberg, N., Fabes, R. A., & Spinrad, T. L. (2007). Prosocial development. In Eisenberg, N. (Ed.), *Handbook of child psychology, vol 3: social, emotional, and personality development* (pp. 646–718).

Fabes, R. A., & Eisenberg, N. (1996). *Meta-analyses of age and sex differences in children's and adolescents' prosocial behaviour*. Unpublished manuscript.

Fabes, R. A., Carlo, G., Kupanoff, K., & Laible, D. (1999). Early adolescence and prosocial/moral behaviour I: the role of individual processes. *The Journal of Early Adolescence, 19*, 5–16.

Fabes, R. A., Martin, C. L., & Hanish, L. D. (2002). *The role of sex segregation in young children's prosocial behaviour and disposition*. Paper presented at the Groningen Conference on Prosocial Dispositions and Solidarity, Groningen, The Netherlands.

Fagot, B. I. (1985). Beyond the reinforcement principle: another step toward an understanding of sex role development. *Developmental Psychology, 21*, 1097–1104.

Galambos, N. L., Almedia, D. M., & Petersen, A. C. (1990). Masculinity, femininity, and sex role attitudes in early adolescence: exploring gender intensification. *Child Development, 61*, 1905–1914.

Gilligan, C., & Attanucci, J. (1988). Two moral orientations: gender differences and similarities. *Merrill-Palmer Quarterly: Journal of Developmental Psychology, 34*, 223–237.

Guest, G., MacQueen, K. M., & Namey, E. (2012). *Applied thematic analysis.* Thousand Oaks, CA: Sage.

Hastings, P. D., Utendale, W. T., & Sullivan, C. (2007). The socialization of prosocial development. In Grusec, J. E., & Hastings, P. D. (Eds), *Handbook of socializaiton: theory and research.* New York and London: The Guildford Press.

Haviv, S., & Leman, P. J. (2002). Moral decision-making in real life: factors affecting moral orientation and behavior justification. *Journal of Moral Education, 31*, 121–140.

Helwig, C. C. (1995). Adolescents' and young adults' conceptions of civil liberties: freedom of speech and religion. *Child Development, 66*(1), 152–166.

Helwig, C. C. (1997). The role of agent and social context in judgments of freedom of speech and religion. *Child Development, 68*, 484–495.

Hill, J. P., & Lynch, M. E. (1983). The intensification of gender-related role expectations during early adolescence. In Brooks-Gunn, J., & Petersen, A. C. (Eds), *Girls at puberty* (pp. 201–228). New York: Plenum Press.

Horn, S. S. (2007). Adolescents' acceptance of same-sex peers based on sexual orientation and gender expression. *Journal of Youth and Adolescence, 36*, 363–371.

Jaffee, S., & Hyde, J. S. (2000). Gender differences in moral orientation: a meta-analysis. *Psychological Bulletin, 126*, 703–726.

Katz, P. A., & Ksansnak, K. R. (1994). Developmental aspects of gender role flexibility and traditionality in middle childhood and adolescence. *Developmental Psychology, 30*(2), 272–282.

Killen, M. (1990). Children's evaluations of morality in the context of peer, teacher-child, and familial relations. *Journal of Genetic Psychology, 151*, 395–411.

Killen, M. (1991). Social and moral development in early childhood. In Kurtines, W. M., & Gewirtz, J. L. (Eds), *Handbook of moral behaviour and development* (pp. 115–138). Hillsdale, NJ: Erlbaum.

Killen, M., & Stangor, C. (2001). Children's social reasoning about inclusion and exclusion in gender and race peer group contexts. *Child Development, 72*, 174–186.

Killen, M., Mulvey, K. L., & Hitti, A. (2012). Social exclusion in childhood: a developmental intergroup perspective. *Child Development*, 1–19.

Leman, P. J., Ahmed, S., & Ozarow, L. (2005). Gender, gender relations, and the social dynamics of children's conversations. *Developmental Psychology, 41*(1), 64–74.

Lennon, R., & Eisenberg, N. (1987). Gender and age differences in empathy and sympathy. In Eisenberg, N., & Strayer, J. (Eds), *Empathy and its development* (pp. 195–217). New York: Cambridge University Press.

Liben, L. S., & Signorella, M. L. (1993). Gender-schematic processing in children: the role of initial interpretations of stimuli. *Developmental Psychology, 29*, 141–149.

Maccoby, E. E. (2002). Gender and group process: a developmental perspective. *Current Directions in Psychological Science, 11*, 54–58.

Martin, C. L. (2000). Cognitive theories of gender development. In Eckes, T., & Trautner, H. M. (Eds), *The developmental social psychology of gender.* Mahwah, NJ: Lawrence Erlbaum.

Martin, C. L., & Halverson, C. F. (1981). A schematic processing model of sex typing and stereotyping in children. *Child Development, 52,* 1119–1134.

Martin, C. L., & Ruble, D. N. (2009). Patterns of gender development. *Annual Review of Psychology, 61,* 353–381.

McHale, S. M., Shanahan, L., Updegraff, K. A., Crouter, A. C., & Booth, A. (2004). Developmental and individual differences in girls' sex-typed activites in middle childhood and adolescence. *Child Development, 75,* 1575–1593.

Opie, I., & Opie, P. (1997). *The Oxford dictionary of nursery rhymes* (2nd ed.). Oxford: Oxford University Press.

Patton, M. Q. (1990). *Qualitative evaluation and research methods* (2nd ed.). Newbury Park, CA: Sage.

Powlishta, K. K. (1995). Gender bias in children's perceptions of personality traits. *Sex Roles, 32,* 17–28.

Powlishta, K. K. (2000). The effect of target age on the activation of gender stereotypes. *Sex Roles, 42,* 271–282.

Powlishta, K. K. (2004). Gender as a social category: intergroup processes and gender-role development. In Bennett, M., & Sani, F. (Eds), *The development of the social self* (pp. 103–133). Hove, East Sussex, UK: Psychology Press.

Radke-Yarrow, M., & Zahn-Waxler, C. (1986). The role of familial factors in the development of prosocial behaviour: research findings and questions. In Olweus, D., Block, J., & Radke-Yarrow, M. (Eds), *Development of antisocial and prosocial behaviour: research, theories, and issues* (pp. 207–233). New York: Academic Press.

Rae Clasen, D., & Brown, B. B. (1985). The multidimensionality of peer pressure in adolescence. *Journal of Youth and Adolescence, 14,* 451–468.

Reed, A., & Aquino, K. F. (2003). Moral identity and the expanding circle of moral regard toward out-groups. *Journal of Personality and Social Psychology, 84,* 1270–1386.

Russell, A., Hart, C. H., Robinson, C. C., & Olsen, S. F. (2003). Children's sociable and aggressive behaviour with peers: a comparison of the United States and Australia, and contributions of temperament and parenting style. *International Journal of Behavioural Development, 27,* 74–86.

Serbin, L. A., Powlishta, K. K., Gulko, J., Martin, C. L., & Lockheed, M. E. (1993). The development of sex typing in middle childhood. *Monographs of the Society for Research in Child Development, 58,* 1–95.

Shigetomi, C. C., Hartmann, D. P., & Gelfand, D. M. (1981). Sex differences in children's altruisitc behaviour and reputations for helpfulness. *Developmental Psychology, 17,* 434–437.

Smetana, J. G. (2006). Social-cognitive domain theory: consistencies, and variations in children's moral and social judgments. In Killen, M., & Smetana, J. G. (Eds), *Handbook of moral development*. New York: Academic.

Smetana, J. G., Killen, M., & Turiel, E. (1991). Children's reasoning about interpersonal and moral conflicts. *Child Development, 62,* 629–644.

Smith, T. E., & Leaper, C. (2006). Self-preceived gender typicality and the peer context during adolescence. *Journal of Research on Adolescence, 16,* 91–104.

Stangor, C., & Ruble, D. N. (1989). Differential influences of gender schemata and gender constancy on children's information processing behaviour. *Social Cognition, 7,* 353–372.

Stoddart, T., & Turiel, E. (1985). Children's concepts of cross-gender activities. *Child Development, 56*(5), 1241–1252.

Theimer, C. E., Killen, M., & Stangor, C. (2001). Young children's evaluations of exclusion in gender-stereotypic peer contexts. *Developmental Psychology, 37,* 18–27.

Turiel, E. (1978). The development of concepts of social structure: social convention. In Glick, J., & Clarke-Stewart, K. A. (Eds), *The development of social understanding*. New York: Gardner Press.

Turiel, E. (1983). *The development of social knowledge: morality and convention*. Cambridge: Cambridge University Press.

Turiel, E. (1998). The development of morality. In Eisenberg, N. (Ed.), *Handbook of child psychology: vol. 3. Social, emotional, and personality development* (5th ed.) (pp. 863–932). New York: Wiley.

Vaish, A., Missana, M., & Tomasello, M. (2011). Three-year-old children intervene in third-party moral transgressions. *British Journal of Developmental Psychology, 29*, 124–130.

Veenstra, R., Lindenberg, S., Oldehinkel, A. J., De Winter, A. F., Verhulst, F. C., & Ormel, J. (2008). Prosocial and antisocial behaviour in preadolescence: teachers' and parents' perceptions of the behaviour of girls and boys. *International Journal of Behavioural Development, 32*, 243–251.

Warden, D., & MacKinnon, S. (2003). Prosocial children, bullies and victims: an investigation of their sociometric statues, empathy and social problem-solving strategies. *British Journal of Developmental Psychology, 21*, 367–385.

Warden, D., Cheyne, B., Christie, D., Fitzpatrick, H., & Reid, K. (2003). Assessing children's perceptions of prosocial and antisocial peer behaviour. *Educational Psychology, 23*, 547–567.

Wark, G. R., & Krebs, D. L. (1996). Gender and dilemma differences in real-life moral judgment. *Developmental Psychology, 32*, 220–230.

Wentzel, K. R. (2002). Are effective teachers like good parents? Teaching styles and student adjustment in early adolescence. *Child Development, 73*, 287–301.

Wentzel, K. R., Filisetti, L., & Looney, L. (2007). Adolescent prosocial behaviour: the role of self-processes and contextual cues. *Child Development, 78*, 895–910.

Whiting, J. W. M., & Whiting, B. B. (1973). Altruistic and egoistic behaviour in six cultures. In Nader, L., & Maretzki, T. (Eds), *Cultural illness and health*. Washington, DC: American Anthropological Association.

Williams, J. E., Bennett, S. M., & Best, D. L. (1975). Awareness and expression of sex stereotypes in young children. *Developmental Psychology, 11*, 635–642.

Zarbatany, L., Hartmann, D. P., Gelfand, D. M., & Vinciguerra, P. (1985). Gender differences in altruistic reputation: are they artifactual? *Developmental Psychology, 21*, 97–101.

6 The gendered self-concept

How implicit gender stereotypes and attitudes shape self-definition

Andrew Scott Baron, Toni Schmader,
Dario Cvencek and Andrew N. Meltzoff

Background

> If women are expected to do the same work as men, we must teach them the
> same things.
>
> Aristotle

As the quote above suggests, the debate over the fundamental similarities and differences between women and men extends at least as far back as Aristotle and underscores the pervasiveness with which the psychological representation of gender as a social category provides a lens through which we perceive others and define ourselves. Across cultures, the development of children's conception of gender is rapid and outpaces their understanding of other locally significant categories including those based on language groups, race, ethnicity, religion, nationality and castes (Bigler & Liben, 2006, 2007; see also, Levy & Killen, 2008; Martin & Ruble, 2004; Martin et al., 2002). Indeed, gender is among the earliest social group distinctions young children make, and soon after children learn to categorize others based on gender, they begin to associate different traits and attitudes with male and female. Once entrenched in long-term memory, these associations can be easily and implicitly activated in the minds of perceivers or targets, acting as an unseen force, pushing and pulling the levers of behaviour to subtly steer men and women to different roles and activities (Croft et al., 2013; Davies et al., 2005; Steele et al., 2002). Existing divisions of behaviour inform developing gender cognitions which then recreate gender differences in behaviour as children develop into adults (Eagly & Steffen, 1984).

The societal costs of persistent gender biases among adults underscore the need to chart its developmental trajectory. Furthermore, advances in social cognition over the past two decades have revealed that implicit associative biases are governed by and thus likely to develop in ways that are distinct from explicit beliefs. The primary goal of the present chapter is to introduce recent evidence from our labs concerning the origins of implicit gender bias in childhood and to demonstrate how data on the developmental trajectory of implicit gender stereotypes and attitudes can inform our theories for the causes and consequences of such biases for a child's developing conception of him or herself. This work will also provide a novel framework for conceptualizing the development of the implicit associative system and highlight new directions for future research.

The benefits of examining the development of gendered cognition at the implicit level

An expanding body of research on young adults reveals the social and cognitive forces that work in concert to carve deep trenches of gender-typical behaviour that get written into our system of cognitive associations. Research reveals the ways in which gender biases disadvantage women from being selected for certain jobs (e.g. Goldin & Rouse, 2000; Moss-Racusin et al., 2012) and influence how men behave toward women during professional interactions (Logel et al., 2009). Furthermore, when women themselves are simply reminded that these gender stereotypes exist, they can show impaired attentional focus and performance resulting from the added concern that their actions might confirm negative stereotypes about their group (Mrazek et al., 2011; Schmader & Johns, 2003; Schmader et al., 2008; Spencer et al., 1999).

Given that these effects of gender biases occur despite explicitly held values for gender equality (Pew Research, 2010), we argue that the implicit processes at work merit special attention and study. In other words, people have cognitive associations linking gender categories with different traits and attitudes and these *implicit associations* are likely to be learned early, unrelated to explicitly endorsed stereotypes and attitudes, and can be activated automatically in ways that bias perception and behaviour. For example, men with stronger implicit stereotypes about women behave in a more dominant and flirtatious way during a professional interaction with a woman (Logel et al., 2009), and women with a stronger implicit association of men with mathematics exhibit poorer performance in mathematics, even among those who are majoring in mathematics-intensive fields (Nosek et al., 2002). From a developmental perspective, then, it is important to consider when and how the implicit associations that underlie these biases develop and how they shape a child's emerging sense of self-definition. Recently, suitable measures of *implicit* processing in young samples have been developed (Baron & Banaji, 2006, 2009; Cvencek et al., 2011a; Dunham et al., 2008; Newheiser & Olson, 2012; Rutland et al., 2005), providing a unique opportunity to examine the developmental trajectory of unconscious cognitions. Understanding when these associations form will speak directly to pathways by which such cognitions can be changed to establish greater gender equality.

The advent of implicit measures avoids several methodological challenges in examining the development of gender bias in childhood. First, compared with their explicit counterparts, measures of implicit associations are generally less susceptible to self-presentational concerns (Banaji, 2001; Nosek, 2007) and avoid some of the interpretive challenges inherent in testing the cognitions of young children (Baron & Banaji, 2006; Dunham et al., 2008). Although measures of explicit gender beliefs can reveal substantial information, these assessment tools also become increasingly susceptible to social desirability as children grow older and become more attuned to the cultural norms for expressing egalitarian attitudes, beliefs and behaviour (e.g. Rutland et al., 2005). For example, whereas children in middle childhood express awareness of mathematics–gender stereotypes (Cvencek et al., 2011b), these children often simultaneously deny endorsing these beliefs (see also Schmader et al., 2004, for evidence with adults). However, it is quite possible that older children and adults possess negative gender stereotypes and attitudes, even if they are reluctant to express them to the interviewer because doing so would be socially inappropriate. By contrast, implicit cognitive measures are relatively free from such social desirability concerns.

In addition, the level of processing that underlies implicit social cognition appears to be continuous across development and thus can be examined independently of an individual's stage of cognitive and language development. The same is simply not the case for explicit processes where at earlier stages of development there are added concerns about whether young children have sufficient introspective access to provide reliable verbal report on what might constitute an attitude or stereotype, not to mention concern as to whether explicit reasoning is even available to such young minds. Children's difficulty with introspection coupled with evidence of preverbal processing of gender categories (Bahrick et al., 1998; Quinn et al., 2002) underscores the need to utilize methods that can assess the more automatic thoughts and associations children hold. As such, the focus on implicit processes provides a broader population to examine.

A third and perhaps most important reason for our focus on implicit associations is that they inform our theories of children's developing sense of themselves seen through the lens of gender. Highlighting an important theoretical distinction between self-reportable *explicit* representations and introspectively inaccessible *implicit* representations (Banaji, 2001; Devine, 1989; Gawronski & Bodenhausen, 2006; Greenwald & Banaji, 1995), research with adults has demonstrated that implicitly held gender attitudes and stereotypes can have a profound influence in daily life, uniquely affecting friendship choices, hiring and voting decisions, and jury verdicts (for a review see Greenwald et al., 2009; for additional evidence of the relationship between implicit processes and behaviour see Nock & Banaji, 2007). These data clearly suggest that implicit cognitions shape behaviour in ways that are independent of the effects of explicit attitudes and beliefs, underscoring the need to understand their developmental trajectory. Indeed, efforts to reduce the deleterious consequences of gender bias among adults will likely require revising the implicit associations that take hold of the developing mind. While there is a vibrant debate in the field concerning the representational nature of implicit and explicit constructs (e.g. Blanton & Jaccard, 2006; Gawronski & Bodenhausen, 2006; Karpinski & Hilton, 2001), the outcome of that debate does not directly bear on the importance of understanding the developmental issues raised here.

The data that we introduce in this chapter examines the development of implicit gender stereotypes and attitudes and provides an emerging framework for understanding how implicit cognitions more generally are shaped by cultural and cognitive forces. We will first consider how implicit associations are learned in general. We will then focus specifically on the development of implicit gender stereotypes about mathematics and science and the development of implicit gender attitudes. We will also examine the ways in which the developing mind may strive to achieve cognitive–affective balance among gender stereotypes and the self-concept (and among gender attitudes and self-esteem). Finally, we will discuss the implications of these findings for theories of the acquisition and development of implicit social cognition more generally, including the timing and method of efforts aimed at *changing* such cognitions.

Theoretical perspectives on the trajectory of implicit associations

The conventional view is that implicit associations are the product of a domain-general computational mechanism that detects patterns of covariation, establishing an implicit association that may be stereotypic (e.g. male = mathematical) or evaluative (e.g. male = good). By virtue of the claim that the learning mechanism is domain-general, it is hypothesized that all associations are learned via the same basic process, regardless of whether they concern stereotypes or attitudes or whether they are in reference to social groups or to non-social categories (Bigler & Liben, 2007; Greenwald & Banaji, 1995). Domain-general associative learning processes can similarly shape associations between the concept gender and children's emerging concept of the self. For example, a child who is praised for learning to count or for demonstrating success with numerical operations might develop an association between the self and numbers/mathematics. Such an association may form directly when one receives praise (linking self with positive performance in the domain of mathematics – '*you are good at mathematics*') as well as from actively noticing one's selective engagement with mathematics activities (e.g. spending more time engaged with mathematics exercises, feeling positive about the self during this engagement, awareness of one's own preference to spend time on mathematics-related activities).

Associations between the self and particular activities (e.g. I can do mathematics) and between the concept gender and those same activities (e.g. girls can do mathematics) can form via independent processes, but they are also importantly linked in one's broader associative network of cognitions. These shared linkages might also influence the magnitude and direction of implicit associations as the developing mind seeks to achieve cognitive balance among associated constructs (Festinger, 1954; Greenwald et al., 2002; Heider, 1946). Within the theoretical framework of balance theory (Heider, 1946), the associations among concepts tend to self-organize on principles of consistency. Thus, if I like John, and John likes Peter, then I will also be inclined to like Peter. Based on Heider's (1946) theory, Greenwald et al. (2002) provided a rigorous statistical approach to test for *balanced identity* among implicit constructs related to the self (Balanced Identity Theory, BIT). The theoretical expectation is that, if a balanced configuration exists among three constructs, any one of the three constructs should be predictable from the multiplicative product of measures of the other two constructs (Greenwald et al., 2002). In other words, when two concepts are associated with the same third concept, the association between those two concepts should strengthen.

Initial evidence of BIT comes from the adult literature. Nosek et al. (2002) showed that among female college students, a balanced configuration of implicit mathematics–gender stereotypes, gender identity and mathematics self-concepts is associated with their negative attitudes towards mathematics and lower performance on the mathematical portion of the Scholastic Aptitude Test. Interestingly, these balanced associations were found even among women majoring in mathematics-intensive fields, pointing to the ways in which these implicit cognitions operate despite more consciously motivated career pursuits. Such findings are informative when found with adults, but only a thorough developmental analysis can reveal whether principles of balance operate across implicit associations (e.g. attitudes, stereotypes and self-identity) from the point of their initial acquisition or whether successful balance among these constructs reflects a major cognitive achievement on the part of the developing child (Cvencek et al., 2011b; Dunham et al., 2007).

With respect to mathematics stereotypes, the idea is that the following set of cognitions forms to create psychological balance: I am female (gender identity), and females in my culture do not do mathematics (a cultural stereotype), then I will not do mathematics (a self-concept). Cvencek et al. (2011b) outlined two ways that cognitions of the self might achieve balance as they are first developing: 1) one's concept of the self with respect to a given domain and given group might shape and inform the development of a broader concept of one's group in that domain, or 2) group stereotypes may be acquired first and subsequently influence mathematics self-concepts for a given domain. The first holds that with a strong gender identity and a given level of self-identification with mathematics (mathematics self-concept), children might generalize/project their own mathematics identification to others of their own gender (mathematics–gender stereotype; for a similar analysis among explicit intergroup attitudes see Patterson et al., 2010). This developmental sequence can be expressed as: Me = Girl; Me $\neq$ Mathematics; *therefore* Girls $\neq$ Mathematics.

An alternative proposal is that children who strongly identify with their gender (strong gender identity) are more likely to internalize cultural stereotypes about their gender (mathematics–gender stereotypes), which in turn influences their mathematics self-concepts. Considered from the perspective of girls, this developmental sequence can be expressed as: Me = Girl; Girls $\neq$ Mathematics; *therefore* Me $\neq$ Mathematics. Children who do not strongly associate self with either male or female might show weaker development of gender-based self-concepts through either mechanism. Evidence for when each leg of this triangle in children's implicit associative network emerges and how they relate to one another will likely speak to the causal processes that result in implicit self-identification with mathematics and its relationship to associated stereotypes and attitudes. Moreover, an examination of principles of cognitive balance among these concepts in children from an Asian culture, in which collectivist societal norms are more salient than the norms for individual cognitions about the self, may also reveal whether or not cognitive balance is a culturally universal mechanism for developmental change in children's social cognition (Cvencek et al., 2013b). In the sections that follow, we will present new evidence from our labs supporting the theoretical claim that cognitive balance in the development of children's stereotypes toward and attitudes about gender groups represents an early emerging and perhaps culturally universal accomplishment that shapes the developmental trajectory of such associations by the eighth year of life.

Evidence for the emergence of implicit gender stereotypes and cognitive balance

Studying the interplay among mathematics–gender stereotypes, mathematics self-concepts and mathematics achievement can help shed light on how the culture's prevailing stereotypes about mathematics ability influences children's emerging mathematics self-concepts and performance. A meta-analysis of gender differences in explicit self-views about mathematics reveals that girls rate their mathematics ability lower than boys do across various cultural contexts (Else-Quest et al., 2010), despite young boys and girls exhibiting similar performance on objective measures of mathematics and science abilities. Thus, the sex differences in explicit mathematics self-concepts observed among older children and adults appear to *precede* rather than follow actual differences in mathematics achievement. The implication of such findings is that, once ingrained, these mathematics self-concepts may exert a developmental influence on children's interest and effort, leading to the gender gap in mathematics-intensive fields such as engineering or computer science that is apparent among adults. If girls develop a lower self-concept of their mathematics ability before they actually underperform in mathematics, the implication is that gender stereotypes affect in some way *how* the self-concept in mathematics first forms. While it is possible that an internalization of cultural stereotypes into children's explicit views of themselves might lead to performance differences in mathematics as children grow older, it is also possible that these performance differences are better explained by changes in gendered cognitions at the implicit level.

Bringing current data to bear on these issues, two of our co-authors conducted two studies with 419 elementary-school children in the US and Singapore that tested the presence of implicit stereotypes about gender, mathematics and the self. Each child completed implicit measures of gender self-concept, mathematics–gender stereotype and mathematics self-concept (Cvencek et al., 2011b, 2013b). Implicit associations were measured using a child-friendly version of the Implicit Association Test (IAT, Greenwald et al., 1998) that measures reaction time during a categorization task to provide an index of the relative association strength among select concepts.

Typical IATs pit two concepts against one another (e.g. gender and self) during which participants are asked to rapidly classify words and or images into their respective categories (e.g. male/female and self/other) using two response keys. For the gender self-concept task this involved categorizing words as either self-related (e.g. me, my, I) or other-related (they, them, their) using separate keys. Further, participants were asked to use those same keys to concurrently classify words as belonging to the category male (e.g. Mike, John, David) or female (e.g. Sarah, Emily, Jen). For half the trials the self-related words and male words shared a single response key (with female and other-related words sharing the second key). For the remaining half of the trials those pairings were reversed such that male and other shared a single response key (while female and self shared the second key). The assumption of this procedure is that the stronger the association among concepts, the faster and more accurate participants should be to categorize them when they share a single response key (e.g. self + male) compared with when they share different response keys (e.g. other + male). For the mathematics self-concept IAT, children were asked to categorize self/other words alongside categorizing words as either mathematics oriented (e.g. numbers, calculator, addition) or reading oriented (e.g. book, literature, library). For the mathematics–gender stereotype IAT, participants were instructed to classify words as either male or female *or* belonging to the category mathematics or reading. The order of these tasks was counterbalanced.

The data show that by eight years of age, children exhibit evidence of implicit gender identity, mathematics-stereotypes and implicit self-beliefs, with boys and girls associating mathematics more with males than females and with boys more strongly associating their concept of self with mathematics than do girls (Cvencek et al., 2011b). In other words, both boys and girls were faster and more accurate in classifying words related to mathematics and words related to male when they shared a single response key. Thus, around the same time that girls begin to exhibit more negative explicit beliefs about their own mathematics ability, they also develop more negative implicit associations of girls with mathematics and a weaker association of self with mathematics, despite no observable differences in performance or ability at this young age. Recent findings demonstrate similar relationships among elementary-school children from Singapore, a country in which girls excel in mathematics (Cvencek et al., 2013b).

This evidence suggests that implicit self-construals, similar to their explicit counterparts, are shaped by the prevailing cultural stereotypes in early childhood. Furthermore, it is noteworthy that mathematics–gender stereotypes were demonstrated in Singaporean culture (Cvencek et al., 2013b), where mathematics performance overall is substantially higher among Singaporean children compared with their American counterparts. In fact, in Else-Quest's cross-national comparison of mathematics performance among 14–16 year old children, boys slightly outperformed girls in the US whereas girls tended to outperform boys in Singapore (Else-Quest et al., 2010). Yet, in spite of these relatively better mathematics outcomes for Singaporean girls, children sampled in our recent study in Singapore exhibited implicit gender stereotypes about gender and mathematics in the same direction as those observed among American youth (mathematics = male), albeit of a somewhat smaller magnitude.

Speaking to issues of cognitive balance among these implicit representations, the results showed that the stronger children identified with their own gender and the stronger they identified their gender with mathematics, then the stronger the association between self and mathematics. Interestingly, the strength of cognitive balance among implicit associations was positively associated with age, suggesting that balance may represent an important accomplishment of the developing mind. This was true in Western individualist cultures and East Asian collectivist ones alike (Cvencek et al., 2013b), and when coupled with similar evidence of cognitive balance found in other domains (e.g. race, Dunham et al., 2007), supports a broader conclusion that the underlying principles of cognitive balance in children's representations of their social–cognitive world may be culturally universal. Whereas cultures may differ on which stereotypes are prominent, the intrapersonal motivation for cognitive balance may apply regardless of the content of the beliefs.

Development of gender stereotypes can impair performance

In addition to illustrating how the development of implicit stereotypes can affect the development of children's self-concept for mathematics, recent evidence also links these implicit stereotypes to actual performance. For example, although recent meta-analyses do not reveal an overall gender gap in mathematics performance among elementary-school-aged children, this gap is more pronounced in some countries than in others (Else-Quest et al., 2010). Moreover, the variation in the gender gap corresponds to variation in children's implicit mathematics stereotypes. In a cross-national comparison of thirty-four countries, country-level measures of mathematics–gender stereotypes predicted country-level gender gaps in eighth-grade mathematics achievement – stronger societal stereotypes against females doing mathematics were correlated with larger gaps between boys' and girls' actual mathematics performance (Nosek et al., 2009).

The relationship between gender stereotypes and a gender gap in mathematics performance is not only found across cultures; it has also recently been shown to exist within cultures as well, as evident by studies of American and German middle-school children and adults. Steffens and colleagues (2010) found that implicit mathematics–gender stereotypes predicted German adolescent girls' (but not boys') mathematics achievement and enrolment preferences in related disciplines. Nosek et al. (2002) found the same relationship among US college students. Taken together, the findings from samples in the US and Germany all show that culturally shared implicit mathematics–gender stereotypes might play a part in creating gender differences in mathematics achievement and mathematics participation, relationships that emerge early in elementary school.

New insights for understanding mathematics achievement gaps

One avenue for future research is to more clearly isolate the process by which implicit gender stereotypes affect girls' mathematics achievement. Specifically, future research is needed to test at least two possible pathways. On the one hand, applying Eccles' expectancy-value hypothesis (Eccles et al., 1983, 1984), these stereotypes decrease young girls' interest and engagement in mathematics because the stereotypes lower their self-confidence and the value they place on that domain. For example, Steffens et al. (2010) found that stronger implicit mathematics–gender stereotypes were particularly predictive of lower achievement among low-achieving girls. They speculated that holding a stereotype that 'mathematics is for boys' plays a role in determining the amount of time girls spend studying mathematics. They observed that if a girl holds a strong mathematics–gender stereotype that girls don't do mathematics, then she may feel that it is not needed, culturally expected or even possible for her to excel in mathematics. From this perspective, implicit gender stereotypes decrease girls' motivation and lead them to avoid mathematics-related pursuits.

Alternatively, the awareness of stereotypes that associate mathematics with male more than female sets the stage for children to experience stereotype threat. Stereotype threat occurs when the concern that one might confirm negative stereotypes about oneself or one's group disrupts performance (Steele & Aronson, 1995). For example, in a recent study of middle-school-aged children, girls evaluated themselves less confidently in mathematics than boys did, despite having equal performance (Muzzatti & Agnoli, 2007). However, when these 10-year-old girls were reminded that females are under-represented in mathematics, the performance of the girls dropped precipitously to become lower than that of boys. Other research has also shown that gender stereotypes about mathematics, if activated, have the potential to create a gender gap in performance (Ambady et al., 2001). The adult literature suggests that these performance impairments induced by bringing stereotypes to mind result from an interrelated set of processes including physiological signs of stress, meta-cognitive monitoring of performance, efforts to regulate emotion and problems of attentional control (Schmader et al., 2008). However, an assumption of stereotype threat theory is that these cognitive impairments stemming from a concern about confirming the stereotype are greatest among those most motivated to do well in the domain. It is not yet known whether any or all of these mechanisms reviewed by Schmader et al. (2008) account for performance impairments that young girls experience when gender stereotypes are primed.

Research is needed to adjudicate between these two possible mechanisms by which implicit gender stereotypes may lead to lower mathematics performance among girls. The first implicates motivational variables like avoidance of mathematics-related tasks and activities as contributing to underperformance. The second implicates impairments in cognitive processing that occur when one is particularly motivated to excel in the domain as a means of disconfirming the stereotype. Although research on the gender gap in mathematics performance among young adults has separately examined each of these mechanisms (Diekman et al., 2010; Forbes & Schmader, 2010; Jamieson & Harkins, 2007), no research has tried to parse the separate effects of motivation versus cognitive interference, especially as predicted by implicit associations among children. Developmentally, the fear of confirming a negative stereotype and the cognitive interference it can create may occur relatively early in development. Indeed, children as young as 3 years of age show a tendency to conform to behaviours stereotypical of their gender (Weinraub et al., 1984), and a motivation to disconfirm negative stereotypes may similarly guide children's behaviours around this period in development. On the other hand, it is not until children are older that they manifest more flexibility in approaching or avoiding mathematics classes and activities. As a result, any motivational differences might not reveal themselves until children experience greater control over their time. The degree to which gender stereotypes shape motivation and induce cognitive interference at younger ages is yet to be examined.

Such research could also explore how manipulating the content of implicit associations uniquely affects these processes. For example, in a series of experiments with undergraduate women, one of our coauthors demonstrated that retraining an implicit association of 'liking' with mathematics led women (but not men) to exert more effort at a mathematics task, especially when gender stereotypes were primed or made salient (Forbes & Schmader, 2010). However, this strengthened tendency to like mathematics did not improve working memory capacity or mathematics performance. Instead, retraining an implicit association of women with mathematics led women to exhibit higher working memory capacity and perform better on a mathematics exam even in the context of stereotype threat cues. Such findings suggest that one's attitude toward a domain might be a stronger predictor of whether one approaches or avoids a task in that domain but that positive stereotypes about your group can specifically shape performance by facilitating more fluid cognition.

Although studies seeking to shape implicit associations have not been done with younger age groups, such data would certainly speak to the causal role that cultural stereotypes about mathematics and gender play in shaping the observed gender differences in performance. We suggest that intervention programmes aimed at targeting such stereotypes before they become engrained might be best aimed at children as young as age six or seven, the earliest ages where evidence of the internalization of cultural stereotypes about gender and ability are observed and prior to the reported developmental increase in strength of cognitive balance among related self-constructs. We return to this general point about changing implicit gendered cognitions later in the chapter.

Evidence for the emergence of implicit gender attitudes

Our recent research demonstrates how the abilities and domains that children come to implicitly associate with males and females might shape their emerging perceptions of the self in or around early childhood. Stepping back we realize that the complex web of gender cognitions extends beyond the relationship between stereotypes and self-definition to include the attitudes, positive and negative, children form toward males and females. In fact, developmentally, gender attitudes emerge prior to gender stereotypes and the awareness of one's own gender identity (Martin et al., 2002). If similar principles of cognitive balance can be applied to the implicit attitudes one develops toward their gender group and themselves, then an examination of implicit gender attitudes could provide an important opportunity to better understand how principles of cognitive–affective balance begin to take hold at even earlier stages of the developing mind. For example, a child's emerging attitude toward the self might be partly shaped by the pressures of cognitive balance stemming from learned attitude associations with his or her gender group. Just as with the insights gained from research on implicit stereotypes, our research has also recently examined the developmental trajectory of implicit gender attitudes to highlight potential pathways and timing for attitude change.

Before presenting our data on the developmental trajectory of implicit gender attitudes, we first summarize alternative hypotheses one might have about how and when these attitudes develop. We will then show how our developmental data has constrained theory building in this domain. First, it might be expected that boys and girls from a young age will simply exhibit a preference for their own gender group. In two classic experiments, Sherif et al. (1961) and Turner et al. (1979) demonstrated that a mere preference for one's in-group may be an automatic consequence of self-categorization processes – once you categorize yourself in a group and identify with that group label you can't help but feel positivity toward it. There is now a wealth of data showing that children and adults tend to prefer the in-group based on sharing the same race or ethnicity (Aboud, 1988), religion (Heiphetz et al., in press), nationality (Barrett, 2007), or language (Kinzler et al., 2007). Indeed, both children and adults even show preferences for previously unfamiliar social groups to which they have been randomly assigned (e.g. Baron & Dunham, 2013; Bigler et al., 1997; Brewer, 1979; Dunham et al., 2011; Greenwald et al., 2002; Nesdale & Flesser, 2001; Nesdale et al., 2003, 2007; Spielman, 2000). Consistent with these findings, Yee and Brown (1994) report that 2 year olds verbally express an own gender preference on explicit attitude measures; little boys like boys and little girls like girls. As such, it might be predicted that boys and girls will exhibit similar levels of implicit own gender positivity once they attain an awareness of their gender identity and associate the self with that gender group. Provided a child's gender identity doesn't change, this own gender preference should be observed across development.

Another possibility, however, is that at an early age, gender labels do not represent abstract categories of males and females in general but rather map on more directly to a child's most salient male and female exemplars (e.g. mum and dad). If this is the case, then we might expect boys and girls to form positive attitudes toward the gender of their primary caregiver. Indeed, research with infants shows that boys and girls illustrate a preference to look at faces of individuals who are matched in gender to their primary caregiver (Quinn et al., 2002). Thus, children raised primarily by their mother show a preference for female faces and those raised primarily by their father show a preference for male faces. Despite improvements in gender equality in the division of labour at home and in the office, women continue to perform the lion's share of child-rearing duties (Croft et al., 2013) and thus it may be expected that a preference for female will similarly shape the gender attitudes of both boys and girls. As such, a role for maternal attachment implicates early-emerging female positivity in both males and females as positive attitudes toward one's mother generalize to positive attitudes toward women in general.

Of course, a preference for one's in-group and a preference for the gender of one's primary caregiver can both exert some combinatory influence over the development of gender attitudes, albeit differently for boys and girls. For girls, both mechanisms would reinforce a strong own gender preference (female = good). For boys, these two forces should act in opposing directions, provided the primary caregiver is female. In this case it might be expected that boys will exhibit a weaker own gender preference relative to females (male = a little good), a significant but weaker preference for female (female = a little good) or the two effects could cancel each other out producing no clear gender preference. This tension for boys should be evident early in development given preverbal children's sensitivity to the gender of their primary caregiver (Quinn et al., 2002) and the fact that the primary caregiver is more prominent in the life experiences of young children.

At a young age, children's developing concepts of 'male' and 'female' can also be shaped by observations that in books and media, males and females often enact different behaviours or embody differentially valenced roles. For example, Rudman and colleagues (Rudman & Goodwin, 2004; Rudman et al., 2007) highlight a tendency to associate men more than women with violence. Although Rudman and colleagues speculate that children might not develop a fear of male violence until adolescence, when a higher propensity for male violence reaches a peak (United States Department of Health and Human Services, 2001), even quite young children are exposed to the potential threat of males through indirect mediums such as television programming where villains are frequently male (Gerbner et al., 1978; Sternglanz & Serbin, 1974; Tedesco, 1974). The salience of such negative and fear inducing imagery might enable a relatively early but strong association of male = bad. For example, studies have shown that even preschoolers have a tendency to assume that males respond to ambiguous situations with more anger than do females (Parmley & Cunningham, 2008). Such information, whether learned directly or indirectly, might simply exacerbate a tendency among girls to prefer their own gender (female = good and male = bad), while again mitigating, cancelling out or even reversing an own group positivity bias among boys.

New empirical insights into the development of gender attitudes

Thus far we have detailed several alternative hypotheses for the development of implicit gender attitudes, depending on different mechanisms that could be involved. Importantly, while each mechanism supports different predictions about the emergence and ontogenesis of implicit gender attitudes among boys and girls, it is certainly possible that multiple mechanisms operate concurrently or even independently across development. Clearly, developmental data is crucial in adjudicating among these contrasting theoretical positions. We next turn to evidence from our labs on the actual developmental trajectory of implicit gender attitudes to provide new insight into which mechanisms shape these attitudes and when during development that influence is exerted.

The earliest developmental examination of implicit gender attitudes to date focused on 4–5 year olds using the Preschool IAT (PSIAT), a child-friendly adaptation of the adult IAT (Cvencek et al., 2011a). Here, children were tasked with categorizing images of boys and girls into their respective categories using either a large green or orange response button connected to the computer. Concurrently, children heard (and saw) affectively positive words (e.g. good, nice) and affectively negative words (e.g. bad, mad) and were similarly asked to classify these words into their respective categories (good or bad) using the same two response buttons. Once again, the average reaction time and error rate to categorize male + good (and female + bad) using the same response key was compared with the average reaction time and error rate to categorize female + good (and male + bad) using the same response key. If children exhibit an implicit preference for their own gender group, then they should be faster and more accurate to categorize images of same gender when those pictures are paired with the same response button used to simultaneously categorize positive words.

Turning to the data, we observed that girls exhibited a strikingly strong implicit preference for female over male, whereas boys exhibited a marginally significant preference for their own gender group (Cvencek et al., 2011a). Thus, children generally exhibited evidence of own gender bias, but this bias was significantly stronger for girls than boys. Even if an own group positivity bias influences implicit gender attitudes at this young age, it appears that other factors could be mitigating the strength of the own gender preference among boys. This discovery of a weaker preference among 4-year-old boys toward their own gender group may reflect an internalization of positive attitudes toward the gender of their primary caregiver (who is most often female). It may also reflect an internalization of a male = violent/angry stereotype. One way to tease these possibilities apart is to collect data on children's primary caregiver and to measure children's implicit gender stereotypes about violence and aggression and examine what role these variables play in shaping implicit gender attitudes at this age.

Moving to an examination of gender attitudes among school-aged children with a specific focus on documenting age and gender differences in attitude, we recently measured the implicit gender attitudes among children aged 5–17 (Dunham et al., 2013). This procedure followed a similar IAT design reported in the preschool study above, whereby children were asked to categorize images of boys and girls into their respective categories along with affectively positive and negative words presented acoustically through headphones into the categories *good* and *bad*. We tested nearly 500 children across this age range with an equal distribution of males and females at each age. As such, we achieved much better power at detecting age and gender related differences in the magnitude and direction of these implicit gender cognitions compared with the prior study by Cvencek and colleagues.

The youngest girls in our sample exhibited an implicit pro-female bias and the magnitude of this bias did not change across the age range studied. This is a remarkable degree of stability in own gender bias for girls throughout childhood and adolescence, seemingly uninfluenced by puberty where notions of masculinity and femininity might be expected to change dramatically. This study also found that boys at the youngest ages in the sample reported a significant implicit own gender preference. This finding provides stronger statistical support for the general conclusion reached by Cvencek et al. (2011a) that males also implicitly evaluate their own gender positively. Moreover, as in Cvencek et al.'s study of preschoolers, the magnitude of this bias was substantially weaker than that shown by their female counterparts. In other words, young girls associated female with good more than young boys associated male with good, even though both showed a significant attitudinal preference for their own gender over the other.

One unique aspect of the Dunham et al. study of implicit attitudes across childhood is the ability to use process dissociation analyses to distinguish between an association of in-group = good and out-group = bad, a distinction that should further disentangle the unique hypotheses raised earlier (Batchelder & Riefer, 1999; Conrey et al., 2005; Sherman et al., 2008). Using these analyses, Dunham and colleagues reveal that a female = good and a male = bad association was observed among girls and the relative strength of each association did not change with age. In contrast, boys only showed evidence of a male = good association that gradually weakens across childhood until no gender preference is observed in or around adolescence. Thus, at no point in development did boys exhibit a female = bad association.

Together, these data are among the first and most convincing to suggest an early emerging role for own group positivity among both boys and girls perhaps in combination with a fear of male violence bias that might model a more negative association with men. Interestingly, our data seem to suggest that girls may learn this male = bad association early on and this association remains stable across development. Among boys, in contrast, their disappearing preference for their own group around puberty hints at the possibility that greater direct exposure to male aggression may help undo this own gender preference. It is also possible that own group positivity bias may operate alongside a maternal attachment bias, thereby increasing positivity toward women. These new findings may explain why males failed to show an out-group = bad association across development. It will be especially important for further research to build off these early findings to evaluate the impact of the male = bad association for males and females at different points during development. Such research could begin to examine the development of implicit gender stereotypes about violence and whether there is evidence of balance among such stereotypes, self-concept and attitudes at some point during development.

Emergence of cognitive balance among gender attitudes, self-concepts and behaviour

Our recent findings suggest that gender biases emerge by the fifth year of life and are largely stable in magnitude across development, at least for girls. We next consider how these emerging biases toward gender concepts interact with a developing sense of self, given the principles of cognitive balance discussed earlier. Recall, according to BIT (Greenwald et al., 2002), people with *high* self-esteem should display stronger in-group bias. This is because people strive to maintain consistent attitudes toward the self and toward their in-groups. Thus, developmentally, BIT allows for a) either self-esteem or in-group bias to precede the other in development or b) for both to develop concurrently. Current research provides both the framework, as well as the methodology, that will allow for a much closer empirical investigation of the developmental course of the interrelationship among these implicit constructs.

Cvencek et al. (2013a) examined evidence of balance among implicit gender self-concept, self-esteem and gender attitudes among 5-year-old children. Once again, they employed a modified version of the PSIAT to measure implicit self-concepts and self-esteem with preschool children. They observed theoretically expected principles of affective–cognitive consistency (Greenwald et al., 2002) operating in children as young as 5 years of age, such that children who had positive self-esteem and strong gender self-concepts also displayed greater positivity toward their own gender. These results now contribute to a growing body of research documenting evidence for principles of cognitive balance operating in children as young as 5 years of age (Cvencek et al., 2011b; Dunham et al., 2007). It is interesting to note that balance among these attitudinal constructs occurs a full three years before documented evidence of balance among the implicit gender stereotypes discussed earlier. Such a finding suggests that the failure to detect balance among younger kids in the domain of gender stereotypes is not the result of a cognitive limitation of the mind in establishing balance, but rather those constructs may take longer to form interconnections. Finally, although implicit self-esteem and in-group positivity appear to be present and developing concurrently by age 5, it is possible that one precedes the other during development. Once more, no studies have examined balance among these constructs with younger samples to date, leaving this an area of considerable interest for further research.

Although the relationship among implicit gender attitudes, explicit gender attitudes and observable behaviour has only recently received developmental examination, there is suggestive evidence of balance among these constructs as well. For example, in the study of preschool children's implicit gender attitudes reported above, Cvencek et al. (2011a) examined the relationship between implicit and explicit gender attitudes and children's gendered play activities. Implicit attitudes were measured using a variant of the PSIAT. Explicit attitudes were measured using a forced-choice preference measure where participants had to choose (across several trials) which gender individual they liked more. Finally, to measure gendered play preference, parents were asked to indicate how frequently during the past month their children played with gender typical toys, engaged in stereotypical activities and exhibited gender typical behaviours.

According to Cvencek et al. (2011a) implicit and explicit measures of gender attitudes correlated significantly with one another, such that the more children implicitly preferred their own gender group, the more they reported an explicit preference for people of that gender. Moreover, both measures predicted variance in parents' reports of their children's gendered play activities. Thus, the more children implicitly preferred one gender over the other, the more likely their parent reported that their child engaged in behaviours typical of that preferred gender.

Pointing to the unique role played by implicit processes in predicting behaviour, children's implicit gender attitudes predicted their play preferences over and above the role played by children's explicit attitudes toward gender groups.

Thus, similar to the developmental emergence of implicit gender stereotypes, children's implicit gender attitudes are shown here to emerge early in development – by the fourth or fifth year of life, and are bound, in some part, by principles of cognitive–affective balance from a young age. These findings in the gender domain parallel recent reports on the early emergence and developmental stability of implicit race attitudes (Baron & Banaji, 2006, 2009; Dunham et al., 2008), underscoring potentially broad signatures of how implicit associations form and develop. While there is considerable research to be pursued, some of which we have outlined here, the evidence is building in support of the important role cognitive balance plays in children's emerging network of associations. Such findings, across measures of gender stereotype, attitude, identity and behaviour, highlight the importance of targeting a vast web of constructs from an early age if one wants to affect positive change for the implicit associations that contribute to gender differences in behaviour and well-being more generally.

A roadmap for change: insights from developmental investigations

Sociocultural learning theories stress the importance of the environment in shaping children's beliefs and attitudes toward social groups. Most learning theories are quite broad, emphasizing the general importance of both direct and indirect experiences. The very nature of these learning mechanisms means individuals will sometimes acquire negative attitudes and stereotypic attributes about themselves and their groups. As such, understanding how to change these implicit associations has received considerable attention, focusing on contact with out-group members as well as direct and indirect forms of exposure to counter-stereotypical and counter-attitudinal information (Dovidio & Gaertner, 1999; Dovidio et al., 2002, 2004; Gaertner & Dovidio, 2005; Gaertner et al., 1999; Gregg et al., 2006; Olsson, et al., 2005; Pettigrew & Tropp, 2006; Tropp & Pettigrew, 2005). Unfortunately, much of this work has revealed that while change is possible, it is also surprisingly difficult to achieve. While many studies share this general conclusion, it is worth noting that all of these examinations have exclusively focused on adult samples. However, recent data on the early emergence of implicit stereotypes, attitudes and cognitive–affective balance from our labs and others discussed here highlights the importance of bringing developmental data to bear on understanding the malleability of implicit associations.

Looking forward, developmental analysis will play a crucial role in understanding when across the lifespan implicit associations are most amenable to change and may help shed light on the challenges faced in changing the minds' of adults. For example, several existing theoretical models produce strikingly different predictions concerning the developmental trajectory of implicit intergroup cognition with implications for when such cognitions would be most flexible.

Only developmental evidence will help adjudicate among these alternatives. On one view, intergroup stereotypes and attitudes are acquired slowly, the result of accumulated experience over the lifespan (Bigler & Liben, 2006; Devine, 1989; Greenwald & Banaji, 1995). This view supports the hypothesis a) that change will become increasingly more difficult with age as there will be a longer period of reinforcement to overcome.

A second view, motivated by the literature on executive function development, suggests that with age comes a global increase in the flexibility of children's thought (Aboud, 1988; Bigler & Liben, 2006; Davidson et al., 2006; Jones et al., 2003; Piaget, 1929; Piaget et al., 1971). Accordingly, this view supports the hypothesis b) that efforts to change implicit associations will be more successful later in development (i.e. adolescence) as the capacity to revise earlier thoughts improves. Both hypotheses predict a gradual change in the flexibility of implicit intergroup cognition across development, albeit in opposite directions.

On a third view, implicit associations are particularly influenced by early life experiences, perhaps akin to a sensitive period, whereby first impressions become particularly difficult to modify. Such a view supports the hypothesis c) that the optimal period to affect change occurs in early childhood at the time these associations first take root (Rudman, 2004; Rudman et al., 2007), with no specific predictions about age-related differences in the capacity for change after this period. The converging evidence from our labs on implicit gender stereotype and attitude development that we have summarized here supports the idea of a sensitive period for the development of implicit associations. Specifically, these studies reveal that such associations are learned surprisingly early during development, and that there is very little change in the magnitude of such associations from age 5 onward. These findings not only parallel what has been observed in the domain of race (Baron & Banaji, 2006; Dunham et al., 2008), but they also underscore the generality of our earlier claims that such associations form early and quickly, relatively unaffected by the wealth of learning opportunities that await the developing mind later in childhood and adolescence. Indeed, given the general stability of these implicit associations across development as well as our presented evidence of cognitive–affective balance that only strengthens over time among school-aged children, we believe that a sensitive period of acquisition appears to take place before or around ages 4–5 for gender attitudes and by age 7–8 for gender stereotypes about mathematics and science (at least among Western societies where formal schooling in these disciplines occurs).

One important implication of our speculation of a sensitive period in the formation of these implicit cognitions is that efforts to change an individual's gender stereotypes or attitudes may be most effective by reaching the child at the very point during development when these associations first take root in the mind. Such a claim runs contrary to the current research focus of investigating adult populations. Examining developmental constraints on the malleability of implicit social cognition can focus on changing the content of the cognition (e.g. we should be instilling that girls do science just as well!) and, based on our findings of cognitive balance, might also minimize the strength of association between self and gender (thereby reducing the likelihood that girls will internalize the stereotype that science isn't for 'me' and that boys will internalize the attitude that 'I' am bad).

One way to approach these questions is to design an experiment with participants who range in age from childhood through adolescence. An initial assessment of an implicit attitude or stereotype should be assessed, followed by a targeted intervention (e.g. direct contact with a counter-attitudinal or stereotypical exemplar such as a female), and then a measure of the implicit association following the intervention period. Age-related differences in how much that initial association changes based on the controlled experience will begin to shed light on the proposals raised earlier.

Other efforts could focus on manipulating the length, quality and type of exposure to counter-attitudinal and stereotypical information. For example, research with young adults has seen some success in predicting weaker implicit gender stereotypes after both short-term and long-term exposure to successful female role models (Stout et al., 2011), but such interventions might be stronger and more long lasting when conducted with young children. One suggestion would be to expose children to early examples of women excelling in mathematics. This could take the form of reading children's books about famous female scholars in the field. Another possibility is to ensure that summer camps and after-school programmes that have mathematics-centred classes for young children have a gender parity requirement. While parents might be subtly influenced by their own gender biases and sign up boys more so than girls for such programmes, the result is that parents' own gender biases reinforce different skills in boys and girls. Another suggestion would be for mothers and fathers to supervise gender atypical courses for their children. Thus, in the case of mathematics and science courses, mums would make more of a concerted effort to review this work with their children while dads focused on other subjects such as reading and writing. This practice would provide children with evidence that counters the prevailing cultural stereotypes. Effects on developing implicit associations of mathematics with gender categories and the self would inform best practices and timing for interventions. Surprisingly, we aren't familiar with any other research focusing exclusively on interventions with young children designed to change implicit gender associations.

Of course, it should also be recognized that our evidence for the stability of implicit gender attitudes and stereotypes from childhood to adulthood does not imply that these associations cannot be changed at later ages. Indeed, while the magnitude of the associations we examined appears fairly stable across development, features of the environment (cultural attitudes and beliefs) are also fairly stable. As such, it is still possible that systematic changes in the cultural messages people receive can lead to changes of various degrees across development in the magnitude of the corresponding implicit associations. Examining this possibility will surely be another important avenue for future research.

Final thoughts on promoting gender equality

In this chapter, we have summarized recent evidence for the early development and ongoing stability of implicit gender biases. We have also argued that an understanding of how gender associations shape children's developing views of themselves points to the need for early intervention for effective change. The findings presented here with elementary-school children reveal that gender-linked academic stereotypes exert an influence on children's mathematics self-concepts much earlier than previously thought. Intervention programmes aimed at changing the ideas of students about gender and mathematics might profitably be directed at very early stages in development. Specifically, interventions based on implicit measurement techniques can be of particular benefit to elementary-school students: by changing young girls' implicit attitudes, stereotypes and self-concepts about mathematics and science, their performance and interest in these domains might also increase. Importantly, exerting such change does not require students to complete a specific curriculum. Implicit measures can also be used to provide diagnostic information about the prevalence of stereotypic biases among students and the effectiveness of approaches that attempt to mitigate these biases. Implicit measures are easily administered, psychometrically sound and sensitive to individual differences. If the lower mathematics achievement in girls can be partially accounted for by those girls' internalization of the cultural stereotype that mathematics is for boys, a method to measure those stereotypes at an early age will provide a useful tool for teachers in assessing their students and designing appropriate intervention strategies.

The developmental trajectory of implicit gender attitudes reported here also raises concern for children's exposure to another cultural association, the male = violent stereotype. The internalization of this association may be diminishing boys' ability to maintain a positive own group preference and fuelling a male = bad association among females. If this causal relationship is borne out through further research, then new consideration must be given to the content of children's (and adults') television programming, especially given evidence of the interrelationship among implicit constructs such as gender identity, gender attitudes and self-esteem. Indeed, the far reach of implicit gender attitudes, shaping attitudes toward the self and one's gender identity through principles of cognitive balance, underscores the need to address this issue quite early in development (Cvencek et al., 2013a).

Gender identity is a foundational way in which we define ourselves. As a result, the associations with gender categories in a child's environment are learned and internalized quite easily. Efforts at reducing gender bias then needs to focus on how environments shape broader cultural information about gender that becomes imprinted onto the minds' of bodies just a few years removed from nappies. Such a conclusion might only be reached from a careful analysis of the developmental trajectory of these implicit associations. Without such enquiry, the window within which such associations form and are considered most malleable would still be wrongly attributed to a period much later in development. We hope researchers who traditionally study the gender cognitions of adults or who focus only on explicit measures of gendered cognitions will increasingly see the value of developmental enquiry in constraining theories of acquisition and change by examining implicit social cognition starting from very early ages.

References

Aboud, F. E. (1988). *Children and prejudice*. New York: Basil Blackwell.

Ambady, N., Shih, M., Kim, A., & Pittinsky, T. L. (2001). Stereotype susceptibility in children: effects of identity activation on quantitative performance. *Psychological Science, 12*(5), 385–390.

Bahrick, L. E., Netto, D., & Hernandez-Reif, M. (1998). Intermodal perception of adult and child faces and voices by infants. *Child Development, 69*, 1263–1275.

Banaji, M. R. (2001). Implicit attitudes can be measured. In Roediger, H. L., III, Nairne, J. S., Neath, I., & Surprenant, A. (Eds), *The nature of remembering: essays in honor of Robert G. Crowder* (pp. 117–150). Washington, DC: American Psychological Association.

Baron, A. S., & Banaji, M. R. (2006). The development of implicit attitudes: evidence of race evaluations from ages 6, 10 and adulthood. *Psychological Science, 17*, 53–58.

Baron, A. S., & Banaji, M. R. (2009). Evidence for the early emergence of system justification in children. *Personality and Social Psychology Compass, 3*(6), 918–926.

Baron, A. S., & Dunham, Y. (2013). Origins of a minimal group bias. Unpublished manuscript. Vancouver, BC: University of British Columbia.

Barrett, M. (2007). *Children's knowledge, beliefs and feelings about nations and national groups*. Hove, East Sussex: Psychology Press.

Batchelder, W. H., & Riefer, D. M. (1999). Theoretical and empirical review of multinomial processing tree modeling. *Psychonomic Bulletin & Review, 6*, 57–86.

Bigler, R. S., & Liben, L. S. (2006). A developmental intergroup theory of social stereotypes and prejudice. In Kail, R. V. (Ed.), *Advances in child development and behavior* (Vol. 34) (pp. 39–89). San Diego, CA: Elsevier Academic Press.

Bigler, R. S., & Liben, L. S. (2007). Developmental intergroup theory. *Current Directions in Psychological Science, 16*, 162–166.

Bigler, R. S., Jones, L. C., & Lobliner, D. B. (1997). Social categorization and the formation of intergroup attitudes in children. *Child Development, 68*, 530–543.

Blanton, H., & Jaccard, J. (2006). Postscript: perspectives on the reply by Greenwald, Rudman, Nosek, and Zayas (2006). *Psychological Review, 113*(1), 166–169. doi:10.1037/0033-295X.113.1.166.

Brewer, M. B. (1979). In-group bias in the minimal intergroup situation: a cognitive-motivational analysis. *Psychological Bulletin, 86*(2), 307–324.

Conrey, F. R., Sherman, J. W., Gawronski, B., Hugenberg, K., & Groom, C. (2005). Separating multiple processes in implicit social cognition: the Quad Model of implicit task performance. *Journal of Personality and Social Psychology, 89*, 469–487.

Croft, A., Schmader, T., Block, K., & Baron, A. S. (2013). Actions speak loader than words: parental beliefs, biases, and behaviors predict children's stereotypic preferences. Unpublished manuscript. Vancouver, BC: University of British Columbia.

Cvencek, D., Greenwald, A. G., & Meltzoff, A. N. (2011a). Measuring implicit attitudes of 4-year-olds: the Preschool Implicit Association Test. *Journal of Experimental Child Psychology, 109*(2), 187–200. doi:10.1016/j.jecp.2010.11.002.

Cvencek, D., Meltzoff, A. N., & Greenwald, A. G. (2011b). Math-gender stereotypes in elementary school children. *Child Development, 82*(3), 766–779.

Cvencek, D., Greenwald, A. G., & Meltzoff, A. N. (2013a). *Implicit self-esteem and self-concepts in preschoolers*. Unpublished manuscript. Seattle, WA: University of Washington.

Cvencek, D., Meltzoff, A. N., & Kapur, M. (2013b). *Cognitive consistency and math-gender stereotypes in Singaporean children*. Unpublished manuscript. Seattle, WA: University of Washington.

Davidson, M. C., Amso, D., Anderson, L. C., & Diamond, A. (2006). Development of cognitive control and executive functions from 4 to 13 years: evidence from manipulations of memory, inhibition, and task switching. *Neuropsychologia, 44*(11), 2037–2078.

Davies, P. G., Spencer, S. J., & Steele, C. M. (2005). Clearing the air: identity safety moderates the effects of stereotype threat on women's leadership aspirations. *Journal of Personality and Social Psychology, 88*(2), 276–287.

Devine, P. G. (1989). Stereotype and prejudice: their automatic and controlled components. *Journal of Personality and Social Psychology, 56*(1), 5–18.

Diekman, A. B., Brown, E. R., Johnston, A. M., & Clark, E. K. (2010). Seeking congruity between roles and goals: a new look at why women opt out of STEM careers. *Psychological Science, 21,* 1051–1057.

Dovidio, J. F., & Gaertner, S. L. (1999). Reducing prejudice: combating intergroup biases. *Current Directions in Psychological Science, 8*(4), 101–105.

Dovidio, J. F., Kawakami, K., & Gaertner, S. L. (2002). Implicit and explicit prejudice and interracial interaction. *Journal of Personality and Social Psychology, 82*(1), 62–68.

Dovidio, J. F., ten Vergert, M., Stewart, T. L., Gaertner, S. L., Johnson, J. D., Esses, V. M., et al. (2004). Perspective and prejudice: antecedents and mediating mechanisms. *Personality and Social Psychology Bulletin, 30*(12), 1537–1549.

Dunham, Y., Baron, A. S., & Banaji, M. R. (2007). Children and social groups: a developmental analysis of implicit consistency among Hispanic-Americans. *Self and Identity, 6,* 238–255.

Dunham, Y., Baron, A. S., & Banaji, M. R. (2008). The development of implicit intergroup cognition. *Trends in Cognitive Sciences, 12*(7), 248–253.

Dunham, Y., Baron, A. S, & Carey, S. (2011). Consequences of 'minimal' group affiliations in children. *Child Development, 82*(3), 793–811.

Dunham, Y., Baron, A. S., & Banaji, M. R. (2013). Development of implicit gender attitudes. Unpublished manuscript. New Haven, CT: Yale University.

Eagly, A. H. & Steffen, V. J. (1984). Gender stereotypes stem from the distribution of women and men into social roles. *Journal of Personality and Social Psychology, 46,* 735–754.

Eccles, J. S., Adler, T. F., Futterman, R., Goff, S. B., Kaczala, C. M., et al. (1983). Expectations, values and academic behaviors. In Spence, J.T. (Ed.), *Achievement and achievement motives* (pp. 75–145). San Francisco, CA: W. H. Freeman.

Eccles, J. S., Adler, T., & Meece, J. L. (1984). Sex differences in achievement: a test of alternate theories. *Journal of Personality and Social Psychology, 46*(1), 26–43.

Else-Quest, N. M., Hyde, J. S., & Linn, M. C. (2010). Cross-national patterns of gender differences in mathematics: a meta-analysis. *Psychological Bulletin, 136*(1), 103–127.

Festinger, L. (1954). A theory of social comparison processes. *Human Relations, 7,* 117–140.

Forbes, C. E., & Schmader, T. (2010). Retraining implicit attitudes and stereotypes to distinguish motivation from performance in a stereotype threatening domain. *Journal of Personality and Social Psychology, 99*(5), 740–754.

Gaertner, S. L., & Dovidio, J. F. (2005). Understanding and addressing contemporary racism: from aversive racism to the common ingroup identity model. *Journal of Social Issues, 61*(3), 615–639.

Gaertner, S. L., Dovidio, J. F., Rust, M. C., Nier, J. A., Banker, B. S., Ward, C. M., et al. (1999). Reducing intergroup bias: elements of intergroup cooperation. *Journal of Personality and Social Psychology, 76*(3), 388–402.

Gawronski, B., & Bodenhausen, G. V. (2006). Associative and propositional processes in evaluation: an integrative review of implicit and explicit attitude change. *Psychological Bulletin, 132,* 692–731.

Gerbner, G., Gross, L., Jackson-Beeck, M. J., Jeffries-Fox, S., & Signorielli, N. (1978). Cultural indicators: violence profile no. 9, *Journal of Communication, 28*(3), 176–207.

Goldin, C., & Rouse, C. (2000). Orchestrating impartiality: the impact of 'blind' auditions on female musicians. *American Economic Review, 90*(4), 715–741.

Greenwald, A. G., & Banaji, M. R. (1995). Implicit social cognition: attitudes, self-esteem, and stereotypes. *Psychological Review, 102*, 4–27.

Greenwald, A. G., McGhee, D. E., & Schwarz, J. L. K. (1998). Measuring individual differences in implicit cognition: The Implicit Association Test. *Journal of Personality and Social Psychology, 74*(6), 1464–1480.

Greenwald, A. G., Banaji, M. R., Rudman, L. A., Farnham, S. D., Nosek, B. A., & Mellott, D. S. (2002). A unified theory of implicit attitudes, stereotypes, self-esteem, and self-concept. *Psychological Review, 109*(1), 3–25.

Greenwald, A. G., Poehlman, T. A., Uhlmann, E., & Banaji, M. R. (2009). Understanding and using the Implicit Association Test: III. Meta-analysis of predictive validity. *Journal of Personality and Social Psychology, 97*(1), 17–41.

Gregg, A. P., Seibt, B., & Banaji, M. R. (2006). Easier done than undone: asymmetry in the malleability of implicit preferences. *Journal of Personality and Social Psychology, 90*(1), 1–20.

Heider, F. (1946). Attitudes and cognitive organization. *Journal of Psychology, 21*, 107–112.

Heiphetz, L., Spelke, E. S., & Banaji, M. R. (in press). Patterns of implicit and explicit attitudes in children and adults: tests in the domain of religion. *Journal of Experimental Psychology: General.*

Jamieson, J. P., & Harkins, S. G. (2007). Mere effort and stereotype threat performance effects. *Journal of Personality and Social Psychology, 93*(3), 544–564.

Jones, L. B., Rothbart, M. K., & Posner, M. I. (2003). Development of executive attention in preschool children. *Developmental Science, 6*(5), 498–504.

Karpinski, A., & Hilton, J. L. (2001). Attitudes and the Implicit Association Test. *Journal of Personality and Social Psychology, 81*, 774–788.

Kinzler, K. D., Dupoux, E., & Spelke, E. S. (2007). The native language of social cognition. *The Proceedings of the National Academy of Sciences of the United States of America, 104*, 12577–12580.

Levy, S. R., & Killen, M. (Eds) (2008). *Intergroup attitudes and relations in childhood through adulthood.* Oxford: Oxford University Press.

Logel, C., Walton, G. M., Spencer, S. J., Iserman, E. C., Von Hippel, W., & Bell, A. E. (2009). Interacting with sexist men triggers social identity threat among female engineers. *Journal of Personality and Social Psychology, 96*(6), 1089–1103. doi:10.1037/a0015703.

Martin, C. L., & Ruble, D. N. (2004). Children's search for gender cues: cognitive perspectives on gender development. *Current Directions in Psychological Science, 13*, 67–70.

Martin, C. L., Ruble, D. N., & Szkrybalo, J. (2002). Cognitive theories of early gender development. *Psychological Bulletin, 128*, 903–933.

Moss-Racusin, C. A., Dovidio, J. F., Brescoll, V. L., Graham, M. J., & Handelsman, J. (2012). Science faculty's subtle gender biases favor male students. *The Proceedings of the National Academy of Sciences of the United States of America, 109*(41), 16474–16479. doi:10.1073/pnas.1211286109.

Mrazek, M. D., Chin, J. M., Schmader, T., Hartson, K. A., Smallwood, J., & Schooler, J. W. (2011). Threatened to distraction: mind-wandering as a consequence of stereotype threat. *Journal of Experimental Social Psychology, 47*(6), 1243–1248.

Muzzatti, B., & Agnoli, F. (2007). Gender and mathematics: attitudes and stereotype threat susceptibility in Italian children. *Developmental Psychology, 43*(3), 747–759.

Nesdale, D., & Flesser, D. (2001). Social identity and the development of children's group attitudes. *Child Development, 72*(2), 506–517.

Nesdale, D., Maass, A., Griffiths, J., & Durkin, K. (2003). Effects of ingroup and outgroup ethnicity on children's attitudes towards members of the ingroup and outgroup. *British Journal of Developmental Psychology, 21*, 177 –192.

Nesdale, D., Maass, A., Kiesner, J., Durkin, K., Griffiths, J., and Ekberg, A. (2007). Effects of peer group rejection, group membership, and group norms, on children's outgroup prejudice. *International Journal of Behavioral Development, 31*(5), 526–535.

Newheiser, A., & Olson, K. R. (2012). White and Black American children's implicit intergroup bias. *Journal of Experimental Social Psychology, 48*, 264–270.

Nock, M. K., & Banaji, M. R. (2007). Assessment of self-injurious thoughts using a behavioral test. *American Journal of Psychiatry, 164*(5), 820–823.

Nosek, B. A. (2007). Implicit-explicit relations. *Current Directions in Psychological Science, 16*(2), 65–69.

Nosek, B. A., Banaji, M. R., & Greenwald, A. G. (2002). Math = male, me = female, therefore math =/= me. *Journal of Personality and Social Psychology, 83*, 44–59.

Nosek, B. A., Smyth, F. L., Sriram, N., et al. (2009). National differences in gender-science stereotypes predict national sex differences in science and math achievement. *Proceedings of the National Academy of Sciences, 106*(26), 10593–10597.

Olsson, A., Ebert, J. P., Banaji, M. R., & Phelps, E. A. (2005). The role of social groups in the persistence of learned fear. *Science, 309*(5735), 785–787.

Parmley, M., & Cunningham, J. G. (2008). Children's gender-emotion stereotypes in the relationship of anger to sadness and fear. *Sex Roles, 58*, 358–370.

Patterson, M. M., Bigler, R. S., & Swann, W. B., Jr. (2010). When personal identities confirm versus conflict with group identities: evidence from an intergroup paradigm. *European Journal of Social Psychology, 40*, 652–670.

Pettigrew, T. F., & Tropp, L. R. (2006). A meta-analytic test of intergroup contact theory. *Journal of Personality and Social Psychology, 90*(5), 751–783.

Pew Research (2010). *Gender equality universally embraced, but inequalities acknowledged.* Pew Research Global Attitudes Project, Washington DC: National Center for Education Statistics.

Piaget, J. (1929). *The child's conception of the world.* London: Routledge & Kegan Paul.

Piaget, J., Green, D. R., Ford, M. P., & Flamer, G. B. (1971). *The theory of stages in cognitive development measurement and Piaget.* New York: McGraw-Hill.

Quinn, P., Yahr, J., Kuhn, A., Slater, A., & Pascalis, O. (2002). Representation of the gender of human faces by infants: a preference for female. *Perception, 31*, 1109–1121.

Rudman, L. A., & Goodwin, S. A. (2004). Gender differences in automatic in-group bias: why do women like women more than men like men? *Journal of Personality and Social Psychology, 87*(4), 494–509. doi:10.1037/0022-3514.87.4.494.

Rudman, L. A. (2004). Sources of implicit attitudes. *Current Directions in Psychological Science, 13*(2), 80–83.

Rudman, L. A., Phelan, J. E., & Heppen, J. (2007). Developmental sources of implicit attitudes. *Personality and Social Psychology Bulletin, 33*(12), 1700–1713.

Rutland, A., Cameron, L., Milne, A., & McGeorge, P. (2005). Social norms and self-presentation: children's implicit and explicit intergroup attitudes. *Child Development, 76*, 451–466.

Schmader T., & Johns, M. (2003). Converging evidence that stereotype threat reduces working memory capacity. *Journal of Personality and Social Psychology, 85*, 440–452.

Schmader, T., Johns, M., & Barquissau, M. (2004). The costs of accepting gender differences: the role of stereotype endorsement in women's experience in the math domain. *Sex Roles: A Journal of Research, 50*, 835–850.

Schmader, T., Johns, M., & Forbes, C. (2008). An integrated process model of stereotype threat effects on performance. *Psychological Review, 115*, 336–356.

Sherif, M., Harvey, O. J., White, B. J., Hood, W. R., & Sherif, C. W. (1961). *Intergroup conflict and cooperation: the Robbers Cave experiment*. Norman, OK: University of Oklahoma Book Exchange.

Sherman, J. W., Gawronski, B., Gonsalkorale, K., Hugenberg, K., Allen, T. J., & Groom, C. J. (2008). The self-regulation of automatic associations and behavioral impulses. *Psychological Review, 115*, 314–335.

Spencer, S. J., Steele, C. M., & Quinn, D. M. (1999). Stereotype threat and women's math performance. *Journal of Experimental Social Psychology, 35*, 4–28.

Spielman, D. A. (2000). Young children, minimal groups and dichotomous categorization. *Personality and Social Psychology Bulletin, 26*(11), 1433–1441.

Steele, C. M., & Aronson, J. (1995). Stereotype threat and the intellectual test performance of African Americans. *Journal of Personality and Social Psychology, 69*(5), 797–811.

Steele, C. M., Spencer, S. J., & Aronson, J. (2002). Contending with group image: the psychology of stereotype and social identity threat. In Zanna, M. P. (Ed.), *Advances in experimental social psychology* (Vol. 34) (pp. 379–440). New York: Academic Press.

Steffens, M. C., Jelenec, P., & Noack, P. (2010). On the leaky math pipeline: comparing implicit math-gender stereotypes and math withdrawal in female and male children and adolescents. *Journal of Educational Psychology, 102*(4), 947–963.

Sternglanz, S. H. & Serbin, L. A. (1974). Sex role stereotyping in children's television programs. *Developmental Psychology, 10*(5), 710–715.

Stout, J. G., Dasgupta, N., Hunsinger, M., & McManus, M. A. (2011). STEMing the tide: using ingroup experts to inoculate women's self-concept in science, technology, engineering, and mathematics (STEM). *Journal of Personality and Social Psychology, 100*, 255–270.

Tedesco, N. S. (1974). Patterns in prime time. *Journal of Communication, 24*(2), 119–124.

Tropp, L. R., & Pettigrew, T. F. (2005). Relationships between intergroup contact and prejudice among minority and majority status groups. *Psychological Science, 16*(12), 951–957.

Turner, J. C., Brown, R. J., & Tajfel, H. (1979). Social comparison and group interest in ingroup favouritism. *European Journal of Social Psychology, 9*(2), 187–204.

United States Department of Health and Human Services. (2001). Youth violence: a report of the Surgeon General. Rockville MD: Office of the Surgeon General.

Weinraub, M., Clemens, L. P., Sockloff, A., Ethridge, T., Gracely, E., & Myers, B. (1984). The development of sex role stereotypes in the third year: relationships to gender labeling, gender identity, sex-typed toy preference, and family characteristics. *Child Development, 55*, 1493–1503.

Yee, M., & Brown, R. (1994). The development of gender differentiation in young children. *British Journal of Social Psychology, 33*, 183–196.

7 Developmental social cognition about gender roles in the family and societal context

Stefanie Sinno, Christine Schuette and Melanie Killen

While family studies research has noted that 70 per cent of all US homes are comprised of dual-earning couples (Raley et al., 2006), and that fathers are increasing their active role in the home (Barnett & Rivers, 2004), women continue to spend more time than men in the role of caretaker (Milkie et al., 2004). Some of the disparities in caretaking roles in the home are related to gender expectations in the workforce, such as hours spent at work and job competency. For example, fathers are often expected to work long hours outside the home and take on the breadwinner role (Palkovitz, 2002; Tamis-LeMonda & Cabrera, 2002). Mothers, in comparison, are often stereotyped as ineffective in the workforce because of the expectation that they are too warm and nurturing resulting in less time at work (Cuddy et al., 2004). Additionally, a woman who has children is seen as less competent in her profession and is often overlooked for training or promotions compared to women without children, which results in spending more time at home (Fuegan et al., 2004).

A foundational developmental question is how do these expectations placed on parents affect the lives of their children, and children's emerging social cognition about gender roles, expectations and aspirations? Research has found that parents who have more egalitarian gender schemas about themselves and society have young children who are less gender stereotypical about careers and occupations (Tenenbaum & Leaper, 2002) and adolescent children who are more tolerant of ambiguity about gender roles (Kulik, 2005). In addition, sons of egalitarian fathers were found to be more accepting of female activities and less likely to associate them with a negative stigma (Deutsch et al., 2001). One reason that these findings might occur is because egalitarian households provide both daughters and sons with diverse experiences related to careers and household responsibilities which, in turn, provide experiential bases to challenge stereotypic expectations and to develop egalitarian expectations for their own lives. Family flexibility influences children's and adolescents' attitudes toward gender-specific tasks and roles and increases opportunities for their own activities and roles.

While there has been an extensive amount of research noting that gender expectations affect adults' beliefs, attitudes and behaviours (see Zosuls et al., 2011) and that children are aware of these gender expectations (Coltrane & Adams, 2008; Fulcher, 2011; Kanka et al. 2011; Weisgram et al., 2010), only recently has developmental research begun to examine children's social cognition about the gendered roles of occupations and parental responsibilities (Fulcher, 2011; Schuette et al., 2012; Sinno & Killen, 2011). The purpose of this research, grounded in social domain theory (see Smetana, 2006; Turiel, 1998), is to understand the social and developmental interpretations of gender role norms and how thinking about these gender expectations affects children's and adolescents' aspirations. Societal expectations that send negative messages about males taking on caretaking roles or egalitarian division of labour have a direct bearing on females' occupational aspirations. To the extent that girls believe that they have to take on the 'lion's share' of parenting and boys believe that they have to be the primary breadwinner, the more limited are their occupational pursuits as they begin thinking about coordinating family and work expectations. What are needed, then, are systematic investigations of how children interpret family roles, and the extent to which their evaluations of parental roles are related to their own career and future family role expectations.

The aim of this chapter is to examine the highly gendered roles of occupations and parental roles in the home, connecting research from social role theory on adults with developmental research about children's social cognition about these adult roles. The chapter will first introduce the theoretical foundation of social role theory and social domain theory and then report new research that focuses on occupations and parental roles. Within each section, the gender norms and expectations for adults will be introduced first followed by research on children's understanding of these norms. Each section will additionally feature new and emerging lines of developmental research to showcase current research directions. The chapter will conclude with a discussion of the implications for developmental processes about family roles.

Theoretical grounding

Research has established that even though there has been a steady increase in the number of women who work outside the home, there is still the prevailing stereotype that women are more nurturing and are more suited for caretaking than men (Gorman & Fritzsche, 2002). Belief in as well as adherence to these gender expectations can limit individuals of all ages in their exploration of viable occupations, such that they may be denied access or may self-select occupations that allow them to focus on being in either the primary breadwinner or caretaker role in their families. This section of the chapter will review research from the social role theory first as it provides foundational evidence of why many adults might adhere to gender expectations within the career and family contexts. The chapter will then introduce and review developmental research grounded in the social domain theory, which moves the adult research further by exploring children's and adolescents' social cognition about these adult roles with the goal of understanding why these gender expectations might continue to exist.

According to research based in the social role theory, adults associate men and women with their primary roles and develop stereotypes based on the characteristics they presume are necessary for each of these roles. Furthermore, gender role ideologies are based on socialization processes and individuals' experiences with roles as they are modelled. In this way, women are more often associated with the caretaker role and the family, and men are more often associated with the role of breadwinner and career (for a review, see Eagly & Wood, 2012).

A further assumption of social role theory is that stereotypes can change as the roles of men and women shift over time (Diekman & Eagly, 2000). Many of the studies about gender roles in the home have been conducted with university-age students or adults and the prevailing finding is that while women expect to work outside the home, they also expect and anticipate having to do more household work and caretaking (Askari et al., 2010; Fetterolf & Eagly, 2011; Kaufman, 2005). Men and women do not differ in their desire for marriage and family (Erchull et al., 2010), yet women anticipate that they will have to balance their careers with child-rearing responsibilities and understand that there may be a conflict between raising a family and having a successful career (Fetterolf & Eagly, 2011). Research has not found that men anticipate this same kind of conflict and many college-age men still express the desire to have a wife who will stay home with the children while they are young (Stone & McKee, 2000). While more researchers are arguing that men's and women's overall workloads are moving towards equality (Bianchi et al., 2006), there is not enough empirical evidence from the social role theory to suggest a change in the societal perception that one of women's primary roles should be to serve as the family's caretaker.

There is some evidence that individuals who hold more liberal beliefs expect a more egalitarian division of labour (Kroska, 2003); however, there is also the emerging belief that the 'good mother' can do it all – have a successful career, marriage and family (Erchull et al., 2010; Gorman & Fritzsche, 2002). Gorman and Fritzsche found that mothers who delayed their careers until their children were school-age were not judged to be less committed to motherhood or less selfless when compared to mothers who stopped working to stay at home to care for their children. Additionally, Erchull et al. (2010) found that adherence to liberal attitudes influences predicted chore participation, and men with liberal attitudes anticipate doing more chores while liberal women expect to do fewer chores. This may represent a shift in societal views regarding mothers who work outside the home out of interest, career aspirations or financial necessity.

Despite these findings, there is a need for more research on which specific liberal views contribute to the development of an equitable distribution of labour, how expectations regarding chores predicts the actual distribution of labour, and studies to explore how to diminish the ideal of the 'superwoman' in place of a shared division of labour (Bianchi et al., 2006). For instance, time diary research has noted that while balance is something that both mothers and fathers try to achieve, mothers 'still shoulder twice as much childcare and housework' (p. 177). Gender inequality is especially evident when parents are asked to justify their time allocation: 'Mothers worry most about adequate time with children, whereas fathers remain focused on providing adequate money for the family' (p. 177). Given that there still exists a gender divide in the home and parents are 'engendering children'

(Coltrane & Adams, 2008, p. 167), it is critical to understand children's social cognition about gender in the family to break the cyclical nature of the gender divide.

Social domain theory has extended research about gender expectations by focusing on individual's reasoning and judgements about these social contexts (Schuette & Killen, 2009; Sinno & Killen, 2009, 2011). Particularly, because the model proposes that children actively participate in their environment and construct their understanding of the social world through interaction (Nucci & Turiel, 1978; Piaget, 1997; Turiel, 1983, 1998, 2006), this work has focused on children's and adolescent's social reasoning about family roles. Research from the social domain theory has found that children's and adolescents' reasoning about social situations that involve gender is often multifaceted (Killen et al., 2007). At times, gender stereotyping or discrimination is rejected because of unfairness (moral). On the other hand, children and adolescents have also been shown to accept exclusion based on gender because it matched cultural standards (social–conventional) or because of the strength of an individual's or group's personal choice (personal).

Social domain theory indicates that children develop concepts of equality and fairness regarding gender equity and discrimination at an early age (Smetana, 2006). Even as young as preschool, when young children are well aware of the stereotype that girls are associated with doll playing, children believe that it is unfair to prohibit a boy from playing with a doll simply because of his gender (Killen et al., 2001). With age, individuals often have difficulty making choices that are compounded by gender expectations as these separate domains of knowledge weigh on their decision. Most of the studies that have examined children's reasoning about gender exclusion have been conducted within the context of peer groups (Killen & Stangor, 2001; Theimer et al., 2001). In general, the studies have consistently found that children reason about gender stereotypic associations from both a moral and a social–conventional perspective. For instance, preschool-aged children's reasoning about exclusion from peer groups engaged in stereotypical play (e.g. a group of girls playing dolls) will elicit moral concerns from some children (e.g. it is not fair to leave someone out of the group if they want to play) as well as social–conventional reasoning from some children with a focus on the gender stereotype (e.g. boys don't like to play with dolls).

Studies from social domain theory have also included measures of stereotype flexibility and tolerance. The constructs of flexibility, the belief that both genders can engage in an activity, and tolerance, a lack of negativity about cross-gender behaviour, are critical to understand because they demonstrate a lack of rigidity about individuals who do not conform to gender stereotypes (Fulcher, 2011; Katz & Ksansnak, 1994; Owen Blakemore, 2003) and may be indicative of an individual's ability to reason about the morality of gender stereotyping. This research has found that while children become more flexible about gender norms with age, children are less flexible about males engaging in cross-gender behaviour (Schuette & Killen, 2009). Furthermore, children are negative about males who participate in stereotypically female activities (such as ballet) and their reasoning centres on gender role norms (Schuette & Killen, 2009).

Less is known, however, about whether children apply this same kind of reasoning to adult roles, more specifically to how flexible and tolerant they are about adult occupational choices and the division of caretaking in the home. Research grounded in social domain theory has just begun to expand on research from the social role theory to shed light on how children's conceptions of fairness and social norms influence their social knowledge concerning the coordination of occupational and parental roles, as shown in the following two sections of the chapter.

Occupational roles

According to the US Census Bureau data (2007), occupations are still divided among traditional gender lines. For example, 72 per cent of men compared to 28 per cent of women hold occupations involving computers and mathematics operations whereas the pattern is almost exactly reversed for education and library occupations (i.e. 27 per cent of men compared to 73 per cent of women). Many researchers have explored the reason behind the under-representation of women in science, technology, engineering and mathematics (STEM) careers and men in non-traditional domains such as nursing, particularly in light of the finding that both genders report higher levels of work satisfaction in masculine-type occupations (Watt, 2010). Several reasons for the occupational gender divide have been proposed: the influence of stereotypes and gender role ideologies, role models, media and the perceived support or lack of support from parents, guidance counselors, peers and teachers (Watt, 2010). Given that there is a stigma associated with males having female-typed occupations and that there is less power and prestige associated with female-dominated careers (Watt, 2010), it is little wonder that there continues to be an occupational divide.

Coupled with the prevalence of gender stereotypical thinking in regard to occupations is the reality that there are fewer role models (males who hold female-typed occupations, or females who hold male-typed occupations), and there is pressure, particularly early in development, for gender conformity (Weisgram et al., 2010). While parents may communicate their egalitarian expectations to their children (Fulcher, 2011), research has found that there are influences such as young women's desire for family-flexible careers (Frome et al., 2008) that prohibit women from succeeding in male-dominated occupations and continue to the 'leaky pipeline' or the exodus of college-age women from male-dominated majors like mathematics and engineering (Frome et al., 2008, p. 196). The cycle thus continues. The consequences are that women's occupations are not as highly regarded as men's, and there continues to be a divide between what is considered 'women's work' and what is considered 'men's work'. Further, compensation and promotion rates are substantially less for women compared to the rates for men (Coltrane & Adams, 2008). An important developmental question is how children interpret this occupational division and to what extent does it bear on their own constructions and expectations about occupational aspirations.

Developmental perspective

With the concern that there is an under-representation of females in STEM careers, there has been a concerted research effort over the past 25 years to explore career aspirations and to encourage girls to pursue their interests and to recognize the problems associated with prevalent gender stereotypes about masculine and feminine-stereotyped occupations (Watt, 2010). In the past, the focus of studies has primarily been on university-age students who are faced with making career development choices. More recently the focus has shifted to studies involving adolescents or school-age children to understand the development of career interests and determine whether there is a need for intervention to counteract the influence of gender role stereotypes about occupations (Fulcher, 2011; Schuette et al., 2012; Weisgram et al., 2010, 2011).

The developmental research has revealed that children as young as preschool associate occupations and activities with gender (Huston, 1985; Owen Blakemore, 2003). For example, when 3-year-old children were asked, 'Who usually plays with a toy kitchen?' and 'Who usually is a nurse?' their responses indicated an understanding of the gender norm (Owen Blakemore, 2003). Furthermore, researchers have identified a list of occupations that children reliably associate with gender (Liben & Bigler, 2002). For example, Liben and Bigler (2002) found that occupations such as doctor, scientist, pilot, mathematician and car mechanic were associated with males more often than females, whereas traditionally female occupations included teacher, hair stylist, librarian, secretary and nurse.

In studies that have included measures of gender stereotype flexibility and tolerance (Carter & Patterson, 1982; Katz & Ksansnak, 1994; Owen Blakemore, 2003; Ruble et al., 2006; Signorella et al., 1993), cross-gender behaviour is judged to be more acceptable for girls than for boys, which broadens the list of occupational pursuits for females but limits the possibilities for males (Schuette et al., 2012). One implication of this asymmetry is that there are more positive messages about moving up the gender hierarchy (girls taking on male-stereotyped occupations) rather than down (boys taking on female-associated occupations). Although asymmetry in gender role flexibility might create more opportunities for young girls, the reality is that when girls begin to aspire for male-stereotyped occupations they may also come to understand the inevitability of social exclusion, stigma and guilt as career and family goals can conflict, negatively impacting their willingness to follow through with these goals.

In the literature with school-age children, the prevailing finding is that there are several factors that influence children's occupational aspirations including the 'traditionality' of parental attitudes (Fulcher, 2011; see Bussey & Bandura, 1999), the prestige of the job (Weisgram et al., 2010) and the stereotypes that are associated with the jobs (Schuette et al., 2012; Sinno & Killen, 2009; Weisgram et al., 2011). For instance, research on career conversations between adolescents and their mothers found that mother–daughter dyads tended to focus on career goals only in the broader sense of keeping options open and maintaining an effective relational context in which decisions can be made at some time in the future. Mother–son dyads, in contrast, were more likely to have conversations that were explicitly about educational achievement and obtaining careers and vocations (Domene et al., 2007). Within this literature there is a gap in understanding children's cognition about these roles, particularly their efficacy beliefs. It is important to understand not only what children think they want to do in their future occupational roles (interests) but also whether they think they can do it (efficacy beliefs). Information about children's efficacy beliefs can help move research forward to understanding their social reasoning about these adult roles.

Research has found that stereotype flexibility increases with age (Ruble et al., 2006) and individuals are more tolerant of cross-gender behaviour for girls than for boys (Turiel, 2006). It is logical that if both factors, stereotype flexibility and tolerance, impact an individual's gender schema of others that they might also be related to one's self schema and efficacy beliefs. Signorella et al. (1993) conducted a meta-analytic review and established that it is important to assess not only stereotype knowledge but stereotype attitudes because there may be a difference between what individuals accept as appropriate for themselves compared to what they accept for others. In other words, a male may think that it is acceptable for men to be nurses, but at the same time hold the view that being a nurse is unacceptable for him. There is a need for research that explores the connection between efficacy beliefs and attitudes regarding stereotypes as both sets of beliefs have implications for children's emerging social role knowledge and career pursuits. If stereotypes potentially influence individual's career self-efficacy and if adherence to stereotypic beliefs results in gender differences in efficacy beliefs, more research should examine career self-efficacy with middle and high school populations to examine whether educational interventions should target their sources of efficacy information to create the same opportunities for both genders (Bussey & Bandura, 1999).

Career self-efficacy and gender expectations in early adolescence

In order to address the gap in the literature noted above and to explore career self-efficacy with pre-adolescents, a survey developed by Schuette and Ponton was administered to a group of middle-school children. The goal of the study was to determine whether there were gender differences in career self-efficacy and interests and to explore the impact of stereotype flexibility and tolerance on their occupational efficacy beliefs. The Career Choices Questionnaire (CCQ) was developed to assess their confidence and interest regarding twenty different occupations and included items to measure their stereotype flexibility and tolerance.

The participants were 147 children in middle school: age 11 ($N = 73$; 28 males, 45 females), age 12, ($N = 46$; 14 males, 32 females), and age 13 ($N = 28$; 12 males, 16 females). Each child completed the CCQ to assess their interest, flexibility and tolerance about twenty occupations of which half were traditionally male occupations (i.e. doctor, scientist, pilot, mathematician, car mechanic, President of the United States, engineer, dentist, computer builder and marine) and half were traditionally female occupations (i.e. school teacher, social worker, interior decorator, dietician, hair stylist, librarian, secretary, nurse, dental hygienist and flight attendant) (Liben & Bigler, 2002).

Children answered several different questions about a list of occupations using a 0–4 Likert scale (0 = not at all, 1= not very much, 2 = sort of, 3 = pretty much, 4 = a lot). The first question asked for their confidence rating about each occupation (e.g. 'How confident are you that you can become the following . . . '), which was the measure of their *career self-efficacy*. Additionally, the children rated their *interest* in each occupation. There were two questions to assess *stereotype flexibility*. The first of these two questions asked for the children to rate how confident they were that a male could have each of the stated occupations whereas the second question asked for the children to rate their confidence in a female having each occupation. The final survey question, which was designed to measure *stereotype tolerance*, required that the children rate how pleased they would be for a female to have each of the traditionally male occupations and to rate how pleased they would be for a male to have each of the traditionally female occupations.

A statistical analysis of the data indicated that there were gender differences for each of the variables (career self-efficacy, interest, flexibility, tolerance). Each gender was more interested in traditional occupations than non-traditional occupations. Similarly, boys judged themselves to be more self-efficacious in traditionally male occupations ($M = 17.13$) than in traditionally female occupations ($M = 8.18$) and the reverse pattern was found for females ($M = 13.19$ for traditionally male occupations; 17.24 for traditionally female occupations) (see Table 7.1). For the flexibility and tolerance findings, while both males and females were more confident that males can have a traditionally male occupation and females can have a traditionally female occupation, both genders were intolerant of males in traditionally female occupations (see Table 7.1). Interestingly, in an overall comparison of self-efficacy, the females in the sample were more efficacious ($M = 15.22$) than the males ($M = 12.67$) (see Table 7.2).

It is a positive finding that females in this middle-school sample were more self-efficacious than males overall. This may represent a shift in societal norms resulting from the advance of women or the increase in the number of women in male-dominated occupations (Stewart & LaVaque-Manty, 2008; Vogt, 2008). On the other hand, the finding that both males and females were more self-efficacious about and interested in stereotypical occupations demonstrates that stereotypes

Table 7.1 Descriptive statistics by gender

Variable	Males		Females	
	M	*SD*	*M*	*SD*
Self-efficacy (TMO)	17.13	7.45	13.19	9.16
Self-efficacy (TFO)	8.18	7.55	17.24	9.38
Interest (TMO)	16.60	7.63	10.37	6.25
Interest (TFO)	6.51	6.64	12.84	7.02
Tolerance (male in TFO)	22.31	11.51	22.79	10.03
Tolerance (female in TMO)	26.05	11.63	27.68	8.97

Note. Range for each variable is 0–40. For males, $n = 55$; for females, $n = 92$.

TMO = traditionally male occupation; TFO = traditionally female occupation.

Table 7.2 T-test results for between gender comparisons

Variable	t	df	p
Self-efficacy (TMO)	2.70	145	.004
Self-efficacy (TFO)	−6.41[1]	133	<.001
Interest (TMO)	5.38	145	<.001
Interest (TFO)	−5.40	145	<.001
Tolerance (M in TFO)	−0.27	145	.395
Tolerance (F in TMO)	−0.89[1]	92	.187

Note. For males, $n = 55$; for females, $n = 92$ with pairwise deletion as needed. A positive t statistic indicates $M_{MALE} > M_{FEMALE}$.

[1]Cell variances statistically unequal; therefore, equal variances not assumed.

TMO = traditionally male occupation; TFO = traditionally female occupation.

are pervasive and still continue to impact adolescents' interests and beliefs about their future options. Interestingly, males and females did not differ in their stereotype flexibility and tolerance in regard to future career pursuits though both genders were less tolerant of males engaging in non-traditional careers.

More research is needed to probe adolescents' stereotypical thinking and raise the question of whether individuals apply the constructs of stereotype flexibility and tolerance discriminately to their judgements of others and not to themselves. These associations have been seen at a young age; however, these aspirations largely mimic the expectations that the larger culture has on men and women, with males choosing jobs in the domains of mathematics and science and females choosing jobs in language arts and those which are also highly agentic (Eccles, 1994). Little research to date has applied a theoretical perspective to examine the influence of children's stereotypes regarding gender related occupations on their understanding of gender roles in the home. Research of this nature is significant, as it will determine whether there is a need for educational interventions to influence efficacy beliefs, to counter stereotypical thinking, and to prevent a disparity in expectations and experiences regarding the household distribution of labour.

Parental roles

According to current research, there remain significant inequalities regarding parental roles and opportunities in the home (Coltrane & Adams, 2008). Societal stereotypes of gender roles persist and continue to limit full gender equality as well as the benefits of full family involvement (Barnett & Rivers, 2004). In particular, the parental roles of primary breadwinner and primary caretaker are still highly differentiated by gender. Although adults' gender attitudes have been found to be related to how they attempt to balance work and family (Barnett & Hyde, 2001; Nomaguchi et al., 2005), 40 per cent of men and 36 per cent of women continue to believe that the family would be better off with a father who works and a mother who stays home to take care of the children (Thornton & Young-DeMarco, 2001).

Fathers, from varying ethnic and economic groups in the US, continue to believe that the primary way to show love for their family is by earning money

(Townsend, 2002), and many mothers and fathers view the wife's income as secondary and therefore her role in the workforce as less important than her role in childcare (Nomaguchi et al., 2005). Additionally, when companies offer employees the option of a flexible work schedule, women are more likely to adjust their schedules to accommodate their children's and partner's lives. Mothers, more than fathers, use non-standard work hours so that they can continue to complete more of the routine physical care and interactive activities with their children (Craig & Powell, 2011).

The decisions involving how to divide roles in the family by gender are complex, and often difficult, for both mothers and fathers, with implications for their children. Women are forced to decide between having a family and pursuing a career (Tiedje, 2004). A man, conversely, may feel pressured to be the breadwinner and to be an 'ideal worker' who spends over forty hours a week at the office (Williams & Cooper, 2004). Many fathers may indeed be highly successful at caretaking, as was found in a study of fathers with sole custody who were as nurturing and loving with their children as mothers (Coltrane, 1996). Wives, however, are left trying to be 'good mothers' and continue to do a majority of the household chores and spend a majority of their time with the children as compared to husbands (Bianchi, 2000; Douglas & Michaels, 2004). Additionally, many women feel pressured to spend less time at work and more time at home, while for men it is the reverse (Holmes et al., 2012). In many cases, women do not have the same opportunities for advancement compared to men because they have fewer hours to dedicate to their work obligations because they must divide their time with their household responsibilities. These expectations and opportunities aid in perpetuating gender inequality as men and women are held to different standards, making it more difficult for them to succeed in counter-stereotypic roles. Such differential standards limit the options that both men and women can have in order to lead truly fulfilling lives.

Developmental perspective

Children witness from early in life that parents often divide roles in the home based on gender (Coltrane & Adams, 2008). Recent research from the social domain theory has begun to investigate how children evaluate the division of labour in the home. As an example, Schuette and Killen (2009) assessed children's judgements about parents' decisions to display a gender preference when requesting that a son or daughter help with a household activity or chore that is typically associated with a gender stereotype. The female-associated chores were vacuuming, cooking, sewing and washing dishes; the male-associated chores were changing the oil in the car, taking out the trash, building a table and mowing the lawn.

Overall, when asked whom a parent should choose, the son or the daughter, to help with the chore, 57–75 per cent of the children chose the child who fit the stereotypic expectation, and this increased with age from kindergarten to fifth grade. During the developmental period when the explicit use of gender stereotypes peaks (3–5 years of age), children were more likely to view chores as gender-neutral activities than they were towards the end of childhood, that is, by 10–11 years of age. Moreover, girls were more likely to make the non-stereotypic choice than were boys, indicating there were no in-group biases displayed. Yet, girls' greater preference for engaging in non-stereotypic chores than boys as early as 10 years of age indicates that the gender gap regarding family roles emerges early in development.

When a counter-probe technique was used in which the interviewer asked the child about the alternative option, children used more moral reasoning and relied less on stereotypes to explain their choice. Thus, children relied on gender stereotypes when that was the only information presented; however, they were more likely to accept cross-gender behaviour when the fairness of the situation was implied (Schuette & Killen, 2009). Children understood the complexity of gender activities and recognized that gender activities involve both gender roles as well as issues of fairness. This research demonstrated that even when children rely on stereotypic expectations (and use social–conventional reasoning) to explain chore assignment, they also perceive and apply their fairness reasoning to the home context, and to parental division of labour in the home. Recent research has expanded this literature to explore children's understanding of parental roles and the negotiation of the work/family balance (Sinno & Killen, 2009, 2011).

From a young age, children differentiate the roles between mothers and fathers. When asked to pose for a photo as a parent with a small baby, preschoolers acted in gender-stereotypical ways: boys moved further away to pose as the father while girls moved closer in to pose as the mother (Reid et al., 1989). Research grounded in the social domain theory has recently found that children also think about the arrangements of parental roles in the home beyond re-enacting stereotypical behaviour. Although children and most adolescents are not themselves in the roles of mother and father, they evaluate the roles of parents by weighing concerns about societal norms and stereotypes, gender equality and fairness, family functioning and personal preferences.

In particular, recent research from the social domain theory has shown that children reason differently about the parental roles of caretaker and breadwinner, based on gender of the parent and the role in question (Sinno & Killen, 2009, 2011). Sinno and Killen (2009) found that children in middle childhood reasoned that mothers had the personal choice to work; however, they judged it more acceptable for mothers to be in the caretaker role. When examining the caretaker role specifically, children reasoned from different domains of knowledge based on the gender of the parent in the role. When the mother was the primary caretaker, children used more personal choice reasoning to support that the mother could decide to stay at home to take care of children or go to work. For fathers who wanted to be the primary caretaker, children used more gender stereotypes to explain why they thought he would not be very competent in the role (e.g. 'He will just lie on the couch and eat potato chips.'). Children's and adolescents' views that both mothers and fathers should be able to have a full-time job if they so desire reflect their social understanding of personal choice and reflect the changing dynamics of dual-earning families (Bianchi et al., 2006).

To further investigate the situation that most US families deal with in terms of two working parents who are attempting to balance occupational and family responsibilities, Sinno and Killen (2011) examined children's and early adolescents' reasoning about second-shift parenting. Second-shift parenting relates to one parent taking on the primary caretaker role after working a full-time job as well (Raley et al., 2006). This study included 10 year olds and 13 year olds who rated hypothetical situations in which both parents were breadwinners but there was an unequal distribution of caretaking among them (Sinno & Killen, 2011). They were asked to rate the situation overall (6-point Likert scale that ranged from 'very bad' to 'very good') and to then provide their social reasoning behind their judgement. Participants again rated it as better for a mother to complete most of the caretaking responsibilities, and they did not expect a father to be in this role because they reasoned that it is unfair for him to be taking on 'double-duty' (Table 7.3). Social reasoning about the father's role was not greatly affected by the child or adolescents' own parents' caretaking responsibilities, highlighting the notion that they think about gender issues within the home context, even those with which they do not have direct experience.

Relationships between gender attitudes, family roles and social reasoning

In order to examine how participants' gender attitudes, their parental occupational status and caretaking responsibilities, and their personal expectations for work and family roles were integrated and linked to social reasoning, a new study was conducted using the paradigm reported in Sinno and Killen (2011). Participants included 102 10 year olds (49 females, 53 males), 98 13 year olds (59 females, 39 males), and 100 19 year olds (52 males, 48 males) from an ethnically diverse, middle income metropolitan area on the east coast of the US. In addition to the social reasoning scenarios presented in Sinno and Killen (2011), participants completed the Attitudes toward Gender Scale (adapted from the Attitudes toward Gender Scale; Leaper & Valin, 1996). Participants rated statements that were targeted towards male and female roles in the home ('In general, the mother should have greater responsibility than the father in taking care of children') on a 6-point Likert scale that ranged from 'strongly agree' to 'strongly disagree'.

Participants also completed a survey indicating their parents' occupations (coded as traditional, non-traditional or neutral based on the US Census Bureau (2007) and Frome et al. (2006)) and which parent was responsible for a variety of

Table 7.3 Means for social reasoning about mothers and fathers in second-shift parental roles

Reasoning	Mums	Dads
Social–conventional	.54 (.37)	.49 (.39)
Moral	.36 (.35)	.43 (.39)
Personal choice	.09 (.20)	.08 (.20)

Note. Standard deviations in ().

caretaking tasks, by indicating 'mostly mother', 'mostly father' or 'both equally'. Finally, participants were asked about their own expectations for their future family life, including whether they expect to have a job when they are older; whether they expect to have a family; whether they expect to work when they have a family; and how much of the caretaking they expect to take on.

Analyses were conducted to determine the interrelations between children's and adolescents' gender attitudes, their parents' occupational and caretaking roles and their own personal expectations for these roles. Similar to research showing children's gender schemas are influenced by their parents' gender beliefs and behaviours (e.g. Ruble et al., 2006), parents' occupational adherence to gendered roles was positively related to participants' personal expectations. Additionally, children and adolescents who perceived that their parents were in less stereotyped occupations were more likely to have egalitarian gender attitudes.

Although a majority of participants expected to have a job and a family, similar to research with adults (e.g. Stone & McKee, 2000), female participants were less likely than males to expect to have a job simultaneous with a family. Additionally, participants with egalitarian attitudes expected to share caretaking of children; however, females more than males expected to get the kids ready for and picked up from day care or school, as well as bathe, discipline, make dinner and comfort children when they are upset. In contrast, for the tasks of taking the kids to the park or to practise, more males than females expected to do all of these tasks. These findings are consistent with past research that has found that although men report that they expect an egalitarian division of labour in the household (Askari et al., 2010), females do not have the same expectations (Fetterolf & Eagly, 2011) and that even before adolescence, girls experience inequality in the distribution of labour in the home from parents' assignment of chores (Coltrane & Adams, 2008).

Regression analyses were then conducted to investigate whether participant gender attitudes, perceptions of their parents' roles, and expectations for their own roles predict participants' judgements and reasoning about hypothetical second-shift contexts. None of these variables were predictive of participants' judgements, or ratings of mothers' or fathers' abilities, to take on more caretaking responsibilities. However, these factors did influence children's and adolescents' social reasoning about parental caretaking. The predictive nature of these factors was dependent upon gender of parent in the second-shift role. When reasoning about a mother in the second-shift role, participants' perception of their parents' occupations was influential. Participants who perceived their mother's occupation as more non-traditional regarding gender norms but their overall family adherence as more traditional were more likely to use social–conventional or practicality reasoning and less likely to provide reasoning that reflected moral concerns or issues of fairness (Table 7.4). Social reasoning about fathers in the second-shift role was not affected by children's and adolescents' perceptions of parental occupations but, rather, by their perceptions of parents' division of caretaking (Table 7.5). For instance, participants whose mothers were more likely to read to them predicted a greater likelihood of using social–conventional reasoning for a second-shift father and predictive of using less moral or fairness reasoning.

Table 7.4 Predictors of reasoning about fathers in the second-shift parenting role

Reasoning	Predictor	Beta	t	p
Social–conventional	Reading to kids	.138	2.05	.04
Moral	Reading to kids	−.197	−2.95	.01
	Bathing kids	.163	2.46	.02
Personal choice	Making dinner	−.141	−2.13	.03
	Bathing kids	−.162	−2.59	.01

Table 7.5 Predictors of reasoning about mothers in the second-shift parenting role

Reasoning	Predictor	Beta	t	p
Social-conventional	Mum's job	.217	2.49	.01
	Family job status	−.177	−1.90	.05
Moral	Mum's job	−.193	−2.21	.03
	Family's job status	.215	2.30	.02

Participants who perceived their own mother taking care of bathing the children were more likely to reason it as unfair for a father to be in the second-shift and predictive of thinking it was not necessarily his personal choice to be in this role. Finally, participants' perception that their own mother made dinner more often was also predictive of thinking that second-shift fathers were not choosing to be in this position. Overall, children and adolescents who were not likely to see their fathers doing more pragmatic and less flexible caretaking tasks, such as bathing the kids and making dinner (Coltrane & Adams, 2008), seem to continue to believe that mothers should be the ones to take on more caretaking, even after work.

In examining the findings of influential factors on children's and adolescents' social reasoning about parental roles, it appears that parents' division of caretaking responsibilities has more of an impact on reasoning about second-shift fathers. In contrast, parents' adherence to gender norms in occupations had more of an impact on reasoning about mothers in the second-shift role. Regardless of gender of parent in the second-shift role, children's and adolescents' perceptions of their own mothers' role seemed to guide social reasoning and in many ways 'carry the weight' of negotiating the balance of work and family life (Craig & Powell, 2011).

Given the percentage of women who work outside the home and the changing depiction of women in the workforce (Martinez, 2005), one might also expect there to be a transformation in societal views about the delegation of caretaking responsibilities. Even though some studies have found that many couples espouse egalitarian views (e.g. Nock, 2001), there is not strong evidence in social reasoning of children and adolescents that there is equality in caretaking tasks. For this reason, more research should continue to explore household functioning and the factors that influence the work and family balance, particularly research involving households in which the couples espouse a shared division of labour or a comparison of traditional and non-traditional families (e.g. male homemakers). Such studies would inform the understanding of the developmental processes of family dynamics and how gender norms influence the work and family balance.

Implications and future research

Understanding how children and adolescents evaluate family roles provides an important window into the factors that help contribute to the goal of providing environments for youth that reflect equality, equity and fairness. Coltrane and Shih (2010) so clearly articulated the illogical nature of the gender inequity in the home, and the continued strength of social conventions, 'If the work is not inherently gendered, why do many people continue to think that most household labor should be performed by women?' (p. 403). The above research about children's and adolescents' understanding of and social cognition about the gendered roles of occupations and parental roles in the home shows children should have opportunities to evaluate fairness in the household domain and to develop their career interests without the pressures of gender conformity. Societal pressures to conform to gender ideologies, and gender expectations for child-rearing bear on the development of children's knowledge, understanding and expectations about gender roles (Fulcher, 2011).

Children's gender role knowledge is complex and is derived from their social experiences (Eagly & Wood, 2012) as well as their reasoning about fairness and conventions of gender norms (Killen & Rutland, 2011; Schuette & Killen, 2009; Sinno & Killen, 2011). Parental support of one another in parenting roles has been shown to enhance a child's well-being (Gable et al., 1995). The more opportunities that children have to witness and evaluate non-traditional households (i.e. stay-at-home or second-shift fathers and parents who share the division of labour), the greater their understanding that concepts of fairness and morality apply to the household domain and that gender does not have to be the sole criteria for role assignment. These findings have implications for individual's healthy social and emotional development as gender norms can limit how children and adolescents make decisions or begin to set aspirations for their adult roles.

To the extent that individuals view caretaking primarily within the mothers' domain and area of competence, children and adolescents may feel restricted in their career choices. Additionally, the expectation that primary roles of breadwinner and caretaker should be divided along gender lines can affect academic endeavours because students might be encouraged to work harder in classes that are more stereotypically gender appropriate (Watt, 2010). Lastly, developing gender bias about adult parental roles could affect children's and adolescents' expectations about the importance of their own anticipated family roles. Although the research presented in this chapter addressed the social cognition of children's and adolescents' understanding of the gendered contexts of occupations and parental roles, there is a great amount of research still left to be conducted about the development of gender expectations as changing family dynamics and community influences have yet to be explored (Tenenbaum & Leaper, 2002).

Although there is research on women/mothers and their attitudes toward negotiating work and family (Fetterolf & Eagly, 2011; Frome et al., 2008), future research should consider more closely examining men/fathers' attitudes. For instance, father involvement has been found to be an important mediating factor between the family and community norms (Tamis-LeMonda & Cabrera, 2002). More specifically, fathers' involvement in routine childcare can predict school attainment in children, can lead to daughters having fewer stereotypical views about adult gender roles, and can led to a more positive rating of parenting skills and satisfaction in relationships later in life (Lewis & Lamb, 2003). However, there is little research particularly investigating how parental attitudes, both mothers' and fathers', affect children's and adolescents' flexibility, tolerance and cognition about the breadwinner or caretaker role.

In addition to including father data in research, it is also imperative for research to move beyond the typical data sets of two-parent, middle-income homes. As noted by research on family dynamics, there are micro-level characteristics of the immediate setting, such as who else is present in the home, that may determine whether parents' gender schemas are activated and motivate sex-typed treatment of children (McHale et al., 2003). It is possible then that the effects of perceptions of their own parents' parental roles in the home on social reasoning may be different if there were more individuals in our sample living in single-parent or same-sex parent homes (Hofferth et al., 2007). For example, lesbian parents held less traditional views about gender related issues and were less likely to decorate physical spaces, such as bedrooms, that brought attention to their child's gender. Lesbian parents also expressed less conservative attitudes about their children's gender related behaviour (Sutfin et al., 2008). It would be interesting for research to examine social cognition about the gendered roles of breadwinner and caretaker in youth whose family dynamic does not lend to a societal expectation for division of these roles.

With the importance of children having the opportunity to see adults in non-stereotypical roles (Fulcher, 2011), more research should explore the use of education interventions to determine whether they help to diminish children's adherence to traditional gender role norms and broaden their occupational aspirations. Furthermore, based on the finding that there is a stigma associated with cross-gender behaviour for males, more interventions should target measures to increase flexibility and tolerance for stereotypically female activities and occupations. As gender stereotypes continue to have a significant impact on children's selection of potential career pursuits, more research should continue to explore ways to increase children's stereotype flexibility and tolerance so that their interests will guide their career paths and their self-efficacy will be shaped by their own achievements rather than the pervasiveness of gender stereotypic beliefs.

Concluding thoughts

Recent research of parental roles has shown that taking on multiples roles in the family can enhance the lives of mothers and fathers as well as their children (Barnett & Rivers, 2004). For mothers, working outside the home in a job that they enjoy allows for a continuation of their individuality in ideas and thoughts and improves their overall well-being. For fathers, an increased role in caretaking allows them to feel more integrated into family life and has mental health benefits for decreasing stress (Barnett & Rivers, 2004). Parents, who share the demands of multiple parenting roles, have been shown to display better moods and have more energy at home. Children from these families, in turn, are developing well, both academically and emotionally, and reinvest their energy back to the workforce and their own families later in life (Barber & Eccles, 1992; Barnett & Rivers, 2004; Galinsky, 2005). Moreover, recent evidence reveals that not only do children do well socially and academically when their parents are involved in work outside the home as well as caretaking roles inside the home, but that they also think about these roles from a fairness and autonomy perspective. Children view fathers' expectations that mothers not work outside the home as unfair, and they value fathers who participate in child-rearing responsibilities.

The topics of parental roles and family and work balance are important in various contexts within the US and around the world. Examining the development of social reasoning regarding the balance of work and family and parental roles can aid in elucidating the developmental trajectory of children's understanding about gender role opportunities and family structures. Additionally, children's understanding of gender roles is related to children's healthy social development, and specifically to social and academic outcomes. Without knowing the reasons why family roles continue to be identified by gender, research cannot offer solutions for making the roles more equitable. Examining age related changes in social reasoning about parental roles, family structures and the division of labour in the home provides insight into decisions that individuals may make for themselves in future contexts of balancing work and family.

References

Askari, S. F., Liss, M., Erchull, M. J., Staebell, S. E., & Axelson, S. J. (2010). Men want equality, but women don't expect it: young adults' expectations for participation in household and child care chores. *Psychology of Women Quarterly, 34,* 243–252. doi:10.1111/j.1471-6402.2010.01565.x.

Barber, B. L., & Eccles, J. S. (1992). Long-term influences of divorce and single parenting on adolescent family- and work-related values, beliefs, and expectations. *Psychological Bulletin, 111*(1), 108–126. doi:10.1037/0033-2909.111.1.108.

Barnett, R., & Hyde, J. (2001). Women, men, work, and family. *American Psychologist, 56*(10), 781–796. doi:10.1037/0003-066X.56.10.781.

Barnett, R. C., & Rivers, C. (2004). *Same difference: how gender myths are hurting our relationships, our children, and our jobs.* New York: Basic Books.

Bianchi, S. (2000). Maternal employment and time with children: dramatic change or surprising continuity? *Demography, 37,* 401–414.

Bianchi, S. M., Robinson, J. P., & Milkie, M. A. (2006). *Changing rhythms of American family life.* New York: Russell Sage Foundation.

Bussey, K., & Bandura, A. (1999). Social cognitive theory of gender development and differentiation. *Psychological Review, 106*(4), 676–713. doi:10.1037/0033-295X.106.4.676.

Carter, D. B., & Patterson, C. J. (1982). Sex roles as social conventions: the development of children's conceptions of sex-role stereotypes. *Developmental Psychology, 18*(6), 812–824.

Coltrane, S. (1996). *Family man: fatherhood, housework, and gender equity.* New York and Oxford: Oxford University Press.

Coltrane, S., & Adams, M. (2008). *Gender and families* (2nd ed.). Lanham, MD: Rowman & Littlefield Publishers.

Coltrane, S., & Shih, K. Y. (2010). Gender and the division of labor. In Chrisler, J. C., & McCreary, D. R. (Eds), *Handbook of gender research in psychology* (Vol. 2) (pp. 401–422). London: Springer Science & Business Media.

Craig, L., & Powell, A. (2011). Non-standard work schedules, work-family balance and the gendered division of childcare. *Work, Employment and Society, 25*(2), 274–291. doi:10.1177/0950017011398894.

Cuddy, A. C., Fiske, S. T., & Glick, P. (2004). When professionals become mothers: warmth doesn't cut the ice. *Journal of Social Issues, 60*(4), 701–718. doi:10.1111/j.00224537.2004.00381.x.

Deutsch, F. M., Servis, L. J., & Payne, J. D. (2001). Paternal participation in child care and its effects on children's self-esteem and attitudes toward gendered roles. *Journal of Family Issues, 22*(8), 1000–1024. doi:10.1177/019251301022008003.

Diekman, A. B., & Eagly, A. H. (2000). Stereotypes as dynamic constructs: women and men of the past, present, and future. *Personality and Social Psychology Bulletin, 26*(10), 1171–1188. doi:10.1177/0146167200262001.

Domene, J. F., Arim, R. G., & Young, R. A. (2007). Gender and career development projects in early adolescence: similarities and differences between mother-daughter and mother-son dyads. *Qualitative Research in Psychology, 4*(1–2), 107–126. doi:10.1080/14780880701473490.

Douglas, S. J., and Michaels, M. W. (2004) *The mommy myth: the idealization of motherhood and how it has undermined all women.* New York: Free Press.

Eagly, A. H., & Wood, W. (2012). Social role theory. In van Lange, P., Kruglanski, A., & Higgins, E.T. (Eds), *Handbook of theories in social psychology* (Vol. 2) (pp. 458–476). London: Sage Publishers.

Eccles, J. S. (1994). Understanding women's educational and occupational choices: applying the Eccles et al. model of achievement-related choices. *Psychology of Women Quarterly, 18*(4), 585–609. doi:10.1111/j.1471-6402.1994.tb01049.x.

Erchull, M. J., Liss, M., Axelson, S. J., Staebell, S. E., & Askari, S. F. (2010). Well . . . she wants it more: perceptions of social norms about desires for marriage and children and anticipated chore participation. *Psychology of Women Quarterly, 34*, 253–260. doi:10.1111/j.1471-6402.2010.01566.

Fetterolf, J. C., & Eagly, A. H. (2011). Do young women expect gender equality in their future lives? An answer from a possible selves experiment. *Sex Roles, 65*, 83–93. doi:10.1007/s11199-011-9981-9.

Frome, P. M., Alfeld, C. J., Eccles, J. S., & Barber, B. L. (2006). Why don't they want a male-dominated job? An investigation of young women who changed their occupational aspirations. *Educational Research and Evaluation, 12*(4), 359–372. doi:10.1080/13803610600765786.

Frome, P. M., Alfeld, C. J., Eccles, J. S., & Barber, B. L. (2008). Is the desire for a family-flexible job keeping young women out of male-dominated occupations? In Watt, H. G., & Eccles, J. S. (Eds), *Gender and occupational outcomes* (pp. 195–214). Washington, DC: American Psychological Association.

Fuegan, K., Biernat, M., Haines, E., & Deaux, K. (2004). Mothers and fathers in the workplace: how gender and parental status influence judgments of job-related competence. *Journal of Social Issues, 60*, 737–754.

Fulcher, M. (2011). Individual differences in children's occupational aspirations as a function of parent traditionality. *Sex Roles, 64*, 117–131. doi: 10.1007/s11199-010-9854-7.

Gable, S., Belsky, J., & Crnic, K. (1995). Coparenting during the child's second year: a descriptive account. *Journal of Marriage and the Family, 57*, 609– 616.

Galinsky, E. (2005). Children's perspectives of employed mothers and fathers: closing the gap between public debates and research findings. In Halpern, D. F., & Murphy, S. E. (Eds), *From work-family balance to work-family interaction* (pp. 219–236). Mahwah, NJ: Lawrence Erlbaum Associates, Inc.

Gorman, K. A., & Fritzsche, B. A. (2002). The good-mother stereotype: stay at home (or wish that you did!). *Journal of Applied Social Psychology, 32*(10), 2190–2201. doi:10.1111/j.1559-1816.2002.tb02069.x.

Hofferth, S. L., Cabrera, N., Carlson, M., Coley, R., Day, R., & Schindler, H. (2007). Resident father involvement and social fathering. In Hofferth, S. L., & Casper, L. M. (Eds), *Handbook of measurement issues in family research* (pp. 335–374). Mahwah, NJ: Lawrence Erlbaum Associates Publishers.

Holmes, E., Erickson, J., & Hill, E. (2012). Doing what she thinks is best: maternal psychological wellbeing and attaining desired work situations. *Human Relations, 65*(4), 501–522. doi:10.1177/0018726711431351.

Huston, A. C. (1985). The development of sex typing: themes from recent research. *Developmental Review, 5*(1), 1–17. doi:10.1016/0273-2297(85)90028-0.

Kanka, M., Wagner, P., Schober, B., & Spiel, C. (2011). Gender-stereotyped attitudes and behavior in kindergarten students. *The International Journal of Learning, 2*, 291–303.

Katz, P. A., & Ksansnak, K. R. (1994). Developmental aspects of gender role flexibility and traditionality in middle childhood and adolescence. *Developmental Psychology, 30*(2), 272–282. doi: 10.1037/0012-1649.30.2.272.

Kaufman, G. (2005). Gender role attitudes and college students' work and family expectations. *Gender issues, 22*, 58–71. doi: 10.1007/s12147-005-0015-1.

Killen, M., & Stangor, C. (2001). Children's social reasoning about inclusion and exclusion in gender and race peer group contexts. *Child Development, 72*, 174–186. doi:10.1111/1467-8624.00272.

Killen, M., & Rutland, A. (2011). *Children and social exclusion: morality, prejudice, and group identity.* New York: Wiley/Blackwell.

Killen, M., Pisacane, K., Lee-Kim, J., & Ardila-Rey, A. (2001). Fairness or stereotypes? Young children's priorities when evaluating group exclusion and inclusion. *Developmental Psychology, 37*, 587–596. doi: 10.1037//0012-1649.37.5.587.

Killen, M., Sinno, S., & Margie, N. (2007). Children's experiences and judgments about group exclusion and inclusion. In *Advances in child development and behavior* (Vol. 35) (pp. 173– 218). San Diego, CA: Elsevier Academic Press.

Kroska, A. (2003). Investigating gender differences in the meaning of household chores and child care. *Journal of Marriage and Family, 65*(2), 456–473. doi:10.1111/j.174 13737.2003.00456.x.

Kulik, L. (2005). Predicting gender role stereotypes among adolescents in Israel: the impact of background variables, personality traits, and parental factors. *Journal of Youth Studies, 8*(1), 111–129.

Leaper, C., & Valin, D. (1996). Predictors of Mexican American mothers' and fathers' attitudes toward gender equality. *Hispanic Journal of Behavioral Sciences, 18*(3), 343–355. doi:10.1177/07399863960183005.

Lewis, C., & Lamb, M. E. (2003). Fathers' influences on children's development: the evidence from two-parent families. *European Journal of Psychology of Education, 18*(2), 211–228. doi:10.1007/BF03173485.

Liben, L. S., & Bigler, R. S. (2002). The developmental course of gender differentiation: conceptualizing, measuring, and evaluating constructs and pathways. *Monographs of the Society for Research in Child Development, 67*(2), vii–147. doi:10.1111/1540-5834.t01-1-00187.

Martinez, S. (2005). Women's intrinsic and extrinsic motivations for working. In Schneider, B., & Waite, L. J. (Eds), *Being together, working apart: dual career families and the work-life balance* (pp. 79–101). Cambridge: Cambridge University Press.

McHale, S., Crouter, A., & Whiteman, S. (2003). The family contexts of gender development in childhood and adolescence. *Social Development, 12*(1), 125–148. doi:10.1111/1467-9507.00225.

Milkie, M. A., Mattingly, M. J., Nomaguchi, K. M., Bianchi, S. M., & Robinson, J. P. (2004). The time squeeze: parental statuses and feelings about time with children. *Journal of Marriage and Family, 66*(3), 739–761. doi:10.1111/j.0022-2445.2004.00050.x.

Nock, S. L. (2001). The marriages of equally dependent spouses. *Journal of Family Issues, 22*(6), 755–775. doi:10.1177/019251301022006005.

Nomaguchi, K. M., Milkie, M. A., & Bianchi, S. M. (2005). Time strains and psychological well-being: do dual-earner mothers and fathers differ? *Journal of Family Issues, 26*(6), 756–792. doi:10.1177/0192513X05277524.

Nucci, L. P., & Turiel, E. (1978). Social interactions and the development of social concepts in preschool children. *Child Development, 49*, 400–407. doi:10.2307/1128704.

Owen Blakemore, J. E. (2003). Children's beliefs about violating gender norms: boys shouldn't look like girls, and girls shouldn't act like boys. *Sex Roles, 48*(9/10), 411–419. doi:10.1023/A:1023574427720.

Palkovitz, R. (2002). Involved fathering and child development: advancing our understanding of good fathering. In Tamis-LeMonda, C. S., & Cabrera, N. (Eds), *Handbook of father involvement: multidisciplinary perspectives* (pp. 119–140). Mahwah, NJ: Lawrence Erlbaum.

Piaget, J. (1997). *The moral judgment of the child.* (trans. by M. Gabian). New York: Free Press Paperbacks. (Originally published in 1932.)

Raley, S. B., Mattingly, M. J., & Bianchi, S. M. (2006). How dual are dual-income couples? Documenting change from 1970 to 2001. *Journal of Marriage and Family, 68* (1), 11–28. doi:10.1111/j.1741-3737.2006.00230.x.

Reid, P. T., Tate, C. S., & Berman, P. W. (1989). Preschool children's self-presentations in situations with infants: effects of sex and race. *Child Development, 60*(3), 710–714. doi:10.2307/1130736.

Ruble, D. N., Martin, C. L., & Berenbaum, S. A. (2006). Gender development. In Damon, W., & Lerner, R. (Series Eds) & Eisenberg, N. (Vol. Ed.), *Handbook of child psychology: Vol. 3. Social, emotional, and personality development* (6th ed.) (pp. 858–932). New York: Wiley.

Schuette, C. T., & Killen, M. (2009). Children's evaluations of gender-stereotypic household activities in the family context. *Early Education and Development, 20*(4), 693–712. doi:10.1080/10409280802206908.

Schuette, C. T., Ponton, M. K., & Charlton, M. L. (2012). Middle school children's career aspirations: relationship to adult occupations and gender. *The Career Development Quarterly, 60*(1), 36–46. doi:10.1002/j.2161-0045.2012.00004.x.

Signorella, M. L., Bigler, R. S., & Liben, L. S. (1993). Developmental differences in children's gender schemata about others: a meta-analytic review. *Developmental Review, 13*, 147–183. doi:10.1006/drev.1993.1007.

Sinno, S., & Killen, M. (2009). Moms at work and dads at home: children's evaluations of parental roles. *Applied Developmental Science, 13*, 16–29. doi:10.1080/10888690802606735.

Sinno, S., & Killen, M. (2011). Social reasoning about second-shift parenting. *British Journal of Developmental Psychology, 29,* 313–329. doi:10.1111/j.2044-835X.2010.02021.x.

Smetana, J. G. (2006). Social-cognitive domain theory: consistencies and variations in children's moral and social judgments. In Killen, M., & Smetana, J. G. (Eds), *Handbook of moral development* (pp. 119–153). Mahwah, NJ: Lawrence Erlbaum Associates

Stewart, A., & LaVaque-Manty, D. (2008). Advancing women faculty in science and engineering: an effort in institutional transformation. In Watt, H. G., & Eccles, J. S. (Eds), *Gender and occupational outcomes: longitudinal assessments of individual, social, and cultural influences* (pp. 299–322). Washington, DC: American Psychological Association. doi:10.1037/11706-011.

Stone, L., & McKee, N. P. (2000). Gendered futures: student visions of career and family on a college campus. *Anthropology & Education Quarterly, 31*(1), 67–89. doi:10.1525/aeq.2000.31.1.67.

Sutfin, E. L., Fulcher, M., Bowles, R. P., & Patterson, C. J. (2008). How lesbian and heterosexual parents convey attitudes about gender to their children: the role of gendered environments. *Sex Roles, 58*(7–8), 501–513. doi:10.1007/s11199-007-9368-0.

Tamis-LeMonda, C. S., & Cabrera, N. (Eds). (2002). *Handbook of father involvement: multidisciplinary perspectives.* Mahwah, NJ: Erlbaum.

Tenenbaum, H. R., & Leaper, C. (2002). Are parents' gender schemas related to their children's gender-related cognitions? A meta-analysis. *Developmental Psychology, 38*(4), 615–630. doi:10.1037/0012-1649.38.4.615.

Theimer, C. E., Killen, M., & Stangor, C. (2001). Young children's evaluations of exclusion in gender-stereotypic peer contexts. *Developmental Psychology, 37,* 18–27. doi:10.1037/0012-1649.37.1.18.

Thornton, A., & Young-DeMarco, L. (2001). Four decades of trends in attitudes toward family issues in the United States: the 1960s through the 1990s. *Journal of Marriage and Family, 63*(4), 1009–1037. doi:10.1111/j.1741-3737.2001.01009.x.

Tiedje, L. B. (2004). Processes of change in work/home incompatibilities: employed mothers 1986–1999. *Journal of Social Issues, 60,* 787–800. doi:10.1111/j.0022-4537.2004.00386.x.

Townsend, N. W. (2002). *The package deal: marriage, work and fatherhood in men's lives.* Philadelphia, PA: Temple University Press.

Turiel, E. (1983). *The development of social knowledge: morality and convention.* New York: Cambridge University Press.

Turiel, E. (1998). The development of morality. In Damon, W. (Ed.), *Handbook of child psychology* (5th ed., Vol. 3: Social, emotional, and personality development) (pp. 863–932). New York: Wiley.

Turiel, E. (2006). Thought, emotions, and social interactional processes in moral development. In Killen, M., & Smetana, J. G. (Eds), *Handbook of moral development* (pp. 7–35). Mahwah, NJ: Lawrence Erlbaum Associates Publishers.

US Census Bureau. (2007). *Occupation by sex and median earnings.* Retrieved on 1 October 2012 from http://factfinder.census.gov/servlet/STTable?_bm=y&-geo_id=01000US&-qr_name=ACS_2007_3YR_G00_S2401&-ds_name=ACS_2007_3YR_G00_.

Vogt, C. M. (2008). The continuing technological revolution: a comparison of three regions' strategies for creating women-inclusive workplaces. In Watt, H. G., & Eccles, J. S. (Eds), *Gender and occupational outcomes: longitudinal assessments of individual, social, and cultural influences* (pp. 323–351). Washington, DC: American Psychological Association. doi:10.1037/11706-012.

Watt, H. (2010). Gender and occupational choice. In Chrisler, J. C., & McCreary, D. R. (Eds), *Handbook of gender research in psychology* (Vol. 2) (pp. 379–400). London: Springer Science & Business Media.

Weisgram, E. S., Bigler, R. S., & Liben, L. S. (2010). Gender, values, and occupational interests among children, adolescents, and adults. *Child Development, 81*(3), 778–796. doi:10.1111/j.1467-8624.2010.01433.x.

Weisgram, E. S., Dinella, L. M., & Fulcher, M. (2011). The role of masculinity/femininity, values, and occupational value affordances in shaping young men's and women's occupational choices. *Sex Roles, 65*(3/4), 243–258. doi:10.1007/s11199-011-9998-0.

Williams, J. C., & Cooper, H. C. (2004). The public policy of motherhood. *Journal of Social Issues, 60*, 849–865. doi:10.1111/j.0022-4537.2004.00390.x.

Zosuls, K. M., Miller, C. F., Ruble, D. N., Martin, C. L., & Fabes, R. A. (2011). Gender development research in *Sex Roles*: historical trends and future directions. *Sex Roles, 64*, 826–842. doi:10.1007/s11199-010-9902-3.

Index